ESSAYS ON DEVELOPMENT ISSUES

INDIA AND THE INDIAN OCEAN REGION

ESSAYS ON DEVELOPMENT ISSUES

INDIA AND THE INDIAN OCEAN REGION

Edited by

R.N. GHOSH

M.A.B. SIDDIQUE • R. GABBAY

ATLANTIC

PUBLISHERS & DISTRIBUTORS

Published by
ATLANTIC PUBLISHERS AND DISTRIBUTORS
B-2, Vishal Enclave, Opp. Rajouri Garden, New Delhi-27
Phones : 5413460, 5429987, 5466842

Sales Office
4215/1, Ansari Road, Darya Ganj, New Delhi-02
Phones : 3273880, 3285873, 3280451
Fax : 91-11-3285873
web : www.atlanticbooks.com
e-mail : info@atlanticbooks.com

ISBN 81-269-0219-1

Typeset at
APD Computer Graphics, Delhi
Printed in India at
Nice Printing Press, Delhi

PREFACE

The idea to produce this volume containing selected essays dealing with different aspects of development with reference to India was conceived in November 2000 in a meeting in Perth, which was attended by primarily academics from Australia, India, South Africa, France and many other countries.

The idea was then floated that development of the heterogeneous countries of the Indian Ocean region could hold the key to our understanding of the factors which might trigger economic change.

Now, India, Australia and South Africa are the three major regional powers in the Indian Ocean region. While Australia is a developed country with a very high level of economic affluence, the South African society's problems are mainly drawn along racial lines. Blacks in South Africa have an overwhelming majority in numbers, and yet most of the black people in South Africa face serious problems of unemployment and poverty. The whites in South Africa have, on the other hand, always enjoyed comfortable standards of living.

India provides the classic example of a developing country that is burdened with overpopulation, communal divisions, gender inequalities, rural poverty, illiteracy and yet it is a country that has the potential to emerge as a great global power in the course of the 21st century. Essays included in this volume were independently reviewed. These essays examine the case of India from various perspectives to demonstrate how the process of economic change in India might have a bearing on the Indian Ocean region as a whole.

As Editors of the Volume, we wish to thank all contributors. Our special thanks are due to Ms Helen Reidy, who was responsible for typing the manuscript. We also thank Dr. K.R. Gupta, Managing Director, Atlantic Publishers and Distributors, New Delhi, for publishing the book at short notice.

—R.N. GHOSH, M.A.B. SIDDIQUE and R. GABBAY
Editors

Business School
The University of Western Australia
Perth

CONTENTS

1

Development Issues: Globalisation, Environment, Gender and Regional Development — An Overview

R.N. GHOSH, M.A.B. SIDDIQUE and R. GABBAY

India occupies a unique position in the Indian Ocean region. Like Australia and South Africa, India is a major regional power, with its GDP exceeding that of Australia, and yet it is one of the poorest countries of the region in terms of the per capita income. Moreover, India faces a critical population problem, both in terms of its current size (in excess of 1 billion) and its annual growth rate (in excess of 1.8 per cent). Nevertheless, India has a great potential for rapid growth in the foreseeable future, as its economy is being forced from governmental intervention and control. Liberalisation and economic reforms, which started in 1991 — although the impetus of the change seems to have come to a halt in more recent years — have now created an environment for potentially dramatic economic growth. India currently enjoys a large reservoir of scientific and technological manpower that has already let to exponential growth in the country's software industries.

If India is successful in achieving rapid economic growth, then it will have considerable impact upon her neighbours in the Indian Ocean region, in particular on South Africa and Australia. Although China is not an Indian Ocean country, its sheer size and rapid industrialisation since the 1980s, are almost certain to have implications for regional development.

The selected essays included in this volume look at India's

emergence as a major power in the context of globalisation. Some of the essays deal with the problems of environmental degradation, gender issues and regional disparities as a result of rapid industrialisation in India and China, and the possibilities of future trade and economic co-operation between India and Australia, on the one hand, and South Africa and Australia, on the other.

In a critical essay, K.C. Roy examines the factors affecting India's emergence as a global power. He compares India's performance with those of other South-East Asian countries in terms of human development indicators. He argues that rural development to remove rural-urban disparities an improvement of the status of women, particularly those who live in rural areas, would hold the key to India's future economic development. Of the major issues affecting Indian women, the issue of property rights has a significant impact on the status of women. Although Indian women seem to have adequate legal rights, these rights are seldom exercised because of the dominance of age-old traditions and customary rights, which tend to condemn women to an inferior status. K.C. Roy critically examines the various inadequacies in the Government of India's rural development policy and then argues that an overall of policy is needed to maintain economic development in India.

In a stimulating paper, Lawson Smith discusses gender issues in relation to certain norms and bargaining in rural India. In rural India, social relations are constrained in an overly rigid, obsolete social system of production that both (1) retards economic growth and (2) purposelessly exacts untold in services and injustices against women, reducing the level of their normal human development and freedom. Lawson Smith endeavours to achieve some insights into gender related bargaining processes in rural India. He argues that a curious juxtaposition of legally prescribed rules and social norm-based activities subject rural women in India to adverse institutional hurdles.

Anita Medhekar-Smith's paper on "Environmental Degradation, Population and Poverty in India" logically follows Lawson Smith's essay on gender issues. Anita Medhekar-Smith examines some aspects of the interrelationship between poverty, population growth and environmental degradation with reference to the Indian experience. Seventy per cent of India's over one billion population live in the rural areas, and the vast majority of them derive a meagre living from the subsistence type of agriculture. Environmental degradation has occurred in India owing to the combined effects of population growth, rural poverty, inappropriate agricultural resource management and technological practices, as well as the failure of the Government's rural development policies. The slow growth of non-agricultural employment has failed to relieve the population pressure on land, thereby leading to land degradation and deforestation. There has also been increasing statisation and privatisation of what were common property resources available to the rural poor. There has also been a failure of the Central and State governments, because of a combination of neglect, misadministration and corruption combined with ineptitude to implement policies that are necessary to curb environmentally degradation.

In a major paper, Rosita Dellios considers the roles of China and India as new *mandalas* of power in 21st Century geopolitics. China and India are two of the World's most populous countries, accounting between them for a third of global population. Yet neither China nor India is regarded as a global power, capable of influencing the international balance of power, despite both being nuclear armed.

However, Chinese military ambition, the strength of Chinese culture, rapid industrialisation and the much touted market of over a billion people, seem to have captivated the global imagination. By comparison, India has not commanded international influence by virtue of being the world's biggest democracy or having a strong compute software industry.

In brief, China is perhaps somewhat feared as having the potential to create instability, but India is not feared enough, despite her nuclear capacity. In her paper, Rosita Dellios uses the concept of *mandalas* or schemas to explore the possibilities for China and India in influencing geopolitics in this Century. A *mandala* — meaning a circle in Sanskrit — was used in the Indian political tradition by Kautilya. She argues that it is possible that both China and India would be able to facilitate the integration of the world into the 21st Century's diverse globalisation.

R. James Ferguson's paper, which follows Rosita Dellios's paper as Chapter 6 in this volume is entitled "India, Multipolarity and Contested Globalisation". Like Rosita Dellios, R. James Ferguson argues that in the current world stage, India suffers from a serious image problems. India's position in world affairs is often presented as that of a 'potential' greater power which remains troubled by internal and regional problems. Despite India's increasing engagement in international financial agencies and WTO processes, public opinion in India remains critical of the American dominated push for globalisation and free trade.

In his provocative paper, R. James Ferguson argues that the external image of India has the risk of stereotyping India as a late comer to the ruling club dominated by developed countries. And yet India can make unique contributions to regional and global developments, particularly in international relations. This can be achieved, according to the author by focusing on the concept of multipolarity. In the past, India has consistently refused to accept a unipolar, or a bipolar world system. Like India, China, France and Russia — among other countries — have argued that several major centres of power need to be recognised on a global basis. On such view, the possibility of hegemonic dominance or preponderance of power by one, or two countries can be avoided. While it is possible to recognise the dangers of multipolarity, including the possibility of conflict and alliance politics among the key powers (now expressed through ideas of 'strategic partnerships' and 'special relationships'), it is also possible to envisage the advantages of a constructive and co-operative multipolarity.

Furthermore, 'multipolarity' can be re-interpreted to indicate different phases of activity that move beyond the tradition 'poles' of military, economic and diplomatic power. On this basis there are a large number of poles of activity that can allow a civilizing and humanising engagement of the forces of globalisation. R. James Ferguson forcefully argues that India can make a conscious use of its cultural and religious diversity (countering many current images created in the Western media), the development and utilization of its scientific, legal and educational infrastructure, and the extension of key concepts such as the principle of non-reciprocity as embodied in the Gujral doctrine. Should India be able to effectively pursue such policy, according to James Ferguson, India will be able not only to extend her international prestige, but also to break out of debilitating geo-political tensions with China, as well as gaining a better normative balance with nations such as the United States of America.

Dhulasi Birundha Varadarajan's paper on "Environmental Globalisation — South-North Relationship" does not specifically deal with any country. But she examines the broad question of what may be called 'environmental globalisation'. Our planet is comparatively small in relation to the size of the human population inhabiting it and the ever-increasing demand for higher standard of living from virtually every person from every part of the world. Long-term sustainable development and inter-generational as well as inter-spatial equity could be achieved only if the present generation was totally committed to avoiding, or at least reducing environmental degradation in terms of both the rapid depletion of the national resources and the pollution of the oceans, waterways and the atmosphere.

Whilst the third world countries are currently tyring to achieve a better standard of living and higher levels of GDP in order to overcome the vicious circle of low income, low savings, low investment and poverty, the richer countries, having already achieved a very high material standard for their population, are still continuing to seek for further development and growth. Such activity from both developed and developing countries lies at the root of our present ecological and environmental crisis.

Problems of Greenhouse gas effect and disposal of toxic wastes — to mention only two of the key environmental issues — cannot be resolved without co-operation between North and South and a constant dialogue between rich and poor countries. The reluctance of the USA to ratify the Kyoto Protocol is a stark example of the rich countries are not prepared to accept their responsibility to reduce Greenhouse gas emissions. In her very interesting paper, Varadarajan examines the various issues involved in what may be called 'environmental globalism'.

M.A.B. Siddique's paper deals with "Some Aspects of Trade Relations between Australia and India". During the past two decades, the direction of Australia's exports had been slowly moving away from the traditional markets of Japan, the U.K. and the U.S.A. to China, South-East Asia and South Asia. Within South Asia, India has now emerged as a major market for Australian exports. In 2001 India was Australia's 15th largest export market, up from 24th in 1980. Bilateral trade with India reached A$3.261 in 2001 (with Australian exports valued at A$2.423 billion and imports at A$0.808 billion). Generally speaking, Australia has over the years enjoyed a significantly favourable balance of trade with India, although the main factor contributing to Australia's favourable balance has been the export of one item, *i.e.*, cooking coal. Indian coal is generally of poor quality, because of its high ash content, so India has to import Coke from Australia.

Australian exports to India increased by 30 per cent between 2000 and 2001. As stated earlier, Australia's largest export to India in 2001 was coal (A$963 million), non-monetary gold and fresh vegetables (A$166 million each) and cotton (A$157 million).

The value of imports from India increased from A$732 million in 2000 to A$808 million in 2001. The largest import item was pearls and gems (A$51 million), followed by textile manufactures (A$50 million), crustaceans (A$40 million), refined petroleum (A$37 million), and footwear and floor coverings (A$24 million each).

The main purpose of Siddique's paper is to examine the patterns and trends of trade between Australia and India during the period 1980-2000, with special emphasis on the possibilities of improving Australia's export performance in India. Siddique has collected a number of statistical tables to highlight some significant aspects of Indo-Australian trade relations, and his paper ends with a brief discussion of the future prospects of bilateral trade between India and Australia — two of the major players in the Indian Ocean region.

The final paper included in this volume on "South Africa and Australia: Possibilities of Economic Co-operation" by R.N. Ghosh and M.A.B. Siddique is the longest paper, which comprehensively discusses how the growing trade, investment and commercial links between these two economics giants of the Indian Ocean region might have a spin-off effect for the region as a whole.

Since the end of the apartheid years, the relationship between Australia and South Africa has improved dramatically. The value of Australian total merchandise exports to South Africa has been increasing at an average of 35 per cent per annum. Investment flows between the two countries have also increased substantially. The first Australia-South Africa Joint Ministerial Commission meeting was held in Pretoria in July 1977. Earlier (December 1996), a Parliamentary Joint Select Committee in Australia published a report dealing with Australia and Southern Africa.

Australia and South Africa have a similar economic structure. They produce and export similar goods and services. Both economies are resource based and have good infrastructures such as roads and railways, and telecommunications. Yet the two countries do not appear to be competitors on the international markets, because their exports tend to be to different geographical areas. There are of course exceptions, such as exports of iron ore to Japan.

It is possible that Australia and South Africa can co-operate in a number of areas. For example, Australia can act as a gateway for South Africa so as to establish joint ventures in Southeast Asia. Similarly, Australia can use the South African experience in Southern African Development Community (SADC) to establish joint ventures in the countries of southern Africa. Two-way exports of manufactured goods between Australia and South Africa also have good prospects. Already by 1994 manufactured goods constituted about 31 per cent of Australian total exports to South Africa. During the same year, manufactured goods made up about 45 per cent of Australia's imports from South Africa.

Estimation of the Revealed Comparative Advantage Index (RCAI) indicates that Australia has relatively high comparative advantage in a number of commodity groups such as crude materials, non-ferrous metals, food and live animals, beverages and tobacco, and mineral fuels. Similarly, RCAI for South Africa indicates that it has relatively high comparative advantage in iron and steel, crude materials and non-ferrous metals. Thus, Australia and South Africa can possibly develop a common marketing strategy (without violating the WTO regulations) in which these two countries have relatively high comparative advantages.

There also exists significant scope for co-operation between Australia and South Africa in the areas of infrastructure projects, tourism, direct investment and joint ventures, health and education, housing, and the transfer of technology.

Development assistance by the Australian government should be aimed at improving manpower resources in South Africa. There is a shortage of skilled labour in South Africa in some areas and this problem will intensify in future with the expansion of economic activities. The achievement of socio-economic objectives documented in the Reconstruction and Development Programme (RDP) and Growth, Employment and Redistribution (GEAR) documents will require the South African economy to grow at about 10 per cent per annum. Such a high growth rate, if achieved, would create additional demand for skilled labour. Careful manpower planning is needed to resolve the anticipated skill shortages in South Africa.

At present, the quality of health and education of a large section of the South African population falls well short of international standards. Policies to improve the standard of housing and health will put enormous pressure on the limited resources of the South African government. Part of the Australian aid may be directed in these areas. For example, many South African blacks do not have the necessary education and skills for economically meaningful employment. Provision of training and education would be an imperative task for the South African government, and Australia has the necessary expertise to assist South Africa in this respect.

Currently, the level of co-operation in education between South Africa and Australia is very limited. Australian academic institutions are just stepping into South Africa. Comprehensive research is needed to understand the complex need for different levels of education in South Africa; and AusAID could play an important role in this respect.

Both Australia and South Africa are likely to significantly gain from economic co-operation. Such economic gains would not remain limited to these two countries, but would spread over the other countries in the Indian Ocean region.

The focus of the essays included in this volume has been on India. Some of the major developmental issues currently discussed and debated in the economic literature such as globalisation, environment, gender and regional development, have all been primarily examined from Indian perspective. These essays have been carefully selected to cover a broad spectrum of both economic and non-economic factors which would tend to have a bearing on economic growth.

Although India had been the focus of this volume, the broader issues such as globalisation and ecology have not been neglected in so far as these have an impact on the Indian Ocean region as a whole, which is somewhat loosely defined in this volume.

The pursuit of the twin goals of economic growth and development has been the main thrust of economic and political agenda in the West since the emergence of Mercantilism in the sixteenth century. The global domination by the West during the colonial era has let to a percolation of the Western economic growth ideology into the political agenda of the newly independent countries in Africa and Asia, in particular, and other countries generally.

Narrowly defined, economic growth refers to an increase of GDP, followed by an increase of *per capita* real income. A continuing economic growth over a longer-term, spanning over several years, would lead to economic development, which is defined to mean for a given population better education, better access to health care, greater urbanisation and industrial development, longer human life expectation, and, more importantly, a more equitable distribution of income and wealth in terms of the triple criteria of inter-class, inter-temporal and inter-spatial distribution. In the final analysis, economic development is expected to raise not only the material standards of living but also the quality of human life ultimately.

It has been argued in the West that poverty, specially appalling poverty, does not prevent human breeding but destroys the quality of life. A positive correlation between material prosperity and human happiness has all along been assumed in the West since the growth of Benthamism and utilitarianism. The Classical Economists used the utilitarian principle to argue that economic growth would reduce poverty and increase economic and social welfare. Furthermore, they believe that the best policy for achieving growth was to reduce government intervention and allow the free market forces to maximise GDP through competition and the profit incentive. Today's globalism as an ideology has its roots in Classical Economics, in so far as it supports free trade, free movement of capital and investment and the withdrawal of restrictive national economic policies.

J.S. Mill was perhaps the first philosopher-come-economist, who (although a passionate believer in individualism and freedom) opposed the goals of a competitive and free enterprise society that seeks to achieve an ever increasing level of GDP through industrialisation and other economic activities. A passage from J.S. Mill's *Principles of Political Economy*, written over 150 years ago is worth quoting at length:

> "it must always have been seen.... That the increases of wealth is not boundless: That at the end of ... the progressive state lies the stationary state, that all progress in wealth is but a postponement of this, and that each step in advance is an approach to it.... I cannot, therefore, regard the stationary state of capital and wealth with the unaffected aversions so generally manifested towards it by political economists of the old school. I am inclined to believe that it would be, on the whole, a very considerable improvement on our present condition. I confess I am not charmed with the ideal of life held out by those who think that the normal state of human beings is that of struggling to get on; that

the trampling, crushing, elbowing, and treading on each other's heels, which form the existing type of social life, are the most desirable lot of human kind, or anything but the disagreeable symptoms of one of the phases of industrial progress."

In more recent years, the goal of free trade free markets and free competition has been relentlessly pushed by the U.S.A., on the one hand, and by the various international funding agencies such as the IMF and the World Bank, and by the World Trading Organisation (WTO). Such policy of globalisation and economic reforms has led to misgivings among many developing countries.

There is the view that the ideology of globalisation, translated into practices, would tend to accentuate the exiting inequalities between rich and poor countries, and that the push for a world-wide economic growth by way of the transfer of the Western industrial mining and farming technology might lend to environmental and ecological crises in many parts of the globe.

WORKS CITED

Drysdale, Peter and David Vines, *Europe, East Asia and APEC: A Shared Global Agenda,* Cambridge University Press, 1998.

Ghosh, R.N. and M.A.B. Siddique, "Some Apsects of Indo-Australian Economic Relations" in *External Powers in the International Relations of the Southern Hemisphere: Political, Military and Economic Dimensions,* edited by R. Gabbay, R. Ghosh and A. Siddique, CMDS, The University of Western Australia, September 1996.

Meadows, Denis, *The Limits of Growth,* Potomac Associates, 1972. www.dfat.gov.au/publications.statistics.html

Mill, J.S., *Principles of Political Economy* (Edited by Donal Winch), Penguin Books, 1970.

Mishan, E.J., *The Costs of Economic Growth.*

SCEP, *Mans Impact on the Global Environment,* M.I.T. Press, 1971 *Australia-India Focus,* Issue 23, March 2002, AIBC, ACT, 2604.

2

Factors Affecting India's Emergence as a Global Power: Women and the Rural Sector in Development

K.C. ROY

SETTING THE SCENE

Some of the countries which have gained the status of global powers are very strong militarily. But their military strength has been contingent on their economic strength. Although countries such as Japan and Germany are only global economic powers, they nevertheless have the capacity to achieve the status of global military powers. In other words, without economic power a country cannot sustain the expenditure necessary to maintain its military strength. But a large developing country cannot attain that economic power unless it achieves a high growth rate consistently over a considerable period of time and places stronger emphasis on human development issues such as education, health, women's welfare etc. and on the rural sector. Poverty is more pervasive in the rural sector than in the urban sector. To reduce the level of rural poverty, attention must be paid to agricultural development. Thus, to maintain a consistently high rate of growth, a country needs to place strong emphasis on the growth of agriculture along with industry and on neglected aspects of human capital. Agriculture provides food to the population and raw materials to the industries. Since the rural sector accommodates the vast majority of the country's population, increase in income in the rural sector generates strong domestic demand for manufactured goods.

The rural sector generates the necessary surplus which can be used for industrial development.

Taiwan achieved a measured annual economic growth rate averaging close to 8 per cent over more than four decades. It grew nearly 10 per cent annually in the widely used bench mark 1965-80 period, higher than any other reported figure. Taiwan was able to record such high growth status due, among other things, to strong emphasis on human development, agriculture and small-scale labour intensive industries located in the rural sector alongside agricultural fields. Land reform which was key to the rural sector's development turned the rural sector into a landholder economy. These were accompanied by well defined property rights.

South Korea followed the same route to development and achieved the status of a developed economy in 1996.

INDIA'S SCENARIO

According to our estimate, India's population which reached 1 billion in May 2000 will increase to 1.02 billion in May 2000. Of this population of 1 billion, 52 per cent or 520 million are males and 48 per cent or 480 million are females. Of the total 1 billion population, 73 per cent or 730 million live in rural areas. Also, roughly about 350.4 million of these 730 million are women. Hence, for India to achieve the status of a global power, it must improve the socio-economic condition in the rural sector. The rural people are poorer than urban people and among the rural population females are poorer than males. Among the total rural population of 730 million, 24.33 per cent or 177.6 million belong to scheduled castes and scheduled tribes. Of these roughly about 85.2 million are females; they are the poorest of the poor in India. Although agriculture accounts for only 25 per cent of GDP, it absorbs 64 per cent of the country's labour force.

POVERTY LEVEL

According to a 1993-94 estimate (GOI 1999), the total population below the poverty line was 320 million. Of these 76 million were in the urban areas and 244 million in the rural areas. In percentage terms, while 32 per cent of the total population were below the poverty line, 23.7 per cent were in the urban areas and 76.3 per cent were in the rural areas. The table 1 illustrates this incidence of poverty and growth rates in India and selected Asian countries.

TABLE 1

Poverty Incidence and Growth Rates in India and Selected Asian Countries (in per cent)

Country	Poverty Ratio 1975	Poverty Ratio 1995	Average GDP Growth 1970-1980	Average GDP Growth 1980-1985
India	54.9	36.0	3.2	5.6
China	59.5	22.2	5.0	11.1
Indonesia	64.3	11.4	7.8	6.6
S. Korea	23.0	5.0	9.0	8.7
Malaysia	17.4	4.3	7.8	6.4
Philippines	35.7	25.5	6.2	1.4
Thailand	8.1	0.9	7.2	7.9

Source: Government of India (1999), Economic Survey 1998-99, New Delhi & Government of India.

It can be seen from the table 1 that in comparison to India, faster economic growth in most of the East Asian countries has contributed to a rapid decline in poverty ratio. China's phenomenal growth of more than 11 per cent for 15 years up to 1995, brought the poverty level down to only 22.2 per cent in 1995 from a high of 59.5 per cent in 1975.

Thailand virtually eliminated poverty by recording a growth rate of more than 7 per cent during a 25-year period. It is, therefore, reasonable to expect that a sustained and long lasting solution to the problem depends on the creation of opportunities for broad-based economic development and higher growth.

In comparison with most other East Asian countries, lower growth in India also has meant lower gains in the most commonly used human development indicators. These are illustrated in table 2.

TABLE 2

Indicators of Human Development of Selected Asian Countries (1997)

Countries	Life expectancy (years) at birth		Infant mortality rate (per 1000 live births)	Adult illiteracy rate (% of people 15 years and above)		Prevalence of child malnutrition (% of children under age 5)
	Male	Female		Male	Female	
India	63	67	71	33	61	53
China	68	71	32	9	25	16
Indonesia	63	67	47	9	20	34
S. Korea	69	76	9	1	4	—
Malaysia	70	75	11	10	19	20
Philippines	60	70	35	5	6	30
Thailand	66	72	33	3	7	—

Source: World Bank (1999), World Development Report 1999-2000, New York: Oxford University Press.

As table 2 shows, the infant mortality rate and prevalence of child malnutrition are higher in India than in other countries listed in the table. Also the adult illiteracy rate in India is significantly higher than in all of the other countries. In India still 61 per cent of females (most of whom live in rural areas) are illiterate compared with only 4 per cent in Korea, 6 per cent in Philippines and 7 per cent in Thailand. A.K. Sen (1997) commented that the most glaring example of failure of successive governments in India had been in the field of primary education, basic health services and land reform. All these had a direct bearing on the economic growth of the country. The empowerment of women was equally a relevant factor in the country's economic growth as it had a direct bearing on education and child nourishment. It was depressing that India would be entering the 21st century with almost 50 per cent of its population still illiterate.

Table 3 illustrates the central government expenditure on human development in total central government expenditure in China, India, South Korea and Thailand. Very strong emphasis on education has been the single most important factor which has contributed to the growth and development of South Korea, Taiwan and Thailand. Central governments' expenditure is an important indicator of the emphasis these countries place on human development.

TABLE 3

Share of Central Government Expenditure on Human Development in Total Central Government Expenditure (in %)

	China				India				South Korea				Thailand			
	Education	Health	Social Security	Total of three	Education	Health	Social Security	Total of three	Education	Health	Social Security	Total of three	Education	Health	Social Security	Total of three
1980																
1981					1.86	1.98	NA	3.84	19.94	1.31	5.96	27.21	18.84	4.17	2.52	25.58
1982																
1983					1.88	2.41	NA	4.29	20.48	1.62	5.15	27.25	20.29	5.01	3.07	28.37
1984																
1985					1.86	2.11	NA	3.97	18.43	1.43	5.65	25.51	19.53	5.69	2.97	28.19
1986																
1987					2.60	1.86	NA	4.46	18.34	2.34	6.43	27.11	19.29	6.08	3.36	28.73
1988																
1989					2.66	1.73	NA	4.39	18.54	2.01	8.33	28.88	19.33	6.27	3.42	29.02
1990	2.14	0.40	0.07	2.61												
1991	2.18	0.40	0.09	2.67	2.20	1.58	NA	3.78	15.76	2.79	13.19	31.74	20.19	7.36	3.54	31.09
1992	2.60	0.38	0.07	3.05												
1993	2.76	0.41	0.05	3.22	1.81	1.70	NA	3.51	21.43	0.95	9.99	32.37	21.77	6.94	3.44	32.15
1994	1.82	0.26	0.14	3.22												
1995	1.64	0.25	0.02	1.91	2.14	1.56	NA	3.70	20.46	0.65	8.70	29.81	21.92	7.96	3.50	32.88
1996	2.07	0.24	0.15	2.46												
1997	2.03	0.23	0.15	2.41	2.26	1.43	NA	3.69	20.50	0.77	10.79	32.06	21.61	8.57	3.74	33.94
1998																

Source: IMF (1990-1999) Government Finance Statistics, Year Book 1990, 1999, Washington D.C.: IMF.

It can be seen from table 3 that in both China and India a very small proportion of central government expenditure has been spent on education, health, social security and welfare. In India the government did not spend anything on social security and welfare. But the total expenditure on education and health in India did not even reach 5 per cent of total central government expenditure. China's record is worse than that of India. In comparison to such meagre expenditure by the two giants of Asia, the total expenditure on these three items as a proportion of central government expenditure has been consistently higher than 25 per cent in both South Korea and Thailand.

Thus, to attain the status of a world power, India needs to do a great deal more in the areas of human development, women's empowerment, agriculture and rural development including land reform and property rights.

DIRECTION OF INDIA'S DEVELOPMENT: GANDHI-NEHRU CONTROVERSY

The essence of the plan that Gandhi prepared for India to adopt after India's independence is as follows (Roy 1986; Roy and Tisdell 1992): Since the vast majority of India's population are poor and live in rural areas, the development of agriculture, rural sector and small-scale labour-intensive industries are the key to the success of India's development efforts. Agriculture and cottage industries must exist side by side to allow the rural worker the opportunity to work for 12 months a year. If the planning is decentralised and the decaying rump economy is revitalised, then the rural sector could provide adequate food, clothing, housing and employment to the growing population. However, Nehru rejected the Gandhian plan and adopted centralisation and large-scale industrial development of the Soviet type by neglecting agriculture, rural sector and small-scale industry in India's planned development which began in 1951. As subsequent events proved, this mistake of Nehru significantly undermined India's capacity to achieve high rates of economic growth over a long period of time thereby affecting India's prospects of becoming a strong economic power.

Nehru, in shaping India's socialist policy and national planning, was greatly influenced by Fabian ideas which emanated from the traditions of English utilitarianism, empiricism and classical thought. Fabian reformism was adopted in the political sphere in the form of a parliamentary democracy.

Nevertheless, it was rooted in Nehru's mind that the greatest good of the greatest number can be achieved only by expanding the role of the public sector, by imposing state control over the means of production and by concentrating production in large-scale industries. By accepting such a process of development, he was implicitly assuming that the income of the poor could be increased this way.

The neglect of the rural sector and agriculture in Nehru's development policy also led to the neglect of the vast majority of rural women whose lives are intimately connected with agriculture.

RELEVANT ISSUES AFFECTING WOMEN'S SOCIO-ECONOMIC STATUS

There are a number of issues relevant to the socio-economic status of rural women in most third world countries. Poor rural women are the major providers of sustenance to their families. Their contributions are not duly rewarded by the society and the government. A number of institutional deterrents impede women's progress towards economic independence and empowerment. Since women spend long hours in household duties, they have less time available to spend on farms and on non-farm activities. Hence, if it is possible to reduce women's time on household tasks, then that time could be spent on income generating activities. Women's access to income is more likely to pay welfare dividends for the community at large (especially for children) than men's incomes. The advantage of targeting women for achieving development goals is that women's productivity and potential for income-generation may be raised with minimum capital outlays (Kandiyoti 1992). Reducing labour times of women on household work does not mean doing away with these jobs. It means doing the same work in a less time-consuming way. The income generating activities also include upgrading those areas in which women are already involved and those newly created opportunities in small scale rural industries such as fruit canning, soap making, textiles, brick making etc.

Increase in women's direct control over resources including cash income is necessary to enhance the immediate welfare of families as well as the health and nutrition status of their children. There is evidence which suggests that the same improvements in welfare may not take place with increase in males' income as considerable part of males' income is usually spent on personal habits, domestic goods and leisure (Roy and Tisdell 1993 a, b; Roy and Tisdell 1996; Hanger and Morris 1973; Palmer 1977; Young 1978).

In Punjab province in India, an average household with a heavy drinker is found to spend 40 per cent less on food per capita and less on clothing, education and medicine as well, than a non-drinker household (Deb 1977 cited in Hariss 1986). A group of women involved in an anti alcoholism campaign in Himachal Pradesh commented:

> "Our men go to market to sell vegetables or spend their days working on the roads but what do we ever see of the money? It all goes on liquor before they reach home in the evening. When they do come back drunk, they beat the children and then complain that there is no food for the evening meal. Where can we get food if there is no money in the house?" (Mahendrapurkar 1987)

This type of situation is also found among women with husbands who regularly migrate to other places to obtain work and among female heads of households who receive very little support from male folks.

In India, although about 10 per cent of all households comprise widowed, divorced, deserted or separated, the estimates of *de facto* female heads which also includes those whose husbands have outmigrated or are invalids appear to be about 8 per cent or more (Agarwal 1989). Region specific studies indicate that the female headed households constitute the highest percentage of the bottom-most income decile of rural households — the poorest of the poor (Viasaria and Viasaria 1985; Parthasarathy 1983).

It is, therefore, important to recognise that women of poor households whether male- or female-headed bear a significant responsibility for family is subsistence. However, the fulfilment of this responsibility is strongly constrained not only by the unequal sharing of the household resources, but also by their unequal access to earning opportunities and to agricultural lands and by the decline in common property and forests. As a response to these problems faced by women, there has also been a shift in policy discussion from an equity oriented approach in matters of assistance to women which stressed the widening gap created by development policies to a poverty oriented approach, which documents the importance of raising the productivity and income of the poor women as a more general growth and poverty alleviation strategy (Kandiyoti 1992). In other words, the implication is that the removal of difficulties faced by women due to unequal sharing of household resources, unequal access to earning opportunities and to agricultural land would reduce poverty and promote growth. Any type of policy measures undertaken to improve women's economic condition should include measures (i) to protect women's existing sources of livelihood; (ii) to eliminate discriminatory legislation in the ownership and control of productive assets; (iii) to ensure equitable access to agricultural inputs, credits, extension services and education; (iv) to provide support of extra household forms of organisation of women's labour; and (v) to provide encouragement for enhancing capacity for political empowerment and organisation (Kandiyoti 1992).

Some Comments

It would not always be easy to protect women's existing sources of livelihood. When a simple and labour-intensive technology which is suited for women is replaced by a complex and labour-saving technology with a larger production scale suitable for men, the women previously employed under old technology become unemployed. In this situation, alternative provision of employment is necessary to protect their livelihood, or a better technology also suitable for women for the same employment needs to be developed.

In the 1950s and 1960s in West Bengal and Orissa in India, and in East Pakistan (currently Bangladesh), in rural areas, a *dheki* was used for husking rice. Two to three women were required to operate a *dheki*. But in the 1960s *dhekis* began to be replaced by rice husking machines which have a much larger production scale and each machine requires one labourer. It is almost universally operated by a male labourer. One such machine can satisfy the rice husking needs of several villages. As a result, the *dhekis* from each village and the women employed in these became redundant. In this situation, to protect women's livelihood, a better technology suitable for women's use should have been developed. For this to happen there is the need for the development of technology suitable for women. The relevant ministry, planning commission and research institutes which have the responsibility of designing technology for women still seem to be oblivious of women's needs.

Adequate access of women to agricultural inputs, credit and services are limited (Ashby 1981; Staudt 1975/76; Berger and De Lancy 1984; Agarwal 1989; Roy and Tisdell 1993a; Roy 1994). Obtaining inputs, credit and services on easy terms is more difficult for women than for men because apart from working in the field women are also engaged in reproductive work and other household duties. Therefore women's productive capacity cannot be increased unless we can reduce the burden of their household duties and responsibilities. Tribal women in hilly areas in India during summer time spend long hours at night in fetching water from distant river beds, thus they work during the day and night almost without any sleep (Roy and Tisdell 1993b). Thus it is suggested that there is the need for extra-supra-familial institutions to organise rural women's productive activities. Organisations such as women's only cooperatives are examples. But there are only a few such organisations currently operating in India and the vast areas of rural hinterland of India are still untouched by such organisations.

To strengthen women's rights of appropriation over resources and access to services what is necessary is a certain measure of political empowerment which enables them to participate in political organisations and pressure groups. One of the important indicators of political empowerment in India is the representation of females in federal parliament, state legislatures and in local self-governments viz., *Anchal Panchayat* and village *Panchayat*. However, although the issue of reservation of seats for women was discussed in the federal Parliament, it was not accepted. At the village level, there are female representatives in some *Anchal* and village *Panchayats*. But from one field survey in three villages in West Bengal we found that these *Panchayats* are dominated by male members and one or two female members cannot exercise any influence on the decision-making process in *Panchayats* (Tisdell and Roy 2000).

Finally, women have very limited access to land and other properties. Legal and customary bottlenecks to women's access to property need to be removed. Land reform can improve women's legal access to land but not the customary access which in rural India is more important than legal right. In a field survey of four villages in West Bengal, the present author found that out of 116 families in 108 of them (or 93% of the total), land titles were held by male members (Roy 1999).

While all the issues raised here are important, the issue of property right assumes crucial importance because the ownership of property strengthens women's economic independence, social status, and improves children's and overall family's welfare. Since the majority of the country's population live in rural areas, improvement in the status of rural women enhances the growth and welfare of the country as a whole.

Property Rights: Legal Rights

For direct access to income, land rights are extremely important. While the creation of other employment opportunities is also necessary for women's access to income, land is a permanent asset and therefore acts as a permanent security against poverty and in cases of divorce, desertion, separation, or widowhood (Agarwal 1984). Furthermore, the women can use a plot of land for many activities such as growing crops, fodder, trees, keeping livestock, practising permaculture or using it as a collateral to obtain loans from the banks (Agarwal 1994). In well-off households it is important for women to have land rights particularly after a marital breakdown. Thus it would seem that even if the plot of land given to a woman is small, on welfare grounds women need to be given land rights.

In rural India while women cultivate land, the land titles are mostly held by men. Outmigration of male labourers to work as hired labour during planting and harvesting seasons forces women to cultivate the family land and act as *de facto* heads. Tribal women cultivate communal land but do not have land titles. Efficient cultivation of land require adequate access to technology, information on productivity increasing agricultural practices and inputs. These are not easily available to women due to bias in the delivery of those (Dasgupta 1977, Byres 1972, Agarwal 1985). Hence on efficiency grounds women deserve land titles.

Furthermore, since the land use patterns of men are more destructive of nature than that of women who are directly concerned with the protection and regeneration of forest for fuel, fodder and other non-timber forest produce, land in women's name will lead to the greater preservation of ecology and environment (Agarwal 1991).

On the efficiency and equity ground, it is also necessary to grant land titles to women. Since gender equity is necessary to achieve social justice, the progress towards gender equity can be facilitated by the granting of land titles to women. The demand for women's land rights is justified as it provides them with economic security and respectability in their marital relations. In absence of land rights, women can sometimes be beaten up and badly treated by their husbands (Manimala 1983). Agarwal (1994) noted that widows with land living with their adult sons were treated with much greater respect and consideration than those without land. While within the family, land titles help women attain equality in status with their husbands, outside their homes, their relationship with the rest of the society also improves (Mises et al. 1986). Land titles also may facilitate women's participation at the village government.

Customary Access to Land

As mentioned before, in India, land titles are held by male members although the property is jointly cultivated by both male and female members. However even if land titles are held by women, exercising these legal rights would require customary access right to land. In other words, for the legal right to be effective, it must not contravene customary or informal right. In rural India customary or informal right which appears to have a greater force than legal or formal right, prevents, in many cases, women from exercising their legal rights. In many cases, even where customary rights do not oppose legal rights, married women living with their husbands at some distance from their marital homes, give up their legal rights to land in favour of their brothers or their male kins for their support in future in times of their sickness, or other unforeseen contingencies. Even if a woman takes some legal actions to enable her to exercise her legal right to land, male members in her natal home may try to find loopholes in their existing legal system or to forge her father's will after his death with a view to preventing her from exercising her legal right (Parry 1979). They may even try to convince the revenue officer of her inability to exercise her legal right because she lives far away from her natal home (Mayer 1960). To force a woman to give up her legal right, her male kins may start expensive legal proceedings against her.

In Bihar there are instances when women have been beaten and even murdered under the false pretext of witchcraft to prevent them from exercising their rights to land (Kishwar 1987). In some rich patrilineal families, women do sometimes have legal rights to land but their effective control over the land was limited because the support of the local communities for the enforcement of such rights was absent. Agarwal (1989) in a study of 145 village communities across all regions of India found that in 131 (or 90.34 per cent of) communities, the land access pattern is patrilineal. Only in 10 communities matrilineal customs determine women's access to land and in only 1 community bilateral custom determines that. These two account for only 8 per cent of total communities. The study further found that only in 5 communities, daughters in son-less families and in 8 communities, wives or widows came into actual possession of land. These account for only 9 per cent of the total communities studied.

Other Difficulties

Even where legal and customary rights are not in conflict women may find it difficult to exercise their right to cultivate the land because of lack of finance to purchase the necessary imports, lack of information about the method of cultivation, and marketing of output etc. Such difficulties are compounded by the fact that being women their movements are also confined within the surroundings of their homes due to the ideology of seclusion. Although santal women are also bound, to some extent, by the ideology of seclusion, they are free to go to the market to purchase imports and to sell their outports. Even village moneylender does not want to lend money to women because men are perceived as having greater capability to repay the loan than women (Agarwal 1989, Roy and Tisdell 1993a).

Extension agents train the villagers in the use of all imports, however the number of villages to be covered by each extension agent is quite large. Hence these villages which are at a considerable distance from the Block Development Office and cannot be reached by normal means of transport usually are deprived of the benefits of extension agents. Most of the extension agents are male and they rarely talk to female cultivators in villages.

There is a particular taboo that women must not plough the land. The force of this taboo is very strong among all communities in all states in India. Among the oraon Tribals it is even believed that if a woman ploughs the field, the whole tribe would suffer from serious consequences (Dasgupta and Maity 1986.) As a result poor women cannot cultivate the land with the help of male labour. But male labourers prefer working for male heads. Hence, labour, plough and other agricultural inputs are not easily available to women, even if they have the financial capacity to obtain them mainly because, it is customary for the owners to supply their factor inputs to male cultivators and male heads first.

Thus even if legal right to cultivate the land exists for a rural woman, the absence of customary right would prevent a woman from exercising that legal right. Sometimes when the customary right does not contravene the legal right, the access to customary right may not be available. Thus, for example, although a woman's customary right to exercise legal right is recognised by the local community, being female, she may not be able to obtain labour, plough, seeds, water supply etc. at the right time of paddy or wheat planting. Again to plant and replant paddy at the right time, if a woman, due to the difficulty of hiring male labourers, decides to plough the land herself, she could be prevented by the village community from doing so because it is against the local custom for a woman to plough the land.

In West Bengal in some santal villages, after the death of the father all sons have the customary right to cultivate the land but the mother, if she is alive, decides which of the sons will have the customary access to customary right. This decision goes in favour of that son who takes care of the mother until her death.[1]

What has the State done?

The state policy for women's empowerment for a long time consisted of a series of stop-gap measure to tackle hunger and malnutrition etc. (Kandiyoti 1992). In the 1950s and 1960s, poor rural families including women were provided with temporary relief work in dry season for a few months during a year. The work consisted mostly of construction of roads, canals in rural areas. But the amount of money spent on such schemes was small and the families covered were few. In the late 1970s and early 1980s, the major schemes implemented for the empowerment of poor families including women were (a) Integrated Rural Development Programme (IRDP); (b) Development of Women and Children in Rural Areas (DOCWRA) and Training of Royal Youths for Employment (TRYSEM).

IRDP

The IRDP was launched in all the blocks in the country on 2 October, 1980 as a major credit linked self-employment

1. This information was obtained from interviews with several families in Piraekata area in Midnapore District in West Bengal during January 2000.

programme for poverty alleviation. The objective of the programme is to identify the rural poor families to argument their income and to cross the poverty line through acquisition of credit based productive assets which would provide self-employment on a sustainable basis. The target group of IRDP consists of families of small and marginal farmers, agricultural labourers and rural artisans whose annual income is below Rs. 11,000 per annum which was the poverty line income as determined in the eighth five year plan. While the credit under the programme is advanced by financial institutions such as commercial banks, co-operative and regional rural banks there is also an element of subsidy by the government. Although IRDP is a centrally sponsored scheme and expenditure is shared equally by the centre and the states, the programme is implemented through the District Rural Development Agency (DRDA).

Performance Evaluation

The IRDP scheme has been running for 20 years but its success does not appear to be impressive. In the early 1980s when the poverty line income was very low (Rs. 6400 per annum), about 54 per cent of total families covered were able to pass the poverty line. But as the poverty line income level continued to rise, the share of families in the total covered continued to fall. Thus this share declined from 54 per cent to 28 per cent in 1982 and from 28 per cent to 15.9 per cent in 1992-93 (Government of India 1999).

Furthermore, to ensure that large number of poor women not only became economically independent but also stay independent, the families covered under IRDP also were needed to be covered under DOCWRA and TRYSEM. As the Government of India Report (1998) notes, in the early 1980s, only 2.09 per cent of families assisted under the IRDP reported that they were assisted under DOCWRA and about 3.02 per cent, of the beneficiaries reported training under TRYSEM. However the question may be asked as to how many women were included in the total beneficiary list.

Unfortunately although 40 per cent was the target, the best result was somewhere around 34 per cent which was reached in 1998. In the total subsidy disbursed, the share of women was only 31 per cent. The share of women in the total credit was also 31 per cent. The Department of Rural Employment and Poverty Alleviation provided the following explanations for the failure to include more women in the beneficiary list:

(i) Women are unable to reap the benefits of the programme due to various social and economic reasons;

(ii) Women were not able to develop required skills to get the requisite Income Capital Output Ratio (ICOR); and

(iii) Agriculture and allied activities which women are predominantly engaged in do not have viable bankability.

These arguments are appalling and unacceptable. Women working in agriculture are landless labourers who would be willing to start any other activity at the very first opportunity. There's also a multi-tier system to monitor and co-ordinate the programme from the federal to the district levels. Naturally the whole process is not efficient.

DOCWRA

The DOCWRA, a sub-scheme of IRDP began in 1982-83 with the primary objective of focusing attention on the women members of rural families below poverty line with a view to providing them with opportunities for self-employment on a sustained basis. A distinguishing feature of DOCWRA is a group strategy as against a family or as a unit of assistance under IRDP. This group strategy was adopted to motivate the rural women to come together to break the forces of the "classic patriarchy" which had denied them income generating and self-fulfilling opportunities. Therefore, DOCWRA has been the single most important programme undertaken by the state exclusively for rural women's empowerment. Started initially on a pilot basis in 50 districts the programme has since been extended to all districts in the country.

Performance Evaluation

Although DOCWRA is the single most important programme for rural women's empowerment, its financial performance has been deteriorating in recent years. While the budgeted outlay remained at Rs. 650 million for three years since 1995-96, the actual expenditure has consistently been less than that. The gap between the budgeted and actual expenditure rose from Rs. 13.5 million in 1995-96 to Rs. 235.5 million in 1997-98. One reason for the shortfall is the non release of funds under second instalment by the relevant ministry as some states might not have released matching amounts against the federal assistance. Performance evaluation of the scheme in 48 districts in 12 states revealed various shortcomings such as inadequate staff, lukewarm attitude to convergence of services, poor use and knowledge of revolving funds, low profit margin from income generating activities, inadequate training and marketing facilities, lack and untimely release of funds etc.

Apart from these shortcomings, the other problem is the inadequacy of forward and backward linkages. Since IRDP, DOCWRA and TRYSEM programmes are implemented by the same department, if intelligent planning had been done by the department, then TRYSEM under which training is imparted to rural youths including women and IRDP would have provided the backward and forward linkages.

Another problem besetting DOCWRA is the lack of adequate marketing facilities for DOCWRA products. The success of the programme and the empowerment of participating women greatly depend on the creation of adequate marketing opportunities and facilities.

Finally the amount of time allocated for this scheme is extremely small when one considers the fact that today about 357 million women and female children live in rural areas of the country.

TRYSEM

It is the oldest of the rural development schemes which are being implemented. The scheme started in 1979 with an initial aim of providing basic technical and entrepreneurial skills to the rural youth below poverty line families to enable them to take up self-employment in the broad fields of agriculture and allied sectors. Subsequently the scope of the scheme was enlarged in 1983 to include taking up wage employment also by the trained youth. The scheme is implemented by the District Rural Development Agency (DRDA) and has a 40 per cent component earmarked for women.

Performance Evaluation

A number of deficiencies have been found in the operation of the scheme:

(i) More than 47 per cent of trainees under TRYSEM have remained unemployed after the training;

(ii) Only 21.5 per cent trainees were provided with tools and equipment instead of 100 per cent;

(iii) The duration of the training period was inadequate;

(iv) More than half of the trainees did not apply for loans under IRDP;

(v) Only 50 per cent of those applied were given loans; and

(vi) Almost 63 per cent of the beneficiaries felt there was no improvement in their socio-economic conditions due to TRYSEM.

Apart from these deficiencies, the other concern is that the total budget allocations since 1995 has remained static at Rs. 950 million, but the annual releases declined from Rs. 750 million in 1995-96 to Rs. 370 million in 1998-99. Similarly the number of youths trained also declined from 3 million in 1995-96 to 2.46 million in 1997-98.

Thus none of the three schemes implemented by the state for rural development and rural women's empowerment appears to have been successful. The Committee on the empowerment of women (GOI 1999) noted that rural women were not aware of the various development schemes launched by the government for their economic and social empowerment. The awareness level even in the rural areas and adjoining metropolitan cities were found to be very low. While the relevant ministries spent huge sums of money but nothing seems to have been done to make the beneficiaries aware of the schemes.

Concluding Remarks

Thus, it is clear from the analysis presented in this paper that in India's development policy, women and rural sectors occupy a place of minor importance. All those countries which placed strong emphasis in their development policies, on women and agricultural sector recorded rapid economic growth and development. In human development indicators, the records of the neighbouring South-East Asian countries are considerably better than that of India.

It is unthinkable that India can attain the status of a strong power without significantly improving the socio-economic condition of nearly 360 million women and female children living in rural India. As we have seen, land titles are mostly held by male members of families. Women certainly need property rights — legal and access rights etc. The state has made very little attempt to change the laws to grant land titles to women. All institutions — legal, political, economic and social are male dominated. These act against the interest of women. We have also seen that in the rural development policies implemented by the state the emphasis placed on women's socio-economic condition and on the rural sector has been very low. Although the growth of agriculture has been slow and the share of agriculture in the GDP has been declining, it still provides employment to the vast majority of rural population and food to 1 billion people. Attempts has been made to direct the state policy to helping women to develop group approach for obtaining loans, procuring inputs, producing goods and for selling them in the market. This is social dynamics. This social dynamics needs to be developed and spread to each village in the rural hinterland. This will help women also in their struggle for property rights. The famous Chipko movement developed from the group approach undertaken by women to protest against the action of the local councillor in a village in Uttar Pradesh in India. The States information network to make women aware of the opportunities available for their employment has not worked effectively. This needs to be improved greatly. Also, the state must undertake a massive programme of community education of adult members of rural families including women. This will raise their consciousness level and act to reduce the force of gender discrimination against women. Lack of emphasis in all these areas will affect India's emergence as a global power.

WORKS CITED

Agarwal, B. (1991), "Engendering the Environment Debate: Lessons from the Indian Sub-Continent", *CASID -- Distinguished Guest Speaker Series No. 8*, Michigan State University, USA.

—— (1994), A field of one's own; Gender and Land Rights in South Asia, Cambridge: Cambridge University Press.

—— (1989), "Rural Women, Poverty and Natural Resources", In *Economic and Political Weekly* 24 (43).

Agarwal, G. (1985), "Women and Technological Change in Agriculture: Asian and African Experience" in Ahmed, I. (Eds), *Technology and Rural Women: Conceptual and Empirical Issues*, London: George Allen and Unwin.

Ashby, J. (1981), "New Models for Agricultural Research Extension: The Need to Integrate Women", in Lewis, B. (Ed), *Invisible Farmers: Women and the crisis in Agriculture*, USAID Office of Women in Development, Washington, D.C.: ICRW, 1986.

Berger, M. and DeLancy, W. (1984), "Bridging the Gender Gap in Agricultural Extension". Report prepared for USAID, Office of Women in Development, Washington D.C.: ICRW, 1984.

Byres, T.J. (1972), "The Dialectics of India's Green Revolution", *South Asia Review*, London, 5 (2).

Dasgupta, S. and Maity, A.K. (1986), "The Rural Energy Crisis, Poverty and Women's Roles in Five Indian Villages", *World Empowerment Programme Technical Report*, Geneva: ILO.

Dasgupta, B. (1977), "Agrarian Change and the New Technology in India", *Report No. 77.2*, Geneva: United Nations Research Institute for Social Development.

Government of India (1999), "Economic Survey 1998-1999", New Delhi: Government of India.

Government of India, Lok Sabha Secretariat (1999), *First Report, Committee on Empowerment of Women*, New Delhi: Lok Sabha Secretariat.

Hanger, J. and Morris, J. (1973), "Women and the Household Economy" in Chambers, R. and Morris, J. (Eds), *Mewa: An Irrigated Rice Settlement in Kenya*, Munich: Welform Verlag.

Hariss, B. (1986), "The Intra-Family Distribution of Hunger in South Asia",

Paper prepared for WIDER project on Hunger and Poverty: Seminar on Food Shortages, Finland: Helsinki.

IMF (1990, 1999), Government Finance Statistics, Year Book, Washington D.C: IMF.

Kandiyoti (1992), "Women and Rural Development Policies: The Changing Agenda", Wilber, C.K. and Jameson, K.P. (Eds), *The Political Economy of Development and Underdevelopment*, Singapore: McGraw Hill.

Kishwar, M. (1987), "Toiling without Rights: Its Women of Birbhum", *Economic and Political Weekly*, January 17, 24, 31.

Mahendrapurkar, S. (1987), "It's About Changing our Lives: Himachali Women Organise", *Manushi*, No. 40.

Manimala (1983), "Zamen kenkar? Jote Onkar: Women's Participation in the Bodhgaya Land Struggle", *Manushi*, 14, January-February.

Mayer, A.C. (1960), *Caste and Kinship in Central India — Village and Its Reform*, London: Routledge and Vegan Paul.

Mises, M. (1986), "Indian Women in Subsistence and Agricultural Labour", Geneva: ILO.

Palmer, I. (1997), "Rural Women and the Basic Needs Approach to Development", *International Labour Review* 115 (1).

Parry, J.P. (1979), *Caste and Kinship in Kangra*, New Delhi: Vikas.

Parthasarathi, G. and Rama Rao (1973), "Employment and Unemployment Among Rural Labour Households", *Economic and Political Weekly* 7 (52).

Roy, K.C. (1994), "Neglected Issues in Technological Change and Rural Development" in Roy, K.C. and Clark, C. (Eds), *Technological Change and Rural Development in Poor Countries: Neglected Issues*, New Delhi: Oxford University Press, 1994.

—— (1986), *Foreign and India's Development*, Ahmedabad: Gujarat Vidyapith.

—— (1999), *ARC Large Grant Field Survey* 1999.

Roy, K.C. and Tisdell, C.A. (1992), "Gandhi's Concept of Development and Nehru Centralised Planning" in Roy, K.C., Tisdell, C.A. and Sen, R. (Eds), *Economic Development and Environment — A Case Study of India*, Calcutta: Oxford University Press.

—— (1993a), "Poverty Amongst Females in Rural India: Gender Deprivation and Technological Change", *Economic Studies* 31 (4).

—— (1993b), "Technological Change, environment and poor women specially tribal women in India", *Savings and Development* 17 (4).

—— (1996), "Women in South Asia with Particular Reference to India", in

Roy, K.C., Tisdell, C.A. and Blomquist, H.C. (Eds), *Economic Development and Women in the World Community*, Praeger: London, CT.

Sen, A.K. (1997), *The Statesman*, Thursday, 12 June.

Smith, S. (1997), *Case Studies in Economic Development*, New York: Addison Wesley.

Staudt, K.A. (1975-76), "Women Farmers and Inequities in Agricultural Services", *Rural Africana* 29.

Tisdell, C.A. and Roy, K.C. (2000), "The Socio-Economics of Gender Issues In Rural India: Results of Interviews In Three Villages and A meeting in Eastern India" — *Working Paper No. 6*, Brisbane: Department of Economics, University of Queensland.

Vasaria, P. and Vasaria, L. (1985), "Indian Households with Female Hands: Their Incidence, Characteristics and Level of Living" in Jain, D. and Banerjee, N. (Eds), *Tyranny of the Household*, Delhi: Vikas Publishing.

World Bank (1999), *World Development Report* 1999-2000, New York: Oxford University Press.

Young, K. (1978), "Modes of Appropriation and Social Division of Labour. A Case Study of Oxxa, Mexico," in Kuhn, A. and Wolpe, A.M. (Eds), *Feminism and Materialism*, London: Routledge and Kegan Paul.

3

GENDER, NORMS AND BARGAINING IN RURAL INDIA

LAWSON SMITH

Introduction

While life no doubt wasn't meant to be easy, nor is society 'a suicide club' (Hart 1961) despite the idiosyncratic and systemic departures from procedural and substantive rationality (Simon 1978; Lonergan 1978; Rabin 1996; Hayakawa 2000) that are evident on the part of individuals, disparate groups and indeed society as a whole. Accordingly, the history of humanity and the ultimate ends of human endeavours and achievements can be typified, in addition to that of mere biological survival (basic life evidently being 'nasty, brutish and short') as comprising the pursuit of human flourishing and well-being (Sen 1995). To be sure, that enduring process — including its recent phase of accelerated socio-economic modernisation and development — has not been one of steady, inevitable progression; on the contrary, periods of reversal have occurred (Denzau and North 1994, p. 22; Lonergan 1978, pp. 228-31). And with the future being equally *contingent,* Fukuyama's (1993) thesis in *The End of History and the Last Man* to the effect that extant western liberal democracy constitutes the end point of mankind's ideological evolution, is one of premature adjudication since life on earth is expected to endure for about five billion years until obliterated by 'a series of unusually large explosions inside the sun' (Dobson 1998, p. 3).

Despite their shortcomings, societies both ancient and modern have largely judged themselves by their level of human flourishing and the good life *vis-à-vis* their contemporaries and own recent history (Adam Smith 1776, 1981; Annas 1993, p. 94 citing Aristotle). Given that human flourishing has a material base (the production and consumption of goods and services) it is unsurprising that in the modern era of increased focus on instrumental rationality, the thrust and deepest motivation of economic analysis and prescription has been the enhancement of living conditions (Sen 1995) to which end development is 'a process of expanding the real freedoms that people enjoy' (Sen 2000, p. 3).

According to a veritable raft of available indicators, modern Indian society — especially in rural areas — has failed badly in its pursuit of human flourishing and well-being, as evident in a comparison with China's achievements (Dreze and Sen 1995; Lipton and Ravallion 1996; World Bank 1997; Sen 2000). India's biomass-based rural economy, on which some 70 per cent of the population is dependent, yields up a meagre precarious living resulting in high levels of (transient and chronic) poverty and income risk (Dasgupta and Maler 1995; Dercon 2000) and attendant low levels of capability and well-being in part due to inept management by successive governments. According to the United Nations' (1999) composite indicator the *human development index*, India ranked a low 132nd out of 174 with an absolute value of 0.545, compared with China's rank of 98th at 0.701. While according to the *gender-related development index*, India did slightly better ranked at 112th, on all social indicators (except life expectancy) females had markedly lower levels of capability and well-being with a literacy rate of only 39.4 per cent (vs. 66.7 per cent for males) and real GDP (PPP$) of $902 compared with $2,389 for males (United Nations 1999, p. 140). Sustained growth, particularly of the backward rural economy, is therefore, necessary to achieve higher sustainable levels of social development (Lipton and Ravallion 1996).

The Government of India has belatedly recognised its past failures in socio-economic development and in August 2000 boldly proclaimed the new decade as a Decade of Development with the primary target of doubling India's per capita income by 2010 — an ambitious but achievable target which as Sachs and

Bajpai (2001, p. 1) note will require total GDP growth of about 9 per cent per year. Moreover, in view of the population's poor present levels of health and education especially in rural areas, Sachs and Bajpai (2001, p. 1) suggested that the Government add the following four explicit human development targets to its primary GDP growth target:

- A decline in infant mortality rates from 80 to 30 per 1000 by 2010;
- A reduction in adult illiteracy rates from 45 per cent to under 20 per cent;
- Universal primary education for children aged 5-14 at a school within 5 kilometres of home; and
- All villages to have basic utility services, road access, a school, health worker and local government by 2010.

These targets have been partly incorporated into the expanded list of 10 monitorable targets as set out in the Planning Commission's (2001) Draft Approach Paper To Tenth Five Year Plan (2002-2007).

The remainder of this paper is structured as follows: Section 1 overviews the general socio-economic state of rural Indian society. In Section 2, there is a macro-level analysis of the multiplicity and redundancy of socio-legal rules and norms. Contrary to assumptions of the overall coherence of a society's *social system of production*, the institutions, norms, rules, customs, social values and organisations of India's rural society have failed to coalesce into a coherent complex social configuration. While Section 3 adopts a micro-level of analysis to explore how bargaining might be undertaken by rural women having regard to their own internalised values, external formal legal rules and social values, and how areas of contestation might be approached with a view to achieving advantageous outcomes. This is further explored in terms of what purposive-rational strategies are available to an ambitious capable rural Indian woman allowing her to deviate from otherwise binding albeit typically suboptimal, obsolete social rules with the object of increasing her level of well-being and agency-freedom.

Section 1: General Socio-economic State of Rural India

Socio-economic development in rural India — accounting for some 70 per cent of the populace — can be readily characterised as being locked in a path-dependent 'long-run low-level equilibrium trap' (Akerlof 1997, p. 1005) owing amongst other reasons to the chronic failure of successive governments in the 50 years since independence to devise and implement the requisite policies to overcome self-replicating poverty, and propel the whole economy through the multi-phase development process (Rostow 1960) thereby facilitating self-sustaining transformative growth.

In his August 2000 Independence Day speech, the President of India (2000, pp. 2-3) spoke directly of 'outmoded social practices retarding the progress of society along modern lines' and also, how whilst (citing a British Administrator in India) the prior experience had been that 'dynasty after dynasty tumbles down but the village communities remain the same', that was no longer acceptable but rather 'today we do not want the village communities to remain fixed in time past, but to change'.

India's rural economy comprises a *social system of production* (SSP) insofar as markets and various other *nonmarket coordinating mechanisms* interact with social systems of production. As Hollingsworth and Boyer (1997, p. 2) explain it, a SSP comprises the manner in which the key institutions and structures of a country or region, including conceptions of capital-labour fairness and justice, customs, traditions, norms, moral principles, rules and laws, are integrated into a social configuration. A pivotal assumption is that of SSP coherence (Hollingsworth and Boyer 1997, p. 2):

> All these institutions, organisations, and social values tend to cohere with each other, although they vary in the degree to which they are tightly coupled with each other into a fully-fledged system. While each of these components has some autonomy ... an institutional logic in each society leads institutions to coalesce into a complex social configuration. This occurs because the institutions are embedded in a culture in which their logics are symbolically grounded....

Hollingsworth and Boyer (1997, p. 3) go on to reject the functionalist, trial and error and neoclassical explanations for how SSPs emerge, adopting instead an institutional rationale, 'we argue that individual action is influenced by the hold that institutions [including idiosyncratic societal customs, traditions and norms] have on individual decision-making'.

While generally adhering to the SSP concept as articulated by Hollingsworth and Boyer, a major point of departure and basis of the following analysis is that India's rural economy comprises *an incoherent and poorly integrated SSP*. That its idiosyncratic excessively autonomous (typically obsolete) norms and social rules governing especially the functioning of nonmarket coordinating mechanisms so important as poverty avoidance, income risk and group insurance mechanisms (Dasgupta 1999; Dercon 2000) frequently compete with typically under-enforced inconsistent formal (substantive and procedural) legal rules with the upshot that the rural socio-economic milieu comprises an over-regulated, over-juridified life-world complex or compound of the rational and irrational which to be understood, 'must be met by a parallel compound of direct and inverse insights, of direct insights that grasp its intelligibility and of inverse insights that grasp its lack of intelligibility' (Lonergan 1978, pp. 628-29).

Much of India's rural biomass-based economy comprises undermarketised subsistence-level activities undertaken by poverty-prone village-level households with under-utilised under-skilled human resources and insufficient low-yielding agricultural land at its command that is farmed far from the production frontier (Hayami and Ruttan 1985; Jayaraman and Lanjouw 1998). Those poor rural households are typically dependent upon a diminishing pool of common property resources (CPRs) for about 12 per cent of their income, and up to 26 per cent in the more arid districts (Beck and Nesmith 2001, pp. 119-28; Dasgupta 1999, p. 12 citing Jodha 1986, 1995).

Consequently a large number of the rural poor are liable to fall under the poverty line at any time *i.e.* suffer *transient poverty* owing to high-income vulnerability due largely to crop fluctuations and the related variable labour demand. For example, 10-year panel data for an ICRISAT village in south India revealed high yearly monetary fluctuations in dominant crop yields — the coefficients of variation being 1.0 for castor, 0.7 for paddy and 0.51 for a sorgum/millet/pea intercrop (Dercon 2000, p. 1 citing Townsend 1994, p. 544). Unsurprisingly, the idiosyncratic or individual/household component of income risk was equally large — up to 75-96 per cent of the total variance of income in the ICRISAT villages. Consequently in those same villages, about 50 per cent of total poverty was transient poverty, with some 25 per cent of households being poor each year, just 12 per cent never being poor and most households being poor at some time (Dercon 2000, p. 6).

Because they live in risky environments, India's poor rural households as elsewhere, have developed livelihood systems designed for their long-run survival and well-being (Dasgupta 1999, pp. 11-16) incorporating risk management (income smoothing) as well as risk-coping strategies that include informal group-based risk sharing or mutual assistance (reciprocity) within extended family and community networks. However, these strategies are imperfect devices, so that 'work on India estimates that transfers amount to less that 10 per cent of the typical income shocks' (Dercon 2000, p. 5).

Furthermore, while Indian governments have set up numerous targeted anti-poverty programmes in addition to more general pro-growth strategies under successive Five Year Plans since independence in 1947, such programmes have failed abysmally due to a host of design and delivery flaws (as well as the usual pervasive problems of bureaucratic and more generalised corruption) to provide much in the way of income smoothing and livelihood diversification for India's rural population (World Bank 1997; 1998).

Since India's rural economy is undermarketised, nonmarket or informal institutions are a major form of economic integration (economic life) and livelihood maintenance although this would clearly differ between and within regions owing to the variable level of agricultural and social development and integration with industrial and consumer markets. In his classic, *The Great Transformation*, Polanyi (1957) proposed that there were four forms of nonmarket integration or modes to access the product of divided labour: reciprocity; householding; barter; and redistribution (cited in Schaniel et al. 1994, p. 2). Various forms of self-sustaining, norm-guided, cooperative *direct reciprocal and indirect reciprocal transactions* (Seinen and Schram 2001, pp. 1-2) occur in the rural economy between households and mostly localised network members motivated by both fairness and *self-interested altruism preferences* (Zywicki 2000, p. 14) enforced by reliance on *implicit contracts* (Arrow 1974) and the threat of *informal sanctions* — 'the key to enforcement of implicit contracts and social norms' (Falk et al. 2000, p. 1).

Nonetheless, in the undermarketised rural economy the rigid caste-based artisanal system is breaking down, labour and land are increasingly treated as commodities and daily wage labour is being increasingly substituted for regular seasonal employment (Pal 1996; Jayaraman and Lanjouw 1998). But as Schaniel and Neale (1999, p. 109) point out, rural labour in India is a mixed case, 'some labour in India is commodified, some not commodified, and some quasi commodified'. Even where it is more or less available as fully commodified, *i.e.* agricultural labour is supplied in the form of cash wage based day labour, farmers still tend to inefficiently treat casual, regular and family labour as close substitutes (Pal 1999) and collude to exploit their bargaining power and pay wage rates — especially to women — at about the family subsistence level, and delay paying the inevitable wage responses to productivity growth (Ramamurthy 1994; Datt and Ravallion 1998). Also, even where mostly commodified, the supply of labour from the household (especially female labour) is subject to a plethora of variable household, village and network-sourced restrictive social rules and norms (*i.e.* suboptimal institutions) that impede the smooth supply of skilled labour, resulting in both inferior labour markets and lower levels of individual capability and well-being.

Land and property rights more generally are less commodified than rural labour. Rural land markets are typically very thin, there being a marked reluctance to part with ancestral land (due to a combination of the *status quo* bias or *endowment effect* (Rabin 1996, pp. 5-6; Nussbaum 2000, pp. 142-44) and over-reliance on land as self-insurance, underpinning long-run livelihood) with less than 1 per cent of agricultural land being available for sale each year, although by contrast the annual turnover in land tenancies is considerable in a dynamic inter-temporal process of assortative (re)selection (Jayaraman and Lanjouw 1998, pp. 6-9). Efforts at land reform have been systematically opposed by land owing classes, so that less than 2 per cent of total cultivated land has been redistributed since independence (Rao 1997, pp. 127-29). Also, endeavours to reform land ownership and tenancy rights have often been counterproductive — land owners at risk responding by redistributing land within their extended households in order to defeat the putative rights of tenants (Jayaraman and Lanjouw 1998, p. 8). Nonetheless, two kinds of land reform — tenancy reform and the abolition of intermediaries — have a strong linkage with poverty reduction, while land reform in general has boosted agricultural wages (Besley and Burgess 2000).

Furthermore, as extensively documented, there is a sizable gap between the formal legal and informal rights of rural women in relation to land, that is, what they're able to actually enjoy as against other members of their households, social networks and male-dominated legal system all of whom typically sanction (as a norm against legal rules, Eggertsson 1999, p. 3) the social norm that women's formal legal rights are subordinate to inconsistent local customs, social rules and norms, *i.e.* they're not recognised and are unenforceable by female social rule/norm-violators in such circumstances (Agarwal 1994, 1997; Moore 1994, pp. 89-93; Nussbaum 2000, Chapter 3).

Section 2: The Multiplicity and Redundancy of Legal Rules and Social Norms

In the western legal tradition, there is a legal and politico-economic doctrine and meta-norm to the effect that a legal system (whether code-based or common law) should comprise a well integrated hierarchical structure of coherent, consistent primary and secondary rules of law (Hart 1961; Detmold 1985; Dworkin 1987) so that, *inter alia,* any given individual/legal entity isn't faced with the impossible task of simultaneous compliance with or enforcement of mutually inconsistent/

exclusive requirements to do X and Y. But because in practice, owing to the mass of law as well as its complexity and frequent amendment, inconsistencies occur systemically, the courts have developed special rules to deal with the contingency of inconsistent (i) formal individual rules and (ii) sources of law (*eg* legislation versus the common law, and common law versus equity). So, a legal system operates, more or less, as an internally consistent dynamic (arguably higher order autopoietic) societal sub-system (Habermas 1998; Teubner 1993).

Furthermore, there is arguably a quite high correlation between formal laws, customs and norms in developed countries. Formal laws frequently merely restate social rules and norms, but equally, reformist laws ("social engineering" measures) are frequently enacted to alter behaviour deemed dysfunctional, or of negative economic utility. Over time those new laws will be internalised by most individuals — generating revised individual endogenous preferences and social values — out of generalised respect for the law and civic values if not from the mere routine of regular compliance.

Indeed, on Hart's (1961) analysis, the two minimum conditions necessary and sufficient for the existence of a legal system are:

- Those rules of behaviours which are valid according to the rule of recognition must be generally obeyed. This doesn't require that private citizens have to (internally) "accept" the primary rules and the rule of recognition, just that they — from whatever motive — obey them, though in a healthy society the rules will be obeyed from the "internal" viewpoint; and
- That officials must accept and apply its rules of recognition, criteria of legal validity, as well as rules of change and adjudication. And that these must be:

> ... effectively accepted as common public standards of official behaviour by its officials ... and [who] appraise critically their own and others deviations as lapses.... Evidence for the existence of a legal system must therefore be drawn from

> two different sectors of social life ... that the rules recognised as valid at the official level are generally obeyed. (Hart 1961, p. 113)

On a strict application of Hart's two conditions it is a moot point whether a legal system exists in much of rural India to the extent that (i) judicial and administrative officers fail to accept as valid and apply basic reformist laws such as the *Dowry Prohibition Act 1961* and a raft of other enactments granting women enhanced real property rights (Agarwal 1994), (ii) such reformist laws are not generally obeyed (from whatever motive) by private citizens, and more generally (iii) the rule of law — formal equality before the law especially relating to women — is systemically flouted in legal processes (Nussbaum 2000, p. 30).

And whilst as Nussbaum (2000, pp. 24-26) points out, 'India's Constitution is a very women-friendly document', there are serious gaps and flaws in the country's array of laws affecting the status of women. Its Uniform Criminal Code is an outdated Victorian relic and there is no Uniform Code of Civil Law:

> ... Civil law remains the province of the various religious systems of law, Hindu, Muslim, Parsi and Christian. There are some individual secular laws of property, marriage and divorce, but they do not form a system and ... it is not easy for individuals to avail themselves of them once they are classified in one of the religious systems. Cases may be appealed from the religious systems to the secular courts, but the lines of authority are extremely unclear, and much difficulty thus ensues.

In a similar vein India's rural *social system of production* exhibits failures in overall coherence and integration. The array of idiosyncratic social rules and norms that function on a localised basis with the added complexity of the remnants of a decaying semi-feudal hierarchical caste system (Gupta 2000, Chapter 1) operate semi-autonomously and at cross-purposes with the western-style formal legal system with its emphasis on individual rights and agency-freedom exercisable by purposive-rational men and women, independently of collectivist goals (Dworkin 1987, p. xi).

In brief, in rural India formal legal rights founded in legislative enactments of state and federal Parliaments relating to land, labour and women's rights in particular, are ignored and tend to be unenforceable where they vary from local custom and social rules. In this way, rural Indian society is over-regulated — there is an over-abundance of competing legal and social rules. In this manner, individuals, social networks and local communities will typically encounter:

- Technically binding but variably enforceable legal rules which theoretically should "trump" inconsistent, inferior social rules; and
- An array of informal social rules and norms including complex stratified, hierarchical caste-based social rules and norms that delimit more or less well the range of activities and upward mobility of individuals in so-called "low castes" and tribal groups (Gupta 2000, Chapter 2) that may be functionally binding even against superior formal legal rules.

Section 3: Social Rules & Norms, Bargaining and Purposive-Rational Deviation Strategies

There has been a centuries long debate in the social sciences, characterised by some scholars as "Das Adam Smith Problem" (Witztum 1999, p. 489) premissed on the supposed inconsistency between his two classics *The Theory of Moral Sentiments* (1759, 1976) and *The Wealth of Nations* (1776, 1981) as to whether individual decision makers are '*homo economicus* guided by independent preferences or *homo sociologicus* guided by social norms' (Hayakawa 2000, p. 1). However, reinterpreted, Adam Smith's supposedly contradictory views of human nature reduce to a single behavioural axiom, 'broadly interpreted, to include the social exchange of goods and favours across time, as well as the simultaneous trade of goods for money or other goods, is sufficient to characterise a major portion of the human and social enterprise' (Vernon Smith 1998, p. 3). Otherwise expressed, the construct of a single behavioural axiom is a composite eclectic "third way" avoiding two extremes of *complete voluntaristic individualism* and *structural determinism* to the effect that 'human behaviour in society rests on a triad of relations involving bounded rationality, the existence of social and cultural norms, and formation of norm-guided preferences' (Hayakawa 2000, p. 26). It is also well articulated in Harsanyi's widely accepted rational choice theory that posits 'self-interested desires for social acceptance side by side with self-interested desires for economic gain' (cited by Pettit 1998, p. 65).

There is a large literature on the nature and prevalence of reciprocal exchange in underpinning social order, how individual behaviour is molded by social and cultural norms, given the constraint of bounded rationality, as 'sources of low-cost heuristics to complex problems and as instruments by which to endow human action with social meaning' (Hayakawa 2000, p. 3). In Beckert's (1996) notion of *intentional rationality* there are four devices of uncertainty-reduction that individuals (groups and societies) can rely on in the absence of more developed, specific instruments: tradition, habit and routines; norms and institutions; structural predispositions of decisions such as social networks, organisational structures and past decisions; and power relations (cited in Hayakawa 2000, p. 4). There is also a variance of opinion as to whether pro-social behaviours such as reciprocal exchange are biologically based or a product of socialisation and learning. Evolutionary psychology suggests that reciprocal exchange is hard-wired in human beings and is one of four bases for cooperation in nature, 'the evolutionary environment for humans is the body of institutions, rules, customs and expectations of others. Thus the fundamental evolutionary difficulty for humans is to solve inherently *social* puzzles as to how to interact with others' (Zywicki 2000, p. 4). The competing view is that there's no need to link social norms with genetic inheritance when, 'cultural transmission and selection will suffice' (Goldspink 2000, p. 14).

Nonetheless, whatever its "true source", reciprocal exchange (and other nonmarket) mechanisms are pervasive, occurring in modern societies besides less marketised and tribal societies, supporting cooperative behaviour in the absence of immediate incentives to cooperate (Arrow 1974; Kranton 1996; Hoffman et al. 1998). And of real relevance to rural India, reciprocal exchange mechanisms and markets interact in interesting ways. While reciprocal exchange can be socially efficient, the opportunity for market exchange can break down the sanctions base of reciprocal exchange and also give rise to new higher value commodities. But it is difficult for markets to emerge and function well when too many people are engaged in reciprocal exchange and the net transfer value is higher (Kranton 1996, p. 831; Stark 1995, p. 14).

And since social norms and the vexed issues of their (dys)functionality loom large in Indian rural society and with respect to reciprocal exchange in particular, it is necessary, finally, to articulate a more or less accurate précis of the social norm phenomenon. Social norms are arguably distinguishable from legal and moral norms. They are a type of basal social routine and behavioural controller that constrain a person's "action repertoires", are typically not discrete but have fuzzy boundaries, and critically are shared with other persons typically in close proximity — households, networks and communities — all of whom imperfectly enforce them by various sanctions of social approval and disapproval. They have the critical feature of not being implicitly outcome oriented (Zsolnai 1998, p. 615 citing Elster 1989) though this does not imply they automatically fail the test of economic rationality, simply that their efficacy is contingent since together with habits, routines and rituals they're, 'maintained on the basis of past contribution rather than prospective relevance' (Goldspink 2000, p. 14). But while they may originate externally and be subject to external enforcement by sanction, norms are best comprehended as internalised obligations and reasons for acting, 'norms become obligations by a process of internalisation that makes them obligatory ... because one comes to accept them as somehow right' (Mitchell 1999, p. 20).

The traditional law and economics approach to norms is somewhat functionalist, viewing norms as arising more or less spontaneously in social groups as efficient "private law" solutions to various problems (Eggertsson 1999), that is an equilibrium-selection norm operating as an effective consensus obligation (*eg* the norm of reciprocal exchange). But there are two further types of social norms — the *rationality-limiting norm* and *preference-changing norm*. The rationality-limiting norm effects a further constraint on a person's feasible set of alternatives, 'the domain over which the rationality calculus applies', while the preference changing norm internalises as a person's preferences, 'what starts out as a norm or custom' (Basu 1998, pp. 2-4). To be sure, while social rules, norms and customs are differentiable, they operate especially in undermarketised rural subsistence economies such as India's as composite interlinked social routines, in which case following Basu (1998, p. 4) the terms social rules, norms and customs are hereafter used somewhat interchangeably although technically, social rules constitute more detailed "regulations" whereas norms comprise more general statements of principle.

In contrast with the traditional law and economics assumption of norms as efficient solutions, the focus of inquiry in New Institutionalism is the linkage between institutions and economic performance — the role of effective rules in shaping economic behaviour — emphasising formal rules of the state and social organisations, social values and norms. As Eggertsson (1999, p. 4) aptly states, 'norms are one of the legs on which the new institutionalism stands'. Indeed, studies in new institutional economics provide a sound theoretical basis for what is otherwise quite apparent — that individual social rules and norms as well as institutional arrangements more generally, can be inefficient, and that owing to the lack of or ineffective social mechanisms for their periodic review (the dialectic of community) may endure from time immemorial (Lonergan 1978, pp. 226-38; North 1996; Eggertsson 1999). As Lonergan (1978, p. 224) mournfully observes:

> Moreover, the course of development has been twisted. The social order that has been realised does not correspond to any coherently developed set of practical ideas. It represents the fraction of practical ideas that were made operative by their conjunction with power, the mutilated remnants of once excellent schemes that issued from the mill of compromise, the otiose structures that equip groups for their offensive and defensive strategies.

These observations are particularly applicable to rural India, where compared with their western counterparts, individuals are typically excessively constrained by inefficient social rules and norms with the upshot that the independence (agency-freedom) of women in particular to make purposive-rational choices to advance their self-interest, is hampered by the 'competing logic of community' (Dhesi 2000, p. 200). This has the unintended consequence as a negative externality, 'of slowing down movements towards socially beneficial equilibria' (Akerlof 1997, p. 1005) given that externalities are especially prevalent, 'where markets and nonmarket institutions co-exist' (Dasgupta 2000, p. 29).

But while India is a collectivist society, expressed at the individual level as a preference for or norm of "psychological collectivism" (Dion and Dion 1993, p. 56) this doesn't infer that women, consciously or unconsciously, uncritically internalise adverse social rules and norms constraining their "action repertoires" (Saam and Harrer 1999, p. 3) so that they have no normative choice at all, albeit sharing 'reasonably convergent mental models, ideologies and institutions' (Denzau and North 1994, p. 3) with significant others.

On the contrary, such a proposition overlooks:

- The contingency of much behaviour (which rule applies and shall I comply?) otherwise stated as the generalised option between conforming and deviance, 'which socialisation inevitably reiterates' (Vanderstraeten 2000, p. 590 explaining Luhmann's theory of autopoietic social systems);
- The difference between objectively observed behaviour and subjectively intended action — the act and the relevant person's volition;
- That there is often an array of closely substitutable social rules and norms of cooperation that can be strategically manipulated in a given situation; and
- The general degree to which micro-level "contractual bargaining" may occur in daily life even in situations where a single norm or social rule applies.

Indeed, there is abundant evidence that rural women in India are intendedly rational, *i.e.* seek to advance their norm-constrained rational choice or what Sen calls "the socio-rational choice" (cited in Zsolnai 1998, pp. 617-18) do not suffer as Sen (1990, p. 126) suggested from a form of "false consciousness" as to their individual interests, and do not unreflexively accept the legitimacy of and internalise their inequality. For as Annas (1993, p. 282) points out it cannot be the case that women who have even very limited prospects cannot conceive of better and happier alternatives, and also that 'women's desires have expanded with the expansion of alternatives open to them'. This is evident for example in the extensive fieldwork carried out by Jeffery and Jeffery (1997) in the Bijnor District of Uttar Pradesh, *inter alia,* with respect to marriage and joint versus separate household arrangements:

> By any simple accounts of these women's lives, none of them had much freedom of action, at least, not of the officially sanctioned sort ... the ambiguities of their situations thus make it hard to see what women can do to enhance their opportunities to exert their agency. As we have argued elsewhere ... this does not mean that [these] women are incapable of seeing the undesirable features of their situation or that they never resist the structures within which they are required to live. (p. 61)

In her treatment of the complex issue of adaptive women's preferences and women's options, Nussbaum (2000, Chapter 2) reaches similar conclusions. In analysing the problem of *preference/desire-deformation* (here, women internalising inferior social rules and norms regarding their well-being and agency-freedom) with reference to the core debate about preferences in social choice, Nussbaum rejects both subjective welfarism and Platonism. Instead, she develops an annexure to the central capabilities construct to overcome problems of the preference-based approach. To the list of "basic goods", she adds access to property rights because of their key role in self-definition, bargaining and self-development, and gives "desire" a pre-eminent independent role apart from choice owing to its role as a heuristic underpinning gains in capability in central areas of human functioning. To be sure, she concedes that there is space for the social deformation of desire. But more importantly, paraphrasing comments by Nehru regarding the apparent acceptance by Indians of their inferior position in the British Colonial system, Nussbaum (2000, pp. 150, 155, 161) emphasises the point that:

> ... to recognise the adaptive nature of one's preferences is the beginning of a search for independence ... [equally] ... for women: recognising the adaptive character of many preferences is a beginning of the search for true self-definition, and the liberties that protect that search are the true opponents of feudal and colonial tyranny.... In case after case [stories of women in self-help groups] we see women quickly dropping habituated preferences and adjusting their aspirations in accordance with a new sense of dignity and equality.

The Scope and Mode of Contractual-style Bargaining Available to Rural Women

In this final part, the issue under consideration is how rural women might instrumentally improve their generalised well-being and agency-freedom by paying close attention to the degree to which insights obtained from education and experience can be applied to commonly encountered socio-economic transactions and major life choices, to (re)negotiate such episodic events via implicit and explicit bargaining, improving individual and collective outcomes. Any transactional gains achieved should result in their increased economic welfare — in Sen's (1981, p. 46) terms, their *endowment (ownership) bundle* and *exchange entitlement set.*

This exposition is premissed on the following points:

India's rural society has a severe deficiency of "social capital" (Dhesi 2000) that is a major constraint on socio-economic development. Educational attainments are low, despite the evident high social returns on investment in education (especially of girls). Trust and pro-social behaviours are at suboptimal levels in view of the reliance in the subsistence economy on nonmarket mechanisms underpinned as they are by norm-guided direct and indirect reciprocal transactions. Also, the social routines (social rules, norms and customs) adhered to with respect to both market and nonmarket transactions typically have dysfunctional and suboptimal socio-economic outcomes. In brief, social failure is pervasive and substantial gains can be derived by individual and group "norm-entrepreneurs" who can overcome the barriers of individual and group bias (the distorted dialectic of community) to disseminate and implement improved social routines. As Lonergan (1978, p. 226) explains, 'technical and material improvements are less subject to the veto of dominant groups than are changes in economic and political institutions'.

Rural Indian women with even a moderate level of education are unlikely to suffer from "false consciousness" but on the contrary, have malleable adaptive preferences and alter such preferences by way of *"Pareto self-improvement"* (Cooter 1998) internalising higher value norms including a resilient moral commitment to pro-social values like honesty, fairness, reliability, a high work ethic and cooperation translating into the "reputation effect" that in cooperative ventures increases productivity and gives those with good character an advantage (Cooter 1998, pp. 3-4) as well as being receptive to improving mundane, routine transactions.

And of critical importance, contrary to perceived wisdom, there is often an array of closely substitutable social rules and norms amenable to strategic manipulation and micro-level "contractual bargaining". While extant social rules and norms in rural India frequently constitute, as elsewhere, inefficient quasi-immutable majoritarian "default rules" that contracting parties adhere by way of inertia owing to uncertainty, loss aversion and anticipatory regret (Korobkin 2000), there is generally scope for individuals either bargaining in the shadow of such norms and default rules etc., or acting unilaterally *vis-à-vis* their first part of direct/indirect reciprocal transactions to devise tailored solutions that improve joint utility that amount to making their own binding commitments or "private ordering" (Mnookin and Kornhauser, 1979). Since default social rules will apply if the parties can't agree, tailored rules will leave them better off, thereby promoting efficiency, in a way that coheres with their internalised values and norms.

Two final points. First in the following stylised but hopefully realistic vignettes, the approach is limited to what extent opportunities exist for pragmatic rural women to improve their well-being and agency-freedom, as opposed to the pursuit of optimal first-best solutions because in most cases, these are simply unattainable. Second and relatedly, in much of the literature (especially Agarwal 1994, 1997) there is excessive stress on the acquisition of direct real property rights as a key factor in enhancing a woman's bargaining powers and *ipso facto,* her generalised welfare. A more cognitively supple approach to women's empowerment is necessary since whilst most rural Indian women do not have or are unable to enforce formal inheritance-sourced land rights, obtaining less formalised "contract-based" access to land is much more feasible, particularly when undertaken in concert with members of her natal or affinal households. This second point is especially salient since the prospect of socio-economic development of rural India presupposes a decoupling or decreasing reliance on direct property rights as sources of livelihood, income and status.

Our idealized young rural woman is a contemporary pastiche loosely modelled on skeletal elements of Tagore's short story "*Haimanti*" concerning an intelligent girl raised 'under the supportive tutelage of a progressive father who respects her intelligence, fosters her education, and treats her as an independent being of worth in her own right' (in Nussbaum 2000, p. 162). This idealisation is necessary because our inquiry essentially reduces to the extent that knowledge and insight can be applied to tailor standardised norms, social rules and routines. Also, utilising the detailed account by Jeffery and Jeffery (1997) of the Jats and Sheikhs in the Bijnor District of the northern state Uttar Pradesh, for convenience, Haimanti is cast as a Hindu Jat woman domiciled in that district, the youngest child and only daughter of her two living parents, and with two brothers whom she is close to. Education is highly valued by the Jat community; her two parents were educated to Year 12 level.

Her eldest brother, Jas, with a Master's degree in Civil Engineering, works in the Civil Service, is married and lives elsewhere in the state. While her second brother, Surinder, with a Master's degree in Agricultural Science, acquired renewable tenancy rights over a sizable piece of land adjacent to his father's property all of which they farm jointly. Surinder supplements his farm income by working almost full time as an agricultural adviser to local farmers. He runs a separate household with his wife and children in quite close proximity to his parents' house. Haimanti is very intelligent and hard working. Funded by a modest scholarship to the State University some 65 kilometres from home, she obtained a three-year Bachelor's degree in Agricultural Economics, residing with her Aunt's family during her study. While supporting Haimanti's higher education, her father, keenly mindful of local marriage customs regarding the age of brides, only agreed to this on the clear understanding that she would return home forthwith on completion with a view to getting her married into an equal or better household that hopefully wouldn't demand too high a dowry, and with the prospect that she might eventually be able to help her brother Surinder expand his agricultural services business.

Episode I: Marriage, Dowry and Household Arrangements

Among the Jats, education does not increase the autonomy of daughters *vis-à-vis* marriage. Also, daughters are not usually married into a family residing in the natal village or nearby, but one some 20-30 kilometres distant, although there are distinct advantages for a daughter living in proximity to her parents. While Haimanti's input into the selection of a spouse was limited she was able to subtly appeal to the self-interest of her brother Surinder and father, and manipulate the selection of a suitable boy (an only son and Secondary Teacher in a nearby State High School, who was not overly interested in farming) from a better-off landed family some 12 kilometres distant, and which was amenable to dowry negotiation rather than a much wealthier family 30 kilometres away demanding a sizable dowry that would have forced her father to either sell one-third of his land or borrow the funds from the local moneylenders at a high interest rate. On Haimanti's suggestion, her two brothers persuaded their father to submit a well-crafted dowry proposal — that her in-laws accepted after much haggling (mindful of Haimanti's reputation as a bright scholar and dutiful daughter) — which reduced the cash component by some 70 per cent in exchange for obtaining through the second brother's advisory network, a renewable five year lease over a piece of good land located near to the in-laws, on their behalf. The net profit would accrue to her in-laws subject to their reimbursing her father the annual tenancy rental as a first charge on the gross profit and a further 15 per cent of the remainder. They also agreed in view of Haimanti's obvious skills as an agricultural economist and budding farm advisor, that under Surinder's supervision she would assist her in-laws in managing their various landholdings with a view to consolidating their activities and increasing profitability.

Also, mindful of its advantages, Haimanti was keen to have a separate household from her in-laws. Surinder had a separate household and Haimanti keenly observed that this had assisted in maintaining smooth harmonious relations between all parties. Although she compliantly lived with her in-laws for the first year after marriage and was able to develop a friendly working relationship with them all, during the second year she was able, owing to an unplanned influx of her in-laws' relations to their house over some months, with good grace and to everyone's satisfaction, to establish a separate household with her husband in a nearby slightly dilapidated dwelling that her father-in-law was clearly reluctant to utilise for his relations.

Episode II: Taking Care of Everyone's Business

In the six years following Haimanti's marriage at 21, besides having two children — with a good deal of support from her natal family during relevant periods — by dint of her diligent application to her various demanding household and other duties, she was able to significantly improve the income and wealth (endowment bundle) of both her natal and affinal families, as well as her own. After much careful analysis and with guidance from her brother Surinder, Haimanti was able to devise and implement a multi-phase risk-adjusted management plan for her in-laws' farming activities including the land obtained as part of the dowry settlement. Over six years, and with only average rainfall, Haimanti was able to:

- Assist them in consolidating their more scattered landholdings by a very careful series of exchanges, sales and purchases of land and leases;
- Introduce more diverse, higher value crops;
- Adjust their inputs of capital and labour to more optimal combinations;
- Rationalise their finances, obtaining a low-interest on-call loan facility from the State Rural Bank that allowed them to purchase additional farm equipment for their expanded cropping operations and avoid recourse to the local moneylenders for high interest seasonal loans in order to finance planting and related activities; and
- Employ a more cost-effective and higher skilled combination of seasonal and daily labour that included, since they required more skilled labour for their higher crops, employing local men and women (rather than itinerant gangs) on an equal basis where possible and paying them what amounted to a premium for reliable good quality work that was typically difficult to accurately monitor. Paying a premium to the more reliable, better skilled labourers gave her in-laws a good reputation as honest decent employers, which in turn guaranteed a much more reliable supply of good workers as required — local women in particular — which proved to her in-laws' great satisfaction, to make operations run far more smoothly and profitably.

As a part of the process of consolidating her in-law's farming activities, Haimanti was able with her husband's support to quite cheaply purchase on a ten year instalment basis, twelve hectares of hitherto very unproductive land (her husband acquiring the title on her behalf paying the first instalment with her funds) that the absentee owner had simply been unable to lease out, but which she was sure had "capabilities". With Surinder's technical assistance, Haimanti was able to accurately diagnose the main causes of its low productivity and devise a remedial five-year programme reliant on a good deal of semi-skilled labour for tree-planting and other rehabilitation work over the first three years. Lacking sufficient funds to hire the necessary labour, Haimanti was nonetheless able to enter into reciprocal exchange arrangements (blessed by the local Priest) with four hardworking skilled landless labourers and their families allowing them to live on the land and cultivate two hectares for a period of ten years in exchange for an agreed amount of free labour in the first five years and preferential hiring as day labourers in her in-laws' expanding farming activities. These arrangements were sanctioned and much admired by Haimanti's in-laws and her husband, and also earned her much respect from their labour force.

Further, with the joint support of her natal and affinal families including her husband, Haimanti was also able to devote some three days of her six working week to helping her brother Surinder build up his farm services business. She eventually became a partner with a one-quarter share (her father and father-in-law were also partners with a one-eighth share respectively and priority rights to income) and agreed that in order to better fund the expanding but undercapitalised business, she would reinvest all her earnings in the firm for at least five years.

Episode III: Improving Water Usage and Cooperation

This episode draws on Aggarwal's (2000) case study of the collective action failures in relation to separate and group-owned wells in two ICRISAT villages over a 10-year period, despite the very clear gains obtained from cooperation. There would seem to be considerable scope for cooperative gains since the Aurepalle village sample group in Aggarwal's case study derived average returns of some 16.5 per cent from investing in group-wells despite often relying on dated technology, failing to take advantage of state financial support for constructing new wells and for failed wells, frequently managing group dynamics quite poorly, and having an average of less than three years education.

At the time of her marriage, the areas where Haimanti's parents and in-laws resided were undergoing somewhat of an agricultural expansion with local farmers endeavouring to shift to higher value more intensive cropping, reliant on higher levels of fertiliser application and irrigation, besides additional farm equipment. Her in-laws relied on 6 separate and 4 ageing group wells for irrigation, while her father and brother Surinder had one separate well and one group-well each and another well shared between them. In each of her parents and in-laws area, there were some 125 farmers with a total of 50 separate and 50 group-wells. There was little cooperation within each group of 125 irrigators to promote their common interests. In fact with water levels declining in some localities, they typically saw themselves as competitors. A number of wells required overdue maintenance as well as the installation of new upgraded pumping equipment to support the agricultural expansion, and 25 new wells were thought to be required. Haimanti also needed a new well for the land she acquired.

Haimanti and her brother Surinder decided that a structured collective approach to managing this common resource was necessary. Through his advisory service network, he was able, after considerable effort, to persuade irrigators in each area to collaborate and establish an Irrigators Cooperative, with localised subgroups formed under the auspices of their respective Panchayat. In recognition of their skills and leadership qualities, Surinder was voted Chairman of the two Cooperatives and Haimanti as Secretary. Through his civil service contacts, Surinder was then able to have the State Department of Agriculture undertake a new geological survey of the two areas to better ascertain the quantity and quality of available groundwater and sustainable consumption rates. Also, through their brother Jas's contacts with the Engineering Department of the State University, they were able to have all wells tested for flow reliability and the attached pumping equipment checked over in a project for final year Engineering and Agricultural Science students, funded by a NGO linked to the University. Also, final year Surveying students were able, under their lecturers' supervision, to produce a series of survey charts denoting the potential for better utilising and recycling irrigation water. These various projects revealed that sustainable water efficiency gains exceeding 40 per cent were readily achievable and if carefully implemented would about support the planned expansion.

To fully explain the collective implications of these various projects and maximise the prospects of ongoing cooperation, Surinder and Haimanti undertook a lengthy series of meetings and on-farm demonstrations, involving where possible, successful irrigators from other areas and some people involved in carrying out the projects. After much further persuasion, irrigators agreed that detailed records for all wells and related irrigation schemes should be drawn up in a standard reporting system to be held by each separate and group-well owner, the local subbranch and Panchayat — where the records would be publicly accessible — as well as centrally by each cooperative. On establishing that standard reporting system, each cooperative was then able, drawing on information from the projects, to draft a management plan for each well and associated irrigation scheme and the estimated costs of any refurbishment and upgrading to be undertaken. That cost estimation exercise was able to draw on recent advances in well and irrigation technology, effecting a one-quarter reduction in well construction costs (reduced further if 3 wells or more could be drilled in one operation), a halving of the chance of a drilling failure, and avoiding the need for multiple pumps in the one well by retrofitting pump upgrade kits and better output devices that could be modified to suit individual irrigator's requirements. Also, to avoid the usual 4-5 year delay in getting an electricity connection to a new well (a major disincentive for new well construction and source of much conflict regarding payment for well construction as between group-owners) it was agreed that a new range of very efficient lower cost multi-purpose portable diesel pumps should be used for all new wells. Furthermore, to avoid the serious ongoing problem of electric pumps sustaining costly damage from all too regular power surges, the cooperatives were able to field test to their complete satisfaction and recommend to irrigators for a retrofit to all pumps, a new upgraded Power Surge Protection Device.

On the basis of these various endeavours, the two

cooperatives were then able to arrange with the State Rural Bank for funding to be made available on a per well and irrigator basis, as and when required. Over the following three-year period, utilising those available funds, almost all existing wells and associated pumping and irrigation equipment were refurbished, repaired and upgraded. And only 10 further new group-wells, funded by the State Rural Bank, were required. Irrigators were also able for the first time to access a long-available state government scheme compensating them up to Rs. 10,000 in the event of a failed well. That was just as well, because in constructing the 10 new wells (undertaken in one single extended operation by a contracting firm, thereby reducing costs by 25 per cent) two drilling failures were experienced.

Concluding Comments

The generally poor socio-economic state of rural India, accounting for some 70 per cent of the population, is the source of endless poverty and human misery owing to the chronic failure of successive governments in 50 years to successfully implement development policies. Moreover, the rural economy is best understood as an incoherent and poorly integrated social system of production comprising a compound of the rational and irrational. And since the rural economy is undermarketised, nonmarket or informal institutions including various forms of self-sustaining norm-guided direct and indirect reciprocal transactions are a major form of economic integration. There is also a direct collision in much of rural India between social rules and norms and formal legislation-based rights relating to land, labour and women's rights in particular with the upshot that to the extent of any conflict, women's legal rights are neither recognised nor enforceable. In an environment in which transactions are typically undertaken with reference to obsolete social routines, rules and norms, individuals are over-socialised and there is the hazard of women experiencing the problem of preference/desire-deformation, one may ponder as to how intelligent women might find areas of contestation in which to promote their legitimate self-interest. However, it is apparent that rural Indian women are as capable as anyone else of articulating informed aspirations for socio-economic advancement, altering their preferences by way of Pareto self-improvement, strategically manipulating the selection of the least disadvantageous social rules and norms available, and in what amounts to a process of contractual bargaining and private ordering, improve the outcomes of social and economic transactions, otherwise regulated by suboptimal default rules and norms.

WORKS CITED

Agarwal, B. (1994), *A Field of One's Own: Gender and Land Rights in South Asia*, Cambridge University Press, Cambridge.

—— (1997), "Bargaining and Gender Rights Within and Beyond the Household", *Feminist Economics* Vol. 3, No.1, pp. 1-51.

Aggarwal, R.M. (2000), "Possibilities and Limitations in Small Groups: The Case of Group-Owned Wells in Southern India", *World Development* Vol. 28, No. 8, pp. 1481-97.

Akerlof, G.A. (1997), "Social Distances and Social Decisions", *Econometricia* Vol. 65, No. 5, pp. 1005-27.

Annas, J. (1993), "Women and the Quality of Life", in M.C. Nussbaum and A. Sen (eds), *The Quality of Life*, Clarendon Press, Oxford, pp. 279-302.

Arrow, K. (1974), *The Limits of Organisation*, Norton, New York.

Basu, K. (1998), *Social Norms And The Law* (http://www.people.cornell.edu/pages/kb40)

Beck, T. and Nesmith, C. (2001), "Building on Poor People's Capacities: The Case of Common Property Resources in India and West Africa", *World Development* Vol. 29, No. 1, pp. 119-33.

Besley, T. and Burgess, R. (2000), "Land Reform, Poverty Reduction and Growth: Evidence from India", *The Quarterly Journal of Economics* Vol. 115, No. 2, pp. 389-430.

Cooter, R. (1998), *Expressive Law and Economics*, Olin Working Paper Series 98-6, Law School, University of California at Berkeley.

Dasgupta, P. (1999), *Poverty Reduction and Non-Market Institutions*, Faculty of Economics and Politics Working Paper, University of Cambridge (http://www.econ.cam.ac.uk/faculty/dasdgupta/index.htm).

—— (2000), *Population, Resources and Welfare: An Exploration into Reproductive and Environmental Externalities*, Faculty of Economics and Politics Working Paper, University of Cambridge, (http://www.econ.cam.ac.uk/faculty/dasdgupta/index.htm).

Dasgupta, P. and Maler, K.G. (1995), "Poverty, Institutions and The Environmental Resource-Base", in J. Behrman and T.N. Srinivasan (eds), *Handbook of Development Economics* Vol. IIIB, Elsevier, Amsterdam, Chapter 39.

Datt, G. and Ravallion, M. (1998), "Farm Productivity and Rural Poverty in India", *Journal of Development Studies* Vol. 34, No. 4, pp. 62-85.

Denzau, A.T. and North, D.C. (1994), "Shared Mental Models: Ideologies and Institutions", *Kyklos* Vol. 47, No. 1, pp. 3-31.

Dercon, S. (2000), *Income Risk, Coping Strategies and Safety Nets*, Centre for the Study of African Economies WPS/2000.26, Department of Economics, Oxford University, Oxford.

Detmold, M.J. (1985), *The Australian Commonwealth: A Fundamental Analysis of its Constitution*, Law Book Co., Sydney.

Dhesi, A.S. (2000), "Social Capital and Community Development", *Community Development Journal* Vol. 35, No. 3, pp. 199-214.

Dion, K. and Dion, K.L. (1993), "Individualistic and Collective Perspectives on Gender and the Cultural Context of Love and Intimacy", *Journal of Social Issues* Vol. 49, No. 3, pp. 53-60.

Dobson, A. (1998), *Justice and the Environment: Conceptions of Environmental Sustainability and Theories of Distributive Justice*, Oxford University Press, Oxford.

Dreze, J. and Sen, A. (1995), *India: Economic Development and Social Opportunity*, Oxford University Press, New York.

Dworkin, R. (1987), *Taking Rights Seriously*, Gerald Duckworth & Co., London.

Eggertsson, T. (1999), *Norms in Economics With Special Reference To Economic Development*, Discussion Paper 10-99, Max Planck Institute for Research into Economic System, Institutional Economics Unit, Jena.

Falk, A., Fehr, E. and Fischbacher, U. (2000), *Informal Sanctions*, Working Paper No. 59, Institute for Empirical Research in Economics, University of Zurich, Zurich.

Fukuyama, F. (1993), *The End of History and the Last Man*, Avon Books, New York.

Goldspink, C. (2000), "Modelling social systems as complex: Towards a social simulation meta-model", *Journal of Artificial Societies and Social Simulation* Vol. 3, No. 2, pp. 1-23. (http://www.soc.surrey.ac.uk/JASSS/3/2/1.html).

Gupta, D. (2000), *Interrogating Caste: Understanding Hierarchy and Difference in Indian Society*, Penguin Books, New Delhi.

Habermas, J. (1998), *Between Facts and Norms: Contributions to a Discourse Theory of Law and Democracy*, The MIT Press, Cambridge MA.

Hart, H.L.A. (1961), *The Concept of Law,* Oxford University Press, Oxford.

Hayakawa, H. (2000), "Bounded rationality, social and cultural norms, and interdependence via reference groups", *Journal of Economic Behaviour and Organisation* Vol. 43, No. 1, pp. 1-34.

Hayami, Y. and Ruttan, V.W. (1985), *Agricultural Development: An International Perspective,* John Hopkins University Press, Baltimore.

Hoffman, E., McCabe, K.A. and Smith, V.L. (1998), "Behavioral Foundations Of Reciprocity: Experimental Economics And Evolutionary Psychology", *Economic Inquiry* Vol. 36, No. 3, pp. 335-52.

Hollingsworth, J.R. and Boyer, R. (1997), "Coordination of Economic Actors and Social Systems of Production", in J.R. Hollingsworth and R. Boyer (eds), *Contemporary Capitalism: The Embeddedness of Institutions,* Cambridge University Press, Cambridge, Chapter 1.

Jayaraman, R. and Lanjouw, P. (1998), *The Evolution of Poverty and Inequality in Indian Villages,* Working Paper No. 1870, The World Bank, Washington DC.

Jeffery, R. and Jeffery, P. (1997), *Population, Gender and Politics: Demographic Change in Rural India,* Cambridge University Press, Cambridge.

Korobkin, R. (2000), "Behavioral Economics, Contract Formation, and Contract Law", in Cass R. Sunstein (ed), *Behavioral Law and Economics,* Cambridge University Press, Cambridge, Chapter 4.

Kranton, R.E. (1996), "Reciprocal Exchange: A Self-Sustaining System", *The American Economic Review* Vol. 86, No. 4, pp. 830-51.

Lipton, M. and Ravallion, M. (1996), "How Important To India's Poor Is The Sectoral Composition Of Economic Growth?", *The World Bank Economic Review* Vol. 10, No. 1, pp. 1-25.

Lonergan, B.J.F. (1978), *Insight: A Study of Human Understanding,* Harper and Row, New York.

Mitchell, L.E. (1999), "Understanding Norms", *University of Toronto Law Journal* Vol. 49, No. 2, pp. 1-57. (http://www.utpress.utoronto.ca/journal/UTLJ/utlj_49_2.htm).

Mnookin, R.H. and Kornhauser, L. (1979), "Bargaining in the Shadow of the Law: The Case of Divorce", *The Yale Law Journal* Vol. 88, No. 5, pp. 950-97.

Moore, (1994), "Law's Patriarchy in India", in M. Lazarus-Black and S.F. Hirsch (eds), *Contested States: Law, Hegemony and Resistance,* Routledge, New York, Chapter 3.

North, D.C. (1996), "Epilogue: economic performance through time", in L.J. Alston, T. Eggertsson and D.C. North (eds), *Empirical Studies In*

Institutional Change, Cambridge University Press, Cambridge, pp. 342-55.

Nussbaum, M. (2000), *Women and Human Development: The Capabilities Approach*, Cambridge University Press, Cambridge.

Pal, S. (1996), "Casual and Regular Contracts: Workers' Self-selection in the Rural Labour Markets in India", *Journal of Development Studies* Vol. 34, No. 2, pp. 133-56.

—— (1999), "Task-based Segmentation of Rural Labour Contracts: Theory and Evidence", *Bulletin of Economic Research* Vol. 51, No. 2, pp. 67-88.

Pettit, P. (1998), "Institutional Design and Rational Choice", in R.E. Goodin (ed), *The Theory of Institutional Design*, Cambridge University Press, Cambridge.

Planning Commission (2001), *Draft Approach Paper: Tenth Five Year Plan (2002-2007)* (http://planningcommission.nic.in/pldraft.htm).

President of India (2000), *Address To The Nation On The Eve Of Independence Day 2000* (http://alfa.nic.in/rb/ind/i20002.htm).

Rabin, M.R. (1996), *Psychology and Economics*, Berkeley Department of Economics Working Paper No. 97-251, University of California at Berkeley (http://elsa.berkeley.edu/econ/index.html).

Ramamurthy, P. (1994), "Patriarchy and the Process of Agricultural Intensification in South India", in Alice W. Clark (ed), *Gender and Political Economy: Explorations of South Asia Systems*, Oxford University Press, New Delhi, Chapter 6.

Rao, J.M. (1997), "Agricultural Development Under State Planning", in Terence J. Byres (ed), *The State, Development Planning and Liberalisation in India*, Oxford University Press, New Delhi, Chapter 4.

Rostow, W.W. (1960), *The Stages of Economic Growth*, Cambridge University Press, Cambridge.

Saam, N.J. and Harrer, A. (1999), "Simulating Norms, Social Inequality and Functional Change in Artificial Societies", *Journal of Artificial Societies and Social Simulation* Vol. 2, No. 1, pp. 1-21. (http://www.soc.surrey.ac.uk/JASSS/2/1/2.html).

Sachs, J.D. and Bajpai, N. (2001), *The Decade of Development: Goal Setting and Policy Challenges in India*, Working Paper No. 62 Centre for International Development, Harvard University, MA.

Schaniel, W.C., Neale, W.C. and Walter, C. (1994), "Comment", *Journal of Economic Issues* Vol. 28 No. 3, pp. 884-89.

Schaniel, W.C. and Neale, W.C. (1999), "Quasi Commodities in the First and Third Worlds", *Journal Of Economic Issues* Vol. 33, No. 1, pp. 95-115.

Seinen, I. and Schram, A. (2001), *Social Status and Group Norms: Indirect Reciprocity in a Helping Experiment*, Tinbergen Institute Discussion Paper TI 2001-003/1 (http://www.tinbergen.nl).

Sen, A. (1981), *Poverty and Famines: An Essay on Entitlement and Deprivation*, New Delhi, Oxford University Press.

Sen, A. (1990), "Gender and Cooperative Conflicts" in I. Tinker (ed), *Persistent Inequalities: Women and World Development*, Oxford University Press, New York, pp. 123-49.

—— (1992), *Inequality Reexamined*, Oxford University Press, Oxford.

—— (1995), "The Concept of Development", in H. Chenery and T.N. Srinivasan (eds), *Handbook of Development Economics*, Vol. 1, Elsevier, North-Holland, Chapter 1.

—— (2000), *Development as Freedom*, Alfred A. Khopf Inc, New York.

Simon, H.A. (1978), "Rationality as Process and as Product of Thought", *American Economic Review* Vol. 68, pp. 1-16.

Smith, A. (1759, 1776), *The Theory of Moral Sentiments*, Liberty Classics Edition, D. Raphael and A. Mactie (eds), Liberty Press, Indianapolis.

—— (1776, 1981), *An Inquiry Into The Nature And Causes Of The Wealth Of Nations* 2 Vols., Liberty Classics Edition, R.H. Campbell, A.S. Skinner and W.B. Todd (eds), Liberty Classics, Indianapolis.

Smith, V.L. (1998), "The Two Faces of Adam Smith", *Southern Economic Journal* Vol. 65, No. 1, pp. 1-19.

Stark, O. (1995), *Altruism And Beyond: An Economic Analysis Of Transfers And Exchanges Within Families And Groups*, Cambridge University Press, Cambridge.

Teubner, G. (1993), *Law as an Autopoietic System*, Blackwell Publishers, Oxford.

United Nations Development Programme (1999), *Human Development Report 1999*, Oxford University Press, New York.

Vanderstraeten, R. (2000), "Autopoiesis and socialisation: on Luhmann's reconceptualisation of communication and socialisation", *British Journal of Sociology* Vol. 51, No. 3, pp. 581-98.

Witztum, A. (1999), "A Study into Smith's Conception of the Human Character: Das Adam Smith Problem Revisited", *History of Political Economy* Vol. 30, No. 3, pp. 489-513.

World Bank (1997), *India: Achievements and Challenges in Reducing Poverty*, The World Bank, Washington DC.

World Bank (1998), *Reducing Poverty in India*, The World Bank, Washington DC.

Zsolnai, L. (1998), "Rational Choice and the Diversity of Choices", *Journal of Socio-Economics* Vol. 27, No. 4, pp. 613-22.

Zywicki, T. (2000), *Evolutionary Psychology and the Social Sciences*, Law and Economics Working Paper No. 00-35, George Mason University School Of Law, Arlington VA.

4

Environmental, Degradation, Population and Poverty in India

ANITA MEDHEKAR-SMITH

INTRODUCTION

This paper addresses the developing country interrelationship between poverty, population growth and environmental degradation with reference to the archetypal Indian experience. The first section describes the typical characteristics of biomass based subsistence economies, and the theoretical and empirical bases of the population-poverty linkage. The second section outlines the incidence and nature of rural poverty in India, the major causes of the mediocre performance of India's agricultural sector to date, and the rural poverty-environmental degradation interrelationship. The third section provides an overview and critique of the policy measures implemented to slow population growth, alleviate poverty, arrest environmental degradation and their interrelationship. The paper concludes with a comment on how the reform-averse political system might be induced to implement and enforce the necessary reform measures.

1. The Characteristics of Biomass Based Subsistence Economies

In low income poor developing countries, about 70-80 per cent of the population is rural based, deriving a meagre living from agriculture which comprises some 30 per cent on average of GDP. This is in marked contrast with industrial market economies that have about 6 per cent of the population engaged in agriculture, which comprises a low 2-4 per cent of GDP. Thus poor developing countries have a very high direct dependence and impact on their natural resources. They are described by Dasgupta and Maler (1995, p. 2373) as 'biomass based subsistence economies'.

The environment has three key functions as stressed by the materials balance models (Ayres and Kneese 1969; Sollner 1997; Turner et al. 1994). It supplies economies with renewable/non renewable resources; it assimilates waste products; and uniquely provides humans with life support natural services. All three functions of the environment have a positive economic value. However, the 'carrying capacity' of the environmental resource-base (soil, soil-cover, water, forests, animals and fisheries) is typically exceeded. That is, environmental degradation occurs especially in poor countries owing to the combined effects of population, rural poverty, inappropriate agricultural and resource management practices, technological practices, institutional failure, and market as well as government failure. Hence, environmental degradation is the cause and consequence of:

> ... accentuated poverty among the rural poor in poor countries ... poverty, high fertility rates and environmental degradation feed upon each other. In fact an erosion of the environmental resource base can make certain categories of people destitutes even while the economy on average grows. (Dasgupta and Maler 1995, p. 2383)

The common characteristics and problems of these mostly biomass-based subsistence economies are as follows:

First, low GNP per capita and widespread poverty. In the underdeveloped world, the low-income economies had an average GNP per capita of just US$350 (as at 1991), with India at US$330, so that about one-third of its population was below the official poverty line. However, the United Nations' (1990) *Human Development Index* (HDI) data for India reveal a more complex outcome; there is considerable inter-state variation even for similar levels of per capita income. For example, the southwest state of Kerala with its low income per capita level but high HDI may well provide the paradigmatic social justice model of sustainable development (Parayil 1996) although its lack of economic growth owes more to poor management than deliberate social choice (Dreze and Sen 1995, pp. 34-38; Ramachandran 1996, pp. 212-24). Its high HDI has occurred despite Kerala's low throughput, 'because of sustained efforts to limit population growth rate and social inequality, and to conserve resources frugally and use them on a shared basis' (Parayil 1996, p. 952).

Second, scarcity of capital, and in India's case falling rural investment (Rao and Storm 1998, pp. 214-26; Duvvury 1998, pp. 226-28). Third, a low level of labour productivity, and in India's case, organised labour dysfunctionally holding sway in a capital-scarce country (Ghosh and Neogi 1996; Misra and Saxena 1997). According to Nurske's (1953) *vicious circle of poverty* theory low income leads to low saving and investment, leading to low productivity which feeds back into low income, thereby completing the vicious circle. Fourth, production techniques in all economic sectors tend to be backward owing to various factors including low capital availability and research and development as well as opposition by organised labour to the adoption of labour-displacing technologies.

Fifth, widespread unemployment and underemployment. In India for example, in 1971 it was estimated that 10.9 per cent and 8.1 per cent of the total rural and urban labour force respectively, were unemployed, while a further 14.9 per cent (27 million) of the total labour force was severely underemployed (Datt and Sundharam 1997, p. 351).

Sixth, there is widespread income inequality. For example, the World Bank in its *World Development Report 1993* (Table 30 at pp. 296-97) reported for India, that the top quintile (20 per cent) derived some 41.3 per cent of national income in 1989-90, and the bottom 3 quintiles (60 per cent) just 37.5 per cent.

Seventh, as noted above, underdeveloped economies are essentially agrarian in nature, with the share of income in agriculture being lower than the share of employment in agriculture reflecting low average productivity in the agricultural sector (Hayami and Ruttan 1985, Chapter 5). Eighth, they are typically inward-looking, with a small participation in foreign trade ("export-pessimism" prevails) which is in any event, dominated by agricultural commodities as a legacy of colonial exploitation by more advanced capitalist countries (Myint 1990, pp. 223-29; Chandra 1992, pp. 5-7; Maheshwari 1971, pp. 107-24).

Ninth, they typically exhibit rapid population growth and a high overall dependency burden owing to high birth rates (World Resources Institute 1998, pp. 141-46; UNFPA 1997, pp. 19-28). India's population in 1951 was 361 million. It then grew at an average 2.13 per cent per annum to reach almost 845 million as at 1991 (Visaria 1992, pp. 273-77) and went on to reach the landmark one billion in 2000.

Tenth, environmental degradation, caused by a rapidly growing rural-based population placing unsustainable demands on land and other natural resources (Laxmi et al. 1997, p. 95; World Bank 1995, pp. 66-101).

The Theoretical Basis of the Population-Poverty Cycle/Linkage

The rapid growth in the world's human population is in the most radical view, the primary cause of most of the world socio-economic and environmental ills. For example so-called radical biologists (*eg* Ehrlich 1968; Ehrlich and Ehrlich 1990) have predicted, on the basis of more sophisticated biological versions of the Malthusian population trap, that unless the 'population explosion' is defused by whatever means necessary then there will be dire irreversible biological consequences — ecological disasters, and the earth will be unable to feed the hungry billions (cf. World Resources Institute 1998, pp. 152-60).

Second, the economic-based population-poverty cycle theory (the PPCT). The essential argument here is, based on Solow's neoclassical growth model (1956, 2000) an extension of the Harrod-Domar model), that population growth simply exacerbates existing socio-cultural and economic difficulties associated with underdevelopment. In the standard production model of:

$$Y = f(K, L, R, T)$$

(where Y = income; K= capital; L = labour; R = resource base; and T = technology),

assuming the resource base is fixed and there are constant returns to scale, the rate of per capita growth (y-1) is proportional to the growth rate of the capital labour ratio (k-l) and the residual effects of technological progress, 'the Solow residual', which is estimated to account for 50 per cent of growth in industrialised countries. With a rising population it is necessary to increase the capital stock growth rate more rapidly just to maintain constant per capita income. And as its likely that the rate of capital growth (*k*) is not independent of the rate of labour force growth, *i.e.* population, the adverse impact of population growth is even more accentuated than the models imply. A further aspect of the PPCT is that while low income families may have additional children to provide cheap labour and old age security (in the typical absence of a welfare system), doing so ultimately causes additional poverty thereby setting up a further self-defeating mechanism in the poverty cycle (Todaro 1997, pp. 216-17).

The Population Explosion and the Population-Poverty Link

Since the industrial revolution, the world's population has grown rapidly. In the 20th century it has taken 35 years to rise from 2 to 4 billion, while the next 2 billion will be added in only about 25 years (World Resources Institute 1994, pp. 27-33). Whether the population is likely to stabilise at about 8 billion in the 21st century is dependent upon the range of government measures undertaken in this adjustment period. The reasons for this continuing high growth are: declining mortality, high fertility (couples in developing countries typically have 5-6 children, and are unlikely to reduce to a sustainable 2), young populations and a low marriage age, and a rapid growth in the number of women in the childbearing age group. The recent history of the population in low-income countries is that crude birth rates fell from 45 to 37 per thousand over 1960-79, and the death rates from 24 to 15 per thousand. Overall, the annual rate of population growth for developing countries has fallen from a peak of 2.4 per cent per annum in 1965 to 2.2 per cent in the late 1980s, though African fertility remains stubbornly high (World Bank 1987, pp. 107-09).

While India has just 2.4 per cent of the world's land area, with a population of 844 million at the 1991 census (1 billion as at 2000) it has to support some 16 per cent of the world's population. Over the 1981-1991 period, the population growth rate was a high 2.11 per cent per annum. Though the death rate has halved from 19.2/1000 to 10/1000 over 1960-1990, the birth rate has only fallen by one-quarter from 41.2/1000 to 29/1000. The changing sex composition of the population from 972 females per 1000 males in 1901 to 929 per 1000 in 1991, is mostly attributed to increased poverty (with 30 per cent higher mortality rates among women of the 15-44 age group than males) with some 37 per cent of the population living below the poverty line in unhygienic conditions with poor or non-existent medical facilities (UNFPA 1997, pp. 53-76) and a socio-economic system which favours the allocation of dietary support and access to medical facilities to male children (Sharma and Vanjani 1994). Over the 1901-91 period, the population density increased sharply from just 77 persons per sq km to 267, though much less than 316 per sq km in the highly industrialised Japan (Datt and Sundharam 1997, pp. 44-50).

The population-poverty link can be summed up as follows:

- Poverty and population are highly interrelated. Attacking poverty which accompanied by poor health, low education, status and job prospects especially for women, is necessary as an end in itself but also as a mechanism to slow population growth;
- Rapid population growth promotes poverty and *immerisation*. Poor families often regard extra children as economically beneficial, though adding to the burden of the family and country, requiring education, housing, health services, adding to the labour pool and stretching existing capital stocks;
- Though a growing labour force boosts total output, when capital and other resources are scarce and unemployment is high, it tends to reduce rather than raise average labour output, and thereby average incomes;
- Besides rapidly slowing down population growth, effective family planning programmes are necessary to stress the point that family size is an issue of choice

while providing the means of allowing that choice (World Bank 1987, pp. 108-10).

2. The Incidence and Nature of Rural Poverty in India

First, despite the growth of non-agricultural sectors in India since independence in 1947, poverty remains essentially a rural phenomenon with 74 per cent of the country's poor in the 1990s, living in rural areas. Urban growth has had little impact on rural poverty especially, since India's development strategy since the 1950s stressed capital-intensive industrialisation in the urban areas of a closed economy. The Kuznets process of economic growth via rural to urban migration has failed to significantly reduce poverty levels. Lipton and Ravallion (1996, p. 19) therefore stress the point of the quantitative importance of the sectoral composition of economic growth. Fostering growth in the rural economy is pivotal to 'an effective strategy for poverty reduction in India'.

Second, statistical details of India's poor. Since the 1950s, there have been numerous studies on Indian rural and urban poverty levels, using various criteria for estimating the poverty. The World Bank's (1991) reporting on Indian poverty used a poverty line, the expenditure level at which a minimum calorie intake and indispensable nonfood purchases are assured. The proportion of the rural population below the poverty line fell from 53 per cent in 1970, to 44.9 per cent in 1983 and 41.7 per cent in 1988, though in absolute terms the number of rural increased from 237 million to 252 million over the same period. The failure of *rural ultra-poverty* levels to decline at the same rate as urban levels indicated that the benefits of economic growth were not 'trickling down' to the rural ultra-poor. The World Bank (1991) report used data from the 38th round of the National Sample Survey (NSS) to calculate the incidence of poverty in different categories of rural household, and found that:

- Persons in wage-dependent households comprised 46 per cent of the rural poor;
- In 1983, 64 per cent of agricultural labour households were below the poverty line;

- Self-employed households (small farmers) were about 38 per cent of the rural poor.

Two main factors accounted for such high rural poverty level. High levels of both unemployment and underemployment, with the failure of minimum wage legislation to deliver decent wages even during employment periods. And secondly, the low asset base of the poor. Essentially, there had been no major change in the rural structure of asset ownership since the 1960s. As Datt and Sundharam (1997, p. 322) observe,

> ... a large proportion of the rural poor remain in poverty, not only because they have very few assets, but also because most of these assets are in the form of durable consumer goods, rather than such assets as land, farm implements, livestock, which increase their productive capacity.

Bhattacharya et al. (1991) reported on their 1986 survey as to the survival strategy of the very poor, and indicators, besides calorific deficiency, of extreme poverty. Their findings included the following:

- the lack of basic needs (*eg* shelter, clothing, bedding and household equipment) was a better indicator of utter poverty than calorific deficiency. For example, half the adult women had no spare clothing, and over 40 per cent of children went naked;
- the poor consumed a wider variety of food than expected, with some food items being collected direct from common property, and small amounts being bought from shops;
- seasonal fluctuations in calorific intake were quite moderate, the average deficiency increasing from 25 per cent to 35 per cent. The most common deficiency range was 30-50 per cent though the value of calorie norms (*eg* 3,900 units for working rural male labourers) was questionable as it was possible to carry out arduous physical work despite a notional 30-50 per cent calorie deficiency;
- most food consumed was not purchased, but obtained freely from nature or by other means;

- there was a high fluctuation in cash transactions; and
- the poor were generally in debt, mostly in the form of consumables purchased on credit from retail shops, and over 40 per cent of households were repaying such loans thereby expending over 10 per cent of their cash income.

Rural poverty in India is also somewhat feminised. As Lipton and Ravillion (1995, pp. 2589-90) explain, young females are typically exposed to excess poverty-related nutritional and health risks, women work longer to obtain the same level of living, they bear the brunt of falling living standards, and they are discriminated against in both educational and work opportunities. According to Dasgupta and Maler (1995, p. 2432), the work-load of women in South Asia is often 150-250 per cent of that of menfolk, with women working up to 15-16 hours per day during the busy agricultural season. They can also spend up to 5 hours per day collecting water in the dry season (accounting for 10-25 per cent of their daytime energy expenditure). Bina Agarwal (1997a, p. 27) highlights the class and gender effects of poverty, and their link with environmental degradation in India:

> ... there is a systematic anti-female bias in the allocation within rural households of subsistence resources controlled by men, including resources used for food, health care, education and other basic needs.

The long hours expended by rural women and children in obtaining water, fuel, wood and food from common property (a burden not shared by men), besides requiring much energy, deprives them of time for educational and other more productive activities, and also exposes them to a variety of health hazards.

The Mediocre Performance of India's Agricultural Sector

The mediocre performance of India's agricultural sector since independence, combined with a rising population, is a major cause of rural poverty. In per capita terms, agricultural income and production has increased just 1 per cent per capita per annum (Datt and Rao 1996, p. 289). Indian agricultural productivity continues to be low: the average yield per hectare in India is below the world average in all crops (Sundharam

1995, p. 141). The causes of this low productivity are: general, institutional and technical (Misra and Puri 1994, pp. 432-34). As Hayami and Ruttan (1985, p. 133) note, 'a prerequisite for agricultural productivity growth is the capacity of the agricultural sector to adapt to a new set of factor and product prices'.

First, the rural socio-cultural atmosphere of low education levels, reluctance to adopt new production techniques and the caste system etc., is an obstacle to agricultural development. Overcrowding in agriculture from population growth has seen the area of land per cultivator decline from 0.43 ha in 1901 to 0.2 ha in 1991 (Misra and Puri 1994, p. 433; Rao 1992, p. 118).

Second, the main institutional causes are the land tenure system and inadequate non-farm services, *eg* the lack of rural credit and marketing facilities. Despite post-independence land reform, the distribution of land ownership is still highly unequal. About three-quarters of the land is owned by one-quarter of land-owning households.

Furthermore, over the 1971-82 period, the average size of operational holdings has declined from 2.28 hectares to 1.84 ha. Also, many holdings are highly fragmented, requiring unproductive highly labour intensive techniques (Roy and Tisdell 1992, p. 77). As Binswanger et al. (1995, p. 2670) note,

> ... under simple technology there are no economies of scale in farming and that independent family farms are economically the most efficient mode of production except for a limited set of plantation crops.

So productivity has suffered from both (i) over-fragmentation of land, and (ii) over-consolidation — the trend to larger landlord managed holdings. The lack of cooperative marketing facilities as well as loans at fair interest rates have also prevented farmers from appropriately increasing the capital intensity of agriculture.

Agricultural capital formation has generally been low, through rising for a period in the 1970s. Also, since the mid-1970s the intersectoral terms of trade have shifted against agriculture (Datt and Rao 1996, p. 289). While the political system in the 1980s directed some 15 per cent of GNP to agriculture as subsidies and concessions in the form of farm-support prices, owing to the failure of land reform, rich farmers (besides industrialists, urban consumers, and exporters) derived most of the benefit. The main technical causes of low productivity are:

- poor outmoded techniques of production (use of wooden ploughs is common while adoption of higher yielding seeds and semi-commercial cropping is slow);
- inadequate irrigation facilities and dependence on unreliable monsoonal rains;
- excessive multiplicity of crops;
- the predominance of small subsistence level farmers;
- large variations in operational holdings (less than 2 ha to 10 ha);
- underemployment of available labour; and
- low levels of general and technical education (Agarwal 1997a; Sundharam 1995, Chapter 7; Hayami and Ruttan 1985, Chapter 6).

Further, the impact of the green revolution has been disappointing. It has been limited to a few crops (notably wheat) and a few regions/states with a sure supply of water, and has generated a growing disparity between regions and classes of farmers. Large farmers with better access to capital benefited most from the green revolution in its first phase, and adopted labour saving practices so labour input per acre declined with the increase in landholdings. Though when smaller farmers were subsequently able to adopt the new seed-fertiliser technology, they obtained a cropping intensity advantage over larger farmers. This indicates that the existing size of holdings was not optimal as regards the capital-labour input ratio, and overall productivity in respect of regions able to adopt green revolution technology (Rao 1992, pp. 116-29). But as Hayami (1990, p. 422) explains it, the rising inequality in the rural sectors of Asian countries including India, 'has been a result not of Green Revolution technology but of insufficient progress of the Green Revolution technology in overcoming growing population pressure on land'.

The slow growth of non-agricultural employment has failed to relieve the rising population pressure on the natural resource base of which only 46 per cent of the land is available for agriculture. As a consequence much semi-arid and fragile land has been brought into production, resulting in some 60 per cent of all agricultural land now being degraded to some extent. Land degradation has also occurred from deforestation and excessive pressure on forests, poor irrigation leading to water-logged soil and salination of one-quarter of irrigated lands, as well as from soil erosion (at a rate of 16.5 tonnes per hectare) caused by poor land management practices. And under 20 per cent of land is under adequate forest cover, compared with the target area of 33 per cent. Further, there has been a sharp decline in common property resources (CPRs) including grazing, forest lands and water courses, whose productivity which is especially important to the landless rural poor, has declined by 30-50 per cent over the last four decades (Datt and Rao 1996, pp. 295-96). Access to CPRs contributes some US $5 billion to the incomes of poor rural Indian households or about 12 per cent of their income — most of which is gathered and used by women and children — so that exclusion from CPRs due to a number of processes, jeopardises their livelihood (Beck and Nesmith 2001, pp. 119-28).

The area prone to flooding has doubled over the 1971-81 period while water stocks are stressed by the uncontrolled sinking of tubewells by the better-off farmers (as part of the green revolution technology), lowering overall water levels, and drying up the drinking water wells of the poor. Also, the lack of forest cover has worsened the soil quality of hill country while the increased run-off, contaminated with fertiliser and pesticides, has contaminated natural water sources damaging fish life and polluting it for human use. Thus the availability of natural resources to the rural poor has declined by two parallel processes: (i) their quantitative and qualitative degradation; and (ii) the increasing statisation and privatisation of what were common property resources (Agarwal 1997a; Hannam 1999, pp. 223-26; Kumar et al. 2000, pp. 12-17). The state monopoly over forests (about 90 per cent of India's 64 million hectares of forests are state owned (Kumar et al. 2000, p. 16)) has increasingly crowded out their subsistence utilisation by the poor. There was a decline in village commons by some 26-63 per cent over 1950-1984. Also, the tapping of common groundwater stocks via tubewells of the better-off farmers effected its inequitable redistribution, crowding out the poor (Agarwal 1997a, pp. 24-26).

Access to village commons in the more arid districts of India has provided some 9-26 per cent of the total income of poor rural households, as well as over 90 per cent of their firewood, and 70-90 per cent of their grazing needs. However as noted above, women and children have borne the major time, income, nutrition, health, social support and knowledge system burdens associated with a marginal rural existence in an over-stressed environment, which includes a diminishing CPR yield (Beck and Nesmith 2001, pp. 119-24). Furthermore, pollution levels inside rural dwellings from using biofuels for cooking are high, causing respiratory infections in children, lung cancers in adults, and adverse pregnancy outcomes (Dev and Ranade 1997, p. 97).

3. The Policy Measures Necessary to Arrest Environmental Degradation and Break the Poverty-Population Link

The Population Policy Imperative

A clear cut effective population policy is needed in India as a key component of overall ecological-economic policy measures. So far, India has followed a piecemeal approach to population control, except for measures adopted during the 1976-77 emergency period, which included: increasing the marriageable age; lifting female education and status; monetary compensation for accepting sterilisation followed by a later compulsory sterilisation policy; and, the virtually free widespread supply of birth control devices.

The Government of India's *Sixth Plan* (1980-85) stressed the need to promote family planning on a voluntary basis, as a peoples' programme, using three methods: sterilisation, IUDs and oral contraceptives. However, the birth rate fell only from 33.8 to 32.7/1000 as a result. By contrast, non-planning measures adopted in such states as Kerala, the Punjab and Gujarat such as raising the mean age of marriage as the consequence of boosting the adult literacy rate of women especially, together with targeted health care for women and children (reducing the child mortality rate) have been more successful. Kerala's birth rate, with its high education levels despite low per capita income, has fallen to a relatively low 9/1000, in contrast to the average Indian rate for 1985-86 of 32.5/1000 (UNFPA 1997, pp. 31-39).

The *Eighth Plan* (1992-97) with its focus on the containment of population growth through peoples' active cooperation and an effective scheme of incentives and disincentives' aimed to reduce the birth rate from 30.2 to 26/1000 by 1997 and infant mortality from 80 to 70/1000 by 1997, thereby achieving a 1.2 per cent annual growth rate by 2006 (compared with the 1.3 per cent annual growth rate achieved by China over 1980-88). In addition, the Eighth Plan proposed to provide adequate attention to 'female literacy, raise the age of marriage, employment opportunities for women and their status in society, improving health and nutrition of pre-school children and providing a comprehensive package of maternal healthier services'. Though the population's annual growth rate is expected to have only declined to 1.74 per cent by 1996 and 1.55 per cent by 2001 which suggests a relative failure of the Eighth Plan's target of 1.2 per cent by 1997. However, the Eighth Plan's mix of both planning and nonplanning measures (as per the successful Kerala model, where government and non-government organisations have worked together) is well conceived but has so far failed to deliver targets owing to:

- The lack of adequate funding and attention to boosting the social indicators (especially education and health) of rural poor women;
- Insufficient political will and promotion; poor incentive structure (based on sterilisation rather than number of children); and
- Excessive stress on contraceptive technology.

The Kerala model demonstrates that lifting the social indicators of women somewhat independently of per capita income is the most effective means of achieving population decline via lower birth rates and infant mortality, and has positive spillover effects. That is, better education and health levels tend to empower rural women, thereby boosting their intrinsic value and income-earning potential, and redressing their power imbalance in the home and local society which enables them to better access available resources. That rural women in Kerala have been socially empowered is confirmed by Kerala's female to male ratio of 1.04 to 1, compared with the Indian average of 0.93 to 1 (Parayil 1996, p. 943).

Poverty Alleviation

Concerning poverty alleviation, Bhagwati (1988) and Ahluwalia (1985) amongst others assert that the 'trickle down' approach has not worked for many reasons, including low agricultural growth and per capita income. Indian governments have initiated a number of direct and indirect poverty programmes since the *Fifth Plan* of 1977-80, with the 'eradication of poverty' being the principal objective. That task was immense given there were over 220 million living below the poverty line, and unemployment and underemployment as well as a low resource base were the main causes of poverty. Various general and specific programmes have been undertaken. General programmes have included: distribution of basic consumer goods (foodgrains and clothing) through government-owned 'Fair Price Shops' at low subsidised prices, and the allocation of free home sites and construction grants. Specific programmes introduced so far include:

- Small Farmers Development Agency (SFDA) and Marginal Farmers and Agricultural Labourers Scheme (MFAL) to provide farming services such as improved seeds, fertilisers, pesticides, irrigation facilities, storage, transportation processing and marketing facilities etc. for small farmers;
- Drought Prone Area Programme (DPAP), infrastructure development to better utilise land, water, livestock and human resources;
- Tribal Area Development Scheme;
- Hill Area Development Programme, with an emphasis

on horticultural development, plantations, animal husbandry, forests, soil conservation, roads and tourism;

- Food for Work Programme (FWP) where underemployed/ unemployed rural labourers are provided work on construction of public works projects (roads and irrigation, drinking water and forest development etc.) and are partly or fully paid through foodgrain supplies from surplus stocks by the central government. This scheme has worked well, by providing work for seasonally unemployed labour, and has lifted the income and nutritional levels of the rural ultra-poor population, especially during drought and famine periods. The FWP is also known as the National Rural Employment Programme (NREP) and has been a major instrument of rural development and employment; and
- the Crash Scheme for Rural Employment (CSRE).

The above listed Fifth Plan programmes for rural development and employment brought about the green revolution making India self-sufficient in foodgrains, however they benefited the bigger farmers and well-developed areas best. They failed to cover the whole country and were ultimately reduced to straight subsidy programmes, lacking a planned approach to elevating the income levels of the rural poor effectively. Therefore in the *Sixth Plan* (1980-85) the emphasis shifted to a direct targeted countrywide assault on rural poverty. The new initiatives included:

- Integrated Rural Development Programme (IRDP) to promote ventures for the self-employed small/marginal farmers, and landless labourers, as they had no productive assets or special skills;
- National Rural Employment Programme (NREP);
- Rural Landless Employment Guarantee Programme (RLEGP) which began in 1983 provided employment to landless labourers, women, scheduled caste and tribal peoples, to undertake public works projects. They were paid partly in cash at minimum wage rates and in kind with subsidised foodgrains.

The *Seventh Plan* from 1989-90, found weaknesses in implementation of the above programmes in terms of:

- worker selection (many were not below the poverty line);
- failure to supply the guaranteed minimum of 100 days employment per annum;
- poor planning, and selection of projects without feasibility studies;
- lack of national integration, having conflicting objectives; and
- open corruption and cheating on the part of contractors and local politicians.

Therefore, in 1989 the NREP and RLEGP were merged into a new programme, the Jawahar Rozgar Yojana programme (JRY), which covered 55 per cent of villages countrywide and expected to benefit 44 million families below the poverty line by employment creating public works projects. However, the JRY programme failed to markedly reduce the degree and incidence of rural poverty due to the failure to reduce population growth, transfer land from rich to landless/small farmers, control inflation, and promote employment in small rural cottage industries. Meanwhile the rural rich became richer, whose agricultural income was exempt from taxation, and ineligible families obtained employment. Various administrative failings and constraints also occurred (Misra and Puri 1994, Chapter 14; Sundharam, 1995, Chapter 30; Mankar 1995, Chapter 11; Dev and Ranade 1997).

The general thrust of the range of direct food support and rural public works project-based job creation programmes is consistent with the policy theory for effectively and efficiently alleviating rural poverty. However, the programmes need to be more comprehensive, as well as better targeted and overall administration improved, to ensure less corruption as much of the benefits are diverted away from the poor. For instance, concerning the Public Distribution System, according to Parikh (1994),

> ... the cost-effectiveness of reaching the poorest 20 per cent of households through PDS cereals is small. For every rupee spent, less than 22 paise (22 per cent) reach the poor in all states except in Goa, Daman and Diu where 28 paise reach the poor. This is not to suggest that PDS does not benefit the poor at all, but only to emphasise that this support is provided at a high cost (as cited by Dev and Ranade 1997, p. 67).

Besides the reform and better management of direct poverty support programmes in conjunction with education, health and nutrition measures (in which India ranks a poor 135 out 174 countries, according to the World Bank's *Human Development Report, 1996*) agricultural productivity needs to be dramatically lifted, in an environmentally sustainable manner.

This requires much additional capital (and commercial expertise as well as financial and marketing facilities) to be injected, through appropriate technology, into the rural sector, the rehabilitation of degraded but potentially productive lands as well as Village Commons and Common Property Resources, and the abandonment of marginal farm lands. Also, the presently unsustainable fiscal level of rural input subsidies for fertilisers and electricity etc. as well as price support (clear evidence of nonmarket failure [Wolf 1993]) which have adverse environmental effects and mostly benefit the better-off farmers, need to be sharply reduced. This would lift foodgrain prices, however the funds saved could be redirected to the rural poor who are net purchasers of food. And free trade in agricultural commodities should be adopted as formal government policy, to equilibrate domestic and world grain prices and encourage India to be a strong export grain producer (Ranade and Dev 1997, p. 114; Rao and Storm 1998, pp. 230-34). This would lift total output through price signalling and significantly boost rural income, besides making nonagricultural sectors pay commercially realistic nonadministered prices for their agricultural (and forest) inputs.

4. The Environment and India's Moribund Political Economy

Finally, the measures outlined above in relation to population control and poverty alleviation need to be underpinned by a series of well-integrated measures designed to stop further environmental degradation and lift the carrying capacity of the natural resource base (World Bank 1995, pp. 66-67; Laxmi et al. 1997, pp. 102-06). There are six main policy options which ought to be adopted by less developed countries such as India and which provide the basis for critically appraising India's performance thus far (Todaro 1997, p. 368):

- proper resource pricing;
- community involvement;
- clear property rights and resource ownership;
- improving economic alternatives for the poor;
- raising the economic status of women; and,
- industrial emission abatement policies.

Poor administration of successive five year economic plans has led to at best careless, and at worst ruthless, exploitation of natural resources resulting in environmental degradation on which failure has occurred. And there has been to date, a serious failure of the government to devise and implement the necessary policies to curb further degradation (thereby limiting the scope of market failure) and remediate existing environmental damage.

Hannam (1999, p. 223) asserts there has been a continuity between colonial and post-colonial forestry policy in India — that of ecological imperialism — so that (citing Gadgil and Guha 1992) the 1952 National Forestry Policy upheld the basic precepts of its 1894 predecessor, reinforcing 'the right of the state to exclusive control over forest protection, production and management'. The 1952, India's Forest Policy declared a target 100 million hectares of tree cover; this has yet to be achieved. While the data on Indian forest cover are inconsistent, by the mid-1990s total forest cover was reduced to about 65 million hectares, most of which was degraded although the rate of decline in tree cover had slowed sharply since the mid-1980s (Kumar et al. 2000, pp. 7-9). Deforestation of some regions had occurred because of the statisation of forest resources by revenue-hungry state governments and their giving precedence to industry's timber demands over peoples' needs for minor forest products. In brief, forestry management has been quite poor. On some estimations, about 1.3 million hectares per annum of forest cover are now being lost, although degradation rather than deforestation is the current concern (World Bank 1995, pp. 71-81; Laxmi et al. 1997, pp. 102-14; Briones and Ramos 2000, p. 243).

The worsening state of forest cover prompted a radical policy reversal in 1988 with the adoption of a *New Forest Policy* (though not legally binding on the central government) under which the forests were first to be treated as an ecological necessity, second as a source of products by the local populace and third as a source of products for industries and other non-local uses. Under the new 1988 Forest Policy:

- the role of tribals in forests was recognised;
- a 'new' target of 100 million ha or 33 per cent of total area in forest was set (really just the old 1952 target recycled);
- forest-based industries were to be discouraged and the system of private forest contractors replaced by a tribal cooperative system;
- joint forest management (JFM) would occur between the Forest Service and local communities with NGOs acting as an interface; and
- forest land was not to be converted to non-forest uses *eg* plantation crops (Kumar et al. 2000; Hannam 1999).

The evidence of progress since the 1988 initiative is somewhat mixed. Some village communities have developed good forest management systems with little help (Chatterji 1999), or alternatively through voluntary participation in general land rehabilitation and poverty elimination programmes run by local and foreign NGOs with limited input from government agencies (Patel 1998). The World Bank over the last 20 years has invested over US$830 million in 16 projects in India's forest sector, strongly supporting the JFM thrust of the new Forest Policy that has been quite successful in Andhra Pradesh and Orissa. However, the recent World Bank review by Kumar et al. (2000, p. 880) concluded that, 'the current strategy India is pursuing in its forest sector is relevant but not sufficient to meet the diverse needs of the sector'. Degradation pressure remains from human and livestock populations, sustainability concerns are not given adequate attention, farm forestry is not being adequately supported and state governments are still supplying products to industry from state forests at often highly subsidized prices, causing serious market distortions and also discouraging private tree plantation (Kumar et al. 2000, pp. 108-12). Further, the paternalistic bureaucratic culture of the Forest Service has been a constraint on JFM implementation with local communities as well as the history of 'mutual hostility and suspicion' between NGOs and the Forest Service (Hannam 1999, p. 228). This unsatisfactory ecological and socio-economic state of affairs is likely to continue unabated unless public pressure forces the corrupt-prone moribund political system to adhere to formal government policy and foreign aid policy requirements in relation to forest management.

Much the same state of affairs applies to government reform attempts in relation to water, soil, air and waste management. Either the necessary reform measures are never devised, or if they are, they are poorly implemented and/or subverted by the corrupt political process in which the major interest groups succeed in capturing government (in what provides a classic example of Stigler's [1971] capture thesis) in collusion with corrupt bureaucrats. The poor track record of India's environmental administrators eventually prompted the judiciary to proactively adopt a quasi-administrative environment oversight role based largely on the legal remedy of the writ petition (Anderson 1998, pp. 199-226). However, *ad hoc* 'court-administered implementation can at best supplement, not replace, the formal agency-dependent enforcement mechanism' (Divan 2000, p. 6).

Conclusion

In the presence of endemic government failure (besides market failure) in relation to environmental policy, there is little point in advocating reform measures that are bound to fail due to entrenched vested interests and their corrupt alliance with individuals in the political system. In these circumstances, a 'grass-roots' self-help network of local communities (Dantwala et al. 1998) and NGOs forming high profile nationwide political pressure groups may well be the sole means of ensuring that the necessary environmental policies are formulated and implemented without being subverted and corrupted. Local communities with women taking an active role (cf. Sivaramakrishnan 2000, p. 448) are well placed to devise and implement their own environmental policies (Agarwal 1997b; Beck and Nesmith 2000). International organisations such as the World Bank, World Trade Organisation and United Nations (with its regional environmental programme) can also bring pressure to bear on Indian politicians otherwise determined to advance their own fiscal and political interests at the expense of the rural poor, and the increasingly degraded environment. India's growing political instability and the rise of small regional parties may unwittingly advance this process as political power becomes more diffuse and therefore more susceptible and accountable to local pressure-groups.

WORKS CITED

Agarwal, B. (1997a), "Gender, Environment and Poverty Interlinks: Regional Variations and Temporal Shifts in Rural India, 1971-1991", *World Development* Vol. 25, No. 1, pp. 23-52.

—— (1997b), "Gender, Resources and Community Action", *World Development* Vol. 25, No. 9, pp. 1373-80.

Ahluwalia, M.S. (1985), "Policy for Poverty Alleviation", *Asian Development Review* Vol. 8, No. 1, pp. 111-32.

Anderson, M.R. (1998), "Individual Rights to Environmental Protection in India" in A. Boyle and M.R. Anderson (eds), *Human Rights Approaches To Environmental Protection*, Clarendon Press, Oxford, Chapter 10.

Ayres, R.U. and Kneese, A.V. (1969), "Production, Consumption and Externalities", *The American Economic Review* Vol. 54, No. 3, pp. 282-97.

Beck, T. and Nesmith, C. (2001), "Building on Poor People's Capacities: The Case of Common Property Resources in India and West Africa", *World Development* Vol. 29, No. 1, pp. 119-33.

Bhattacharya, N., Chakraborty, P., Chattopadhya, M. and Rudra, A. (1991), "How Do the Poor Survive?", *Economic and Political Weekly*, February 16, 1991, pp. 373-79.

Bhagwati, J.N. (1988), "Poverty and Public Policy", *World Development* Vol. 16, No. 5, pp. 539-55.

Binswanger, H.P. Deininger and Feder, G. (1995), "Power, Distortions, Revolt And Reform In Agricultural Land Relations" in J. Behrman and T.N. Srinivasan (eds), *Handbook of Development Economics* Vol. IIIB, Elsevier, Amsterdam, Chapter 42.

Briones, A. and Ramos, C. (2000), "Market forces and food security: The Case of Developing Asia" in P.S. Chasek (ed), *The global environment in the twenty-first century: Prospects for international cooperation,* United Nations University Press, New York, Chapter 12.

Chandra, B. (1992), "The Colonial Legacy" in B. Jalan (ed), *The Indian Economy: Problems and Prospects,* Penguin Books India, New Delhi, Chapter 1.

Chatterji, A. (1999), "Forest Reform in India", *Earth Island Journal,* Fall 1999, pp. 29-30.

Dantwala, M.L., Sethi, H. and Vasaria, P. (eds) (1998), *Social Change Through Voluntary Action,* Sage Publications, New Delhi.

Dasgupta, P. and Maler, K-G. (1995), "Poverty, Institutions And The Environmental Resource-Base", in J. Behrman and T.N. Srinivasan (eds), *Handbook of Development Economics* Vol. IIIB, Elsevier, Amsterdam, Chapter 39.

Datt, A.K. and Rao, J.M. (1996), "Growth, Distribution and the Environment: Sustainable Development in India", *World Development* Vol. 24, No. 2, pp. 287-305.

Datt, R. and Sundharam, K.P.M. (1997), *Indian Economy,* 36th revised edition, S. Chand and Co. Ltd., New Delhi.

Dev, S.H. and Ranade, A. (1997), "Poverty and Public Policy: A Mixed Record" in K.S. Parikh (ed), *India Development Report 1997,* Oxford University Press, Delhi, Chapter 4.

Divan, S. (2000), "Judicial Juggernaut: Environment Protection Through the Indian Courts", *National Environmental Law Association National Conference,* Freemantle.

Dreze, J. and Sen, A. (1995), *India: Economic Development and Social Opportunity,* Oxford University Press, Delhi.

Duvvury, N. (1998), "Women and Agriculture in the New Economic Regime", in M. Krishnaraj, R.M. Sudarshan and A. Shariff (eds), *Gender, Population and Development,* Oxford University Press, Delhi, Chapter 10.

Ehrlich, P.R. (1968), *The Population Bomb,* Ballantine Books, New York.

—— and Ehrlich, A.H. (1990), *The Population Explosion,* Simon and Schuster, New York.

Ghosh, B. and Neogi, C. (1996), "Liberalisation in India: Quality Differentials Between Public and Private Companies", *The Developing Economies* Vol. 34, No. 1, pp. 61-79.

Government of India, 1976, *Fifth Five-Year Plan*, Planning Commission, New Delhi.

——, 1981, *Sixth Five-Year Plan*, Planning Commission, New Delhi.

——, 1985, *Seventh Five-Year Plan*, Planning Commission, New Delhi.

——, 1992, *Eighth Five-Year Plan*, Planning Commission, New Delhi.

Hannan, K. (1999), "Environmental Management in India: Recent Challenges to the Indian Forest Service" *Journal of Environmental Planning and Management* Vol. 42, No. 2, pp. 221-33.

Hayami, Y. (1990), "Assessment of the Green Revolution" in C.K. Eicher and J.M. Staatz (eds), *Agricultural Development in the Third World, 2nd edition*, John Hopkins University Press, Baltimore, Chapter 26.

—— and Ruttan, V.W. (1985), *Agricultural Development: An International Perspective*, John Hopkins University Press, Baltimore.

Kumar, N., Saxena, N., Alagh, Y. and Mitra, K. (2000), *India: Alleviating Poverty Through Forest Development — Evaluation Country Case Studies*, The World Bank, Washington DC.

Laxmi, V., Parikh, J. and Parikh, K.S. (1997), "Environment: Can Neglect No Longer" in K.S. Parikh (ed), *India Development Report 1997*, Oxford University Press, Delhi, Chapter 6.

Lipton, M. and Ravillion, M. (1995), "Poverty and Policy", in J. Behrman and T.N. Srinivasan, *Handbook of Development Economics* Vol. IIIB, Elsevier, Amsterdam, Chapter 41.

Lipton, M. and Ravillion, M. (1996), "How Important to India's Poor Is the Sectoral Composition of Economic Growth?" *The World Bank Economic Review* Vol. 10, No. 1, pp. 1-25.

Maheshwari, B.P. (1971), *Industrial and Agricultural Development of India since 1914*, S. Chand & Co., New Delhi.

Mankar, V.G. (1995), *Economic Policy and Planning*, 2nd edition, New Age International Publishers, New Delhi.

Misra, S.K. and Puri, V.K. (1994), *Indian Economy: Its development experience*, 12th edition, Himalaya Publishing House, Bombay.

Misra, S.D. and Saxena, K.K. (1997), "Structural Change in Cost Shares of Primary Inputs of Indian Industries: An Input-Output Approach", *The Indian Journal of Economics* Vol. 77 Part 4, pp. 443-72.

Myint, H. (1990), "Exports and Economic Development of Less Developed Countries" in C.K. Eicher and J.M. Staatz (eds), *Agricultural*

Development in the Third World, 2nd edition, John Hopkins University Press, Baltimore, Chapter 13.

Nurske, R. (1953), *Problems of Capital Formation in Underdeveloped Countries*, Blackwell, Oxford.

Parayil, G. (1996), "The Kerala model of development: Development and sustainability in the third world", *Third World Quarterly*, Vol. 17, No. 5, pp. 941-57.

Patel, P. (1998), "Participatory Experiences in Adivasi Villages: Experiences of NIRID, 1979-1997" in M.L. Dantwala, H. Sethi and P. Visaria (eds) (1998), *Social Change Through Voluntary Action*, Sage Publications, New Delhi, Chapter 7.

Ramachandran, V.K. (1996), "On Kerala's Development Achievements" in J. Dreze and A. Sen (eds), *Indian Development: Selected Regional Perspectives*, Oxford University Press, Delhi, Chapter 4.

Ranade, A. and Dev, S.M. (1997), "Agriculture and Rural Development: Stocks, Subsidies and Food Security" in K.S. Parikh (ed), *India Development Report 1997*, Oxford University Press, Delhi, Chapter 7.

Rao, C.H.H. (1992), "Agriculture: Policy and Performance", in B. Jalan (ed), *The Indian Economy: Problems and Prospects*, Penguin Books: New Delhi, Chapter 4.

Rao, J.M. and Storm, S. (1998), "Distribution and Growth in Indian Agriculture" in T.J. Byres (ed), *The Indian Economy: Major Debates Since Independence*, Oxford University Press, Delhi, Chapter 5.

Roy, K. Tisdell, C.A. and Sen, R.K. (1992), *Economic Development: A Case Study of India*, Oxford University Press, New Delhi.

Sharma, M. and Vanjani, U. (1994), "Engendering Reproduction" in A.W. Clark (ed), *Gender and Political Economy: Explorations of South Asian Systems*, Oxford University Press, Chapter 2.

Sivaramakrishnan, K. (2000), "Crafting the public sphere in the forests of West Bengal: democracy, development and political action", *American Ethnologist* Vol. 7, No. 2, pp. 431-61.

Sollner, F. (1997), "A reexamination of the role of thermodynamics for environmental economics", *Ecological Economics*, Vol. 22, No. 3, pp. 175-201.

Solow, R.M. (1956), "A Contribution to the Theory of Economic Growth", *Quarterly Journal of Economics* Vol. 70, pp. 5-94.

—— (2000), *Growth Theory: An Exposition*, 2nd edition, Oxford University Press, New York.

Stigler, G.J. (1971), "The Theory of Economic Regulation", *Bell Journal of Economics and Management Science* Vol. 2, No. 1, pp. 1-21, in

G.J. Stigler (ed) (1988), *Chicago Studies in Political Economy*, The University of Chicago Press, Chicago, Chapter 6.

Sundharam, K.P.M. (1995), *Introduction To Indian Economy: A Descriptive Analysis*, 30th edition, R. Chand & Co., New Delhi.

Todaro, M.P. (1997), *Economic Development*, 6th edition, Longman, New York.

Turner, R.K., Pearce, D. and Bateman, I. (1994), *Environmental Economics: A Elementary Introduction*, Harvester Wheatsheaf, London.

UNFPA (1997), *India: Towards Population and Development Goals*, Oxford University Press, Delhi.

Vasaria, P. (1992), "Population" in B. Jalan (ed), *The Indian Economy: Problems and Prospects*, Penguin Books India, New Delhi, Chapter 10.

Wolf, C. (1993), *Markets or Governments: Choosing Between Imperfect Alternatives*, 2nd Edition, The MIT Press: Cambridge, Massachusetts.

World Bank, (1987), *World Development Report*, Oxford University Press, New York.

—— (1991), *World Development Report: Poverty*, Oxford University Press, New York

—— (1993), *World Development Report*, Oxford University Press, New York.

—— (1995), *India: Recent Economic Development and Prospects*, The World Bank, Washington DC.

—— (1996), *World Development Report: From Plan to Market*, Oxford University Press, New York.

World Resources Institute (1994), *World Resources 1994-95*, Oxford University Press, New York.

—— (1998), *World Resources 1998-99: A Guide to the Global Environment*, Oxford University Press, New York.

5

China and India: New *Mandalas* of Power in 21st Century Geopolitics

ROSITA DELLIOS

I. Introduction: 21st Century *Mandalas* of Power

A *mandala* — meaning circle in Sanskrit — is a mystic diagram representing the cosmos. Composed of circles, squares and sometimes other geometrical shapes, it looks like a palace floorplan with gates from the outer to the inner chamber where the monarch is enthroned. In Buddhism and Hinduism is it used as a meditational aid to reach a higher state of consciousness. One needs to progress through such human causes of suffering as selfishness, greed, ignorance and intolerance, before entering higher states of being as one centre. Besides its spiritual meaning, the *mandala* is also a geopolitical expression to describe the conduct of relationships of power among ancient kingdoms in India and later in Hinduised Southeast Asia (see, for example, Dellios, 1997a, 1997b, 1999). These two meanings are not necessarily mutually exclusive, particularly in the present age when moral and material power are pursued simultaneously.

The present world *mandala* is largely American-inspired but two emerging regional *mandalas* are those of China and India. Both have sizable continental and maritime dimensions, generally unchallenged except where they meet in the trans-Himalayan and Ganges-Mekong sectors. The mountain sector is less volatile than the water domain further south, where each comes face to face with the other's traditional spheres of influence and vulnerability to invasion. If India expands its influence into the South China Sea via Indochina,[1] and likewise China does so into the Indian Ocean via Burma,[2] instability is likely to arise if this is perceived as a negation of the values of the retreating power, and hence loss of its 'charismatic' attraction.[3]

In the 21st century, both China and India represent great cultural nations that are endeavouring to become great political powers. They must do this within the prevailing conditions of global connectivity and competitiveness in the knowledge industry, and not only by traditional means of a strong armed force and economy. While respecting the sovereign equality of states, they are not likely to settle for 'middle power' status, except in terms of a temporary hardship. India is already distinguished as "a high-tech leader, with the second largest computer software industry, the largest being in the US" (Sheridan 2000). China, in having succeeded in joining the WTO in 2001, can better access global markets while profiting from the benefits of competition in its own market. With progress in these and other related areas already underway, it is well within the realms of speculation to anticipate new *mandalas* — or schemas — of power in 21st century geopolitics, based on the Chinese and Indian power centres. The language and signification of *mandala,* drawn from Indian political tradition (the *raj-mandala* of Kautilya) as well as Chinese *mandala* formations during the Middle Kingdom's height of power in dynastic times, is a fitting device for providing a culturally regional perspective. The use of *mandala* here is not directly

1. In November 2000, India formed a formal grouping with five Southeast Asian countries for cooperation in culture, education, human resources and other areas, called the Ganges-Mekong Cooperation Organisation.
2. Burma is widely viewed as a client state of China. See, for example, International Institute for Strategic Studies, 2000a.
3. Traditional geopolitical *mandalas* were based on the politics of a charismatic centre, with its attraction of "deference and obligations" from other power centres through a demonstrated "ability to win allies and overtake enemies" (Higham, 1989: 240).

Kautilyan, but a significantly modified concept to account for 21st century geostrategic conditions.

II. The Narrative of Power as it Travels East from Western Gateways

China and the India — Asia's two great civilisational states — are also the world's most populous nations. Their combined populations of 2.3 billion represent a third of humankind. They are among the poorest of people with per capita GNP, for many, at below US$200. In view of their widespread material poverty, neither country can be considered a truly great power, not even China whose permanent membership of the UN Security Council confers international influence beyond its economic and strategic reach. As Lee Kuan Yew, Singapore's respected senior minister, once remarked: "At present [1997], when people refer to China as a great power, it is more diplomatic courtesy than reality" (Richardson 1997).

Perception of power and the power of perception

More pointed has been the appraisal of the late Gerald Segal, acerbic analyst of Chinese power and former director of studies at London's influential International Institute for Strategic Studies (IISS). Writing in *Foreign Affairs* in 1999, under the telling title of 'Does China Matter?', he found that the Middle Kingdom was really only a middle power (Segal, 1999). Applauding China for its theatrical performance in convincing the world of its illusionary power, Segal concluded that the statistics of power — both economic and military — did not support the perception of China as great. "Beijing is a seriously overrated power," he claimed. "China made up a mere 3 per cent of total world trade in 1997, about the same as South Korea and less than the Netherlands" (p. 26). He also singled out Foreign Direct Investment (FDI) into China as another myth which did not withstand statistical scrutiny, in that China accounted for only about 10 per cent of global FDI (p. 28). As to China's military credentials, these he dismissed as "second-rate":

> . . . China is a second-rate military power — not first-rate, because it is far from capable of taking on America, but

> not as third-rate as most of its Asian neighbours. China accounts for only 4.5 per cent of global defense spending (the United States makes up 33.9 per cent) and 25.8 per cent of defense spending in East Asia and Australasia. (p. 29)

While Segal's statistically-backed arguments are plausible, so are those in support of China's greatness. Illustrative is a speech to Beijing University in the same year cited above, 1997, by the then director-general of the World Trade Organisation (WTO), Renato Ruggiero. He spoke of "the reality that China is already a leading power in an ever more interdependent global economy", and went on the provide supporting evidence:

> This reality is emphasized by the sheer force of China's rise in the world. During the last decade, output has been expanding by an average of 10 per cent a year, while merchandise export volume has been growing even faster, at about 15 per cent. In two decades, the value of China's merchandise exports has expanded more than twenty-fold, reaching US$151 billion last year. China is already the world's fifth largest trading power, and the second largest recipient of foreign investment. Today the Chinese economy represents between 5 to 10 per cent of global output, depending on the method used to calculate national production. (Ruggiero 1997)

While there is some disparity in the statistics cited by an academic of international repute and an equally reputable trade organisation director, for a range of reasons,[4] there is no doubt

---

4. These reasons may include methodology of calculation, the inclusion or exclusion of Hong Kong, the reliability of China's state-issued statistics, or even the authenticity of FDI data. With regard to the first, a better known alternative method of calculation is 'purchasing power parity' (PPP). Its acceptance is reflected in its inclusion the World Bank's 'World Development Indicators'. Thus PPP GNP is defined as "gross national product converted to international dollars using purchasing power parity rates. An international dollar has the same purchasing power over GNP as a U.S. dollar has in the United States" (World Bank, 2000). Or, as the East Asia Analytical Unit (1996: 111) elaborates, PPP "refers to a method of comparing the size of economies using international price comparisons to reflect the relative domestic purchasing powers of currencies. Traditional ways . . . simply convert

that each of these influential commentators was more concerned with perception of power. Each had an argument to make, and it mattered not whether a country which was responsible for (only) three per cent of world trade was the equivalent of the world's fifth largest trading power. What did matter was the light in which economic and military statistics were seen, and hence the perception which was being created or reinforced.

Given the importance of generating impressions of power, it is with some interest that Segal should conclude his essay on 'Does China Matter?', with the following observation: ". . . until China is cut down to size in Western imaginations and treated more like a Brazil *or an India*, the West stands little chance of sustaining a coherent and long-term policy toward it" (p. 36, emphasis added).

In choosing India as an example of a lesser power with which China should compare, a great deal is revealed about perceptions of India. While both China and India, as large but poor nations, could legitimately be painted as middle powers, they could equally be considered in the category of great powers — particularly from a Southern hemisphere and equatorial

national figures on the size of a given economy, expressed in the local currency, to foreign exchange (usually US dollars) at the prevailing official exchange rate. This method has well-known shortcomings, including the fact that prices of services and other non-traded goods tend to be much lower in developing economies. As a result, PPP measures of developing economies are frequently higher than estimates based on exchange-rate calculations." With regard to the second reason for statistical sources of difference, Hong Kong Special Administrative Region of the PRC functions as a separate Customs territory and hence does not automatically come under PRC trade figures. Complicating the matter further, however, is the conduct of a proportion of Chinese trade through Hong Kong. Under careful analysis, this can be discerned through *China's Customs Statistics* (see EAAU, 1996: 145). As to reliability of China's statistical data, the fourth reason noted above, even the central government might be misled by enterprises seeking to exaggerate their productivity to avoid being targeted for reform. Finally, the questionable authenticity of FDI data derives from Chinese mainland investments sometimes being disguised as FDI when entering via Hong Kong. The purpose of this ploy is to qualify for tax concessions (see Segal, 1999: 28).

point of view. In the Western Pacific and Indian Ocean regions, greatness resides in Japan, China and India. Yet India, in terms of dominant Western (Northern hemisphere) perception, surely suffers from the opposite condition of China. Rather than being an inflated power, it is in all probability a decidedly deflated power. Why might this be so? As I have written elsewhere:

> . . . India is not well understood by the rest of the world. Its preoccupations are not the world's preoccupations. Neither rivalry with Pakistan in foreign relations nor the complexity of Indian socio-political affairs internally are international staples.
>
> . . . China is also not generally well understood, but the world is acutely aware of it. Indeed China itself ranks as a global preoccupation. (Dellios 1999: 5)

'Is it better to be feared than loved if you cannot be both?'

India appears to be underestimated as a potential great power, largely because *it fails to inspire fear, awe or avariciousness* in the world beyond. (These are typical testing grounds in the outer frames of a *mandala*.) China, by comparison, has succeeded. Chinese military ambition (as distinct from capability), the strength of Chinese culture, and the much touted market of a billion people, have captivated the global imagination. Even China's critics are at their harshest when discussing human rights issues, Tibet and Taiwan. India, by comparison, is not feared for being the world's biggest democracy or having a strong computer software industry. Its nuclear weapons status as of 1998 has not primarily inspired fear, but condemnation or ridicule for perceived 'gung-ho' behaviour. In short, where China is perhaps unreasonably feared, given its lack of capability or even sufficiently demonstrated intent, India is not feared enough. And while that famed Florentine strategist, Nicholi Machiavelli (1469-1527), thought it was better to be both loved and feared, he recognised both do not always coincide, and that human experience has taught that it is safer to be feared if a prince (in current times, a state) is to be influential. Hence the following words of caution have been proffered:

> . . . it is far better to be feared than loved if you cannot be both. . . . The bond of love is one which men, wretched creatures that they are, break when it is to their advantage to do so; but fear is strengthened by a dread of punishment which is always effective.
>
> . . . The prince must nonetheless make himself feared in such a way that, if he is not loved, at least he escapes being hated. For fear is quite compatible with the absence of hatred; . . . [and with the presence of respect].
>
> . . . So, on this question of being loved or feared, I conclude that since some men love as they please but fear when the prince pleases, a wise prince would rely on what he controls, not on what he cannot control. (Machiavelli, *The Prince:* XVII).

Machiavelli's thinking was formulated within the competitive political climate of Renaissance Italy, but the power-politics which he studied are of universal import. Forms of political realism, or *realpolitik,* may be recognised from European antiquity (Thucydides' history of the Peloponnesian War) through to diverse cultural settings, including Chinese legalist and Indian Kautilyan traditions.[5] 'Realism' is a political currency with which the world is long acquainted and which in many respects still holds sway unto the current era.

The power of attraction

That which is feared often inspires awe, and not only in its power of punishment but also in its cultural identity. American

5. Greek historian Thucydides (460 BC—400 BC) is famed for his history of the Peloponnesian War, which he attributed to threat perception and power politics. Chinese legalism refers to a school of classical thought which, when put into practice, brought about the unification of China in 221 BC. It supported standardisation, centralisation, severe punishments, and the effectiveness of military power. In China, the first dynasty's legalist rule was thought to be so severe as to sow the seeds of its own downfall. In India, during the Mauryan era, the renowned strategist Kautilya (4th century BC), through the *Arthasastra* (*Book of the State*), developed a complex system of international relations based on relationships of power.

culture may be said to be as powerful and awesome as its fighter jets; oftentimes it is just as feared. China has long used culture as a defining feature of civilisation and state strength. In Reischauer and Fairbank's (1970) apt summation, the "Chinese state was regarded as coterminous with Chinese culture" (p. 293). The Middle Kingdom's traditional tributary system of international relations was based on the notion of cultural superiority. Lesser nations would pay tribute to the Chinese emperor in an atmosphere of elaborate ritual. That 'barbarians' represented China's uncivilised 'other' is testimony to the important place accorded to culture in Chinese constructions of power.

Culture — and with it, religion — may be seen as the positive face of power. It is the 'carrot' to attract love and respect, as distinct from the 'stick', or negative face of power, which is used to compel or deter through coercion. The 'stick', while inducing fear, can also lead to hatred. Hatred, as Machiavelli warned, is a condition the astute ruler must avoid when deploying the power of fear. Organised hatred of the government may lead to rebellion within, and justify intervention from without. History, including that of the late 20th century, has furnished abundant examples of this. Thus there are pragmatic and not only moral reasons for the avoidance of tyranny. The *Arthasastra* or *Book of the State* from India's Mauryan empire concurred when it stated: "a king of unrighteous character and of vicious habits will, though he is an emperor, fall prey either to the fury of his own subjects or to that of his enemies" (Kautilya 1: 259). Chinese political philosophy is a ready source of warnings against tyranny as, for example, found in the *Mencius*:

> Confucius said: 'There are but two ways to follow, that of humanity and that of inhumanity.' A ruler who oppresses his people to the extreme will himself be slain and his kingdom will perish. If he oppresses not to the extreme, even then his life will be in danger and his kingdom will be weakened. (*Mencius* 4A:2 in Chan 1963: 73)

Not only was humane government to be practised within the state, but 'the power of attraction' was held in high esteem in traditional Chinese foreign policy. To quote China's pre-eminent Master, Confucius, when asked about government: "Ensure those who are near are pleased and those who are far away are attracted" (*Analects* XIII: 16). Irrespective of the ethical reasons for humane government (and these figured prominently in Confucianism), Chinese deployment of culture was of strategic import. Through the principle of *laihua,* which means 'come and be transformed', China's *modus operandi* as a state was to attract the world rather than conquer it. This meant that the 'barbarian' tribute bearers to the Chinese capital were represented as being drawn to civilisation (the *mandala* centre), not cowed into submission. While there is little to link Machiavelli to Confucius philosophically, it is worth mentioning Machiavelli's viewpoint on this matter, and perhaps in doing so linking ethics to pragmatism, like *yin* to *yang, dharma* to *artha* (soft and hard power, ethical and material power). Machiavelli regarded propaganda as one of "two principal instruments at the disposal of the prince" (Jones 1969: 29), the other being force. He considered religion to be a prime propaganda technique. "Whoever reads Roman history attentively," Machiavelli wrote in the *Discourses on the First Ten Books of Titus Livius* (Vol. II, Bk. I), "will see in how great a degree religion served in the command of the armies, in uniting the people and keeping them well conducted, and in covering the wicked with shame" (Jones 1969: 31). The propaganda power of religion was also used effectively against the Romans, as evidenced by the rebellious Christians.

Present-day secular India is well aware of the political potency of religion. 'Partition' and 'demolition' are politically-charged terms in Indian discourse.[6] 'Partition' — the division of British India into a secular state with a Hindu majority (India) and an Islamic state with a Muslim majority (Pakistan) — was accompanied by much bloodshed (at least 500,000 perished) and bitterness as the opposing religious groups fought during the mass exodus to their respective states. 'Demolition' was also accompanied by inter-communal violence — though not on the

6. As evident in the diversely-sourced essays found in Silvers and Epstein, 2000, for example.

scale of partition — when Hindu fanatics tore down a 16th century mosque in Ayodhya in 1992. The fanatics believed that the mosque, called the Babri Masjid, had been built by the founder of the Moghul dynasty on the birthsite of Lord Ram. China, too, is no stranger to the pitfalls of religiously-based movements. Its banning of, and police action against, the Falun Gong sect provides only the latest example of the Chinese state versus religious cult politics — the most famous being the 'Boxer Rebellion' during the Qing dynasty.

But to return to the awe-generating potential of culture, and China's refinement of the art, there is yet another power element to which it is related. In addition to tribute relations equating with a symbolic submission to civilisation (China), this form of traditional foreign policy which China practised also entailed attractive rewards, both in terms of trade opportunities and the conditions of peace in which they could be pursued. Here the 'barbarian's' avariciousness comes into play.

The power of greed

Gerald Segal, in his abovementioned essay questioning China's credentials as a great power, speculated that "China is better understood as a theoretical power — a country that has promised to deliver for much of the last 150 years but has consistently disappointed" (p. 24). It is true that the vast Chinese market has not fully materialised, largely because it has not been fully developed. Poverty prevented a large proportion of the Chinese population from becoming consumers — except for opium, owing to 19th century British commercial avarice and political expedience. There were also restrictive Chinese government policies on trade when it was demanded by the 'foreign devils' as a right, rather than conferred as a consequence of proper tributary relations. Indeed it was an imbalance of trade, in China's favour, that led the British to resort to the sale of opium, grown in India, to open the China market. When they could not succeed by subversive means, because of a concerted clampdown on the illegal opium trade, the British imperialists openly employed force. This became known as 'gunboat diplomacy' during the Opium Wars of 1842 and 1860.

China's subjugation to British trade interests demonstrates the power of greed when it is turned against you. Beijing has learnt this lesson well and opened up, on its own terms, the same treaty ports — as well as many other areas — more than a century after the Opium Wars. Long prized for its luxury consumer products that included silk, tea, and porcelain, China is now courted once again by business interests the world over. Because of the much celebrated China market, Beijing is exempt from the more censorious extremes of American and allied foreign policy. Even for the USA, the celebrated 'land of the free', ideology is not the sole — nor always the primary — 'criterion of truth'. The United States and India, the world's two largest democracies, have seen little of each other during the Cold War when strategic alignment held higher value as an indicator of worth than constitutional, freely elected, government. Like China, the United States well understands the language of power — markets, military might and global diplomatic impact.

Given the weight of American business and stability-promoting interests, neither democratic Taiwan nor Tibet as an international *cause celebre* can sway Washington into taking punitive action against China. NATO's use of force in Kosovo in 1999 is unlikely to be replicated in the Strait of Taiwan or in the Himalayan plateau, let alone across the less publicised region of Xinjiang from which calls for an independent 'East Turkistan' issue. Beijing acts like a beacon to international investors, particularly with its recent admission to WTO. It controls a credible and constantly modernising nuclear arsenal, as well as the world's largest armed force. While Beijing reserves its smiles for investors, it readily displays a belligerent attitude as the occasion demands, particularly on issues of sovereignty.

China's flexibility of forces

In a world which has become far more interdependent (the integrating function of *mandala*) but no less wedded to power as an *exclusive value* — that is, "Since one's own power is relative to others' lack of it, the pursuit of power for oneself implies the denial of power to others" (Jones 1969: 26) — finding one's preferred place in the hierarchy involves skills relevant to both conditions (becoming more integrated as one travels to the centre in the *mandala* but also manipulating the demons of human appetites). Power as a *common value* — "in the sense it could be shared without loss" (*ibid.*) — refers here to the (productive) economic and cultural power of attraction (*laihua*). It also includes China's much publicised 'strategic partnerships' with various countries, including the USA and Russia. These are fluid partnerships of power rather than entrenched struggles for power that characterised 19th century diplomacy and 20th century Cold War politics. 'Strategic partnerships' may prove to represent a shrewd diplomatic device for defusing a competitor's exclusive pursuit of power. Power as a *common value* accords with global interdependence. However, the quest for a preponderance of power characterises the power-maximising activities of nations wishing to reduce their vulnerabilities and maintain a credible capacity to enforce claims or threaten punishment when interests are compromised.

In the light of the above, China may be said to have performed its fear-inducing and awe-inspiring — not to mention, greed-invoking — role rather better than India. Western 'realism' may well be misreading both centralised, 'Communist' China (which is popularised as a potential threat to the established order), and democratic, 'chaotic' India (which is not). In turn, Beijing and New Delhi may also have only themselves to congratulate or blame, as the case may be, for misleading the West and possibly themselves. In a word, neither China nor India is sufficiently appreciated for its inherent capacities. Their current *mandalas* are not fully formed. In China, whatever the appearance, power no longer grows out of 'the barrel of a gun'.[7] Indeed, the military is among the least of China's assets — *unless* it is deployed to extramilitary ends — and can be among its worst enemies if it is not.

By this is meant that Chinese military power should not be

7. A famous Mao dictum, which was included in the *Little Red Book*, was that 'political power grows out of the barrel of the gun'. Its historical context was that the Chinese Communist Party needed its army to win the revolutionary war; but the army was expected to obey the party and not *vice versa*.

used or threatened to be used in any situation which could advance the image of China as a brutal power,[8] as in case of Taiwan's reunification or in an internal security role, lest China's campaign of economic and cultural attraction (a contemporary version of *laihua*) turns to repulsion. This, of course, occurred most vividly in response to the use of the People's Liberation Army (PLA) against students in Tiananmen Square in June 1989. Military power is best used when held in abeyance as a deterrent to aggression or as psychological ballast for advancing its diplomacy — in other words, being able to negotiate from a position of strength. If we are to understand that, in Henry Kissinger's words, "the United States is the only superpower in only one field of activity, and that is the military" (Kissinger 1998: 2), then China has a great deal of room to maneuver. With its portfolio of forces, including economic attraction and partnership diplomacy (especially in US President Bush's 'war against terrorism'[9]), it can set out to modify US behaviour, and not only compete in kind — that is, militarily.

Avoidance of outright military competition will save China money and 'face', in that its inadequacies will not be under constant scrutiny. If China attempted to match the US, the cost would be prohibitive. Avoidance of even the appearance of an arms race will also save it from continued suspicion of its intentions. Meanwhile, the psychological ballast of credible defence capability must be maintained — especially in the conventional weapons sector. Undue reliance on the nuclear threat is fraught with the risk of (a) *use* in the event that deterrence fails and conventional forces are inadequate; (b) *non-use* and hence capitulation (like the Cuban missile crisis when the Soviet Union backed down in the face of US nuclear threats); and (c) *provoking or providing a pretext* for US deployment of missile defence systems. This would considerably diminish China's nuclear credibility (see the International Institute for Strategic Studies 1999a, 1999b).

8. For example, former British Ambassador to China, Sir Percy Craddock, is quoted in MacFarquhar (2000: 165) as describing the Chinese as 'thugs'.
9. This theme is developed in Dellios and Field (2002).

China's geostrategic advantage is that it is the largest and always has been the largest polity in East Asia, much of which came under its suzerainty for two millennia. This, coupled with the China's attractiveness to futurists and optimists who invest in emerging world orders, provide the People's Republic with sufficient flexibility to arrange its power portfolio as circumstances demand. When Mao Zedong addressed the question of how does a weak army fight a strong one, his answer then has not lost any of its salience. The answer was to gain psychological ascendancy over the opponent so as to minimise his comparative advantage in material power. At the time, Mao's strategy was called People's War and involved guerilla tactics — "The enemy advances, we retreat; the enemy camps, we harass; the enemy tires, we attack; the enemy retreats, we pursue" (Mao 1966). As I have written elsewhere: "Such guerilla tactics naturally favour fluid rather than fixed battle lines. The purpose is to avoid engaging the enemy force on its own self-serving terms — an example of the wider principle of denying the adversary its concepts of warfare" (Dellios 1989: 13).

China has a rich and robust history of strategic endeavour. Mao, like Confucius, was a creative transmitter of tradition, mining China's cultural resources for answers to contemporary predicaments. It is said that nothing is wasted in China. Its use of history and culture attests to this. In questions of war and peace, Mao revived such classical strategists as Sunzi, just as Confucius addressed the militarism of his times by invoking the humane way of the sages. China has a flexible and diverse range of power factors at its disposal. Because these are often 'value added' by circumstance or convergence with one another, they are not readily measured. However, it would be unwise to underestimate this form of power while overestimating the significance of arms acquisition programmes and forays into the South China Sea.

India's Diversionary Power

India's greatness lies in its wide-ranging talents for losing itself in the world and finding its presence in almost any philosophy, religion and social condition, while retaining the recognisable *rasa* or flavour of 'Indian' civilisation.

> All the convergent influences of the world run through this society: Hindu, Moslem, Christian, secular; Stalinist, liberal, Maoist, democratic socialist, Gandhian. There is not a thought in the West or East that is not active in some Indian mind. (Historian E.P. Thompson quoted in Sen 2000: 101)

India's capacities are underestimated in terms of their diversionary power; it is therefore a case of watch what India says, not what it does. What is India saying in what it is doing? Interpreting India, and hence its potentialities, is perhaps even more important than interpreting China which is, ironically for a relatively secretive polity, more revealing of itself. China's concerns are highly focused: domestic economic reform; vigilance against American containment; and defence of Westphalian sovereignty to prevent interference in the upkeep and pursuit of Chinese state unity.[10] China's preoccupations read like a career path to great power status.

India, by comparison, is more evocative in its approach to the conduct of state affairs. For example, the otherwise fear- and awe-inducing act of nuclearisation is verbally juxtaposed with smiling Buddhic serenity. India's civilisational greatness, the birthplace of Buddhism and home of Hinduism, was brought home to the modern world with a 'bang rather than a whimper', to borrow from T.S. Elliot's suitably titled poem, *The Wasteland.* Upon the testing of India's nuclear device in 1974, its success was conveyed to Indira Gandhi, the then prime minister, with the code term: 'Buddha is smiling'. That test was conducted on Buddha Poornima Day (or *Wesak,* Buddha's birthday). On the 24th anniversary of the first test came another. It was codenamed, 'Buddha smiles again'. One scientist, on witnessing the underground explosion of three nuclear devices was reported in *India Today* (May 1998) as saying: "I can now believe stories of Lord Krishna lifting a hill" (in Roy 2000: xvii). The 1974 test had been described as a peaceful explosion. Its sequel in 1998

10. Thus, for example, in 1992, China passed legislation declaring sovereignty over the disputed Spratly, Paracel and Diaoytai (or Senkaku) island groups and also reserved the right — as it did with Taiwan — to use military force to assert its claims.

came with a government assurance that India continued to be "committed to the global elimination of nuclear weapons" (*Deccan Herald* 1998). In this regard, it is ironic that among the official reasons given for the test was 'exposing Western hypocrisy'.

The 1998 test was presided over by a Bharatiya Janata Party (BJP) Hindu nationalist prime minister, Atal Bihari Vajpayee, who was politically embattled at the time — just as Indira Gandhi had been in 1974. As Pankaj Mishra (2000: 228) observed: "India's first nuclear test in 1974 came in handy for Indira Gandhi when she was facing a crippling railway strike (the first of the political challenges that eventually led her to suspend civil rights in 1975)." The second demonstration of nuclear power gave a new lease of political life to Vajpayee, just as the first had done so for Mrs Gandhi: "The tests removed a feeling of 'national weakness' among Indians, a BJP spokesman said. This is why criticism of the Prime Minister virtually ceased for a while after the tests: he was now praised, even by his recent opponents, for being courageous and decisive . . ." (Mishra, 2000: 231). Indian public acclaim for heroic deeds on the part of its leaders links into god-king and mother-goddess attributes. Indeed, Pankaj Mishra (2000: 238) relates how after India's defeat of Pakistan in 1971, Indira Gandhi was hailed as the Hindu goddess Durga, consort of Shiva. The tale of a BJP leader, L.K. Advani, dressing up like Lord Rama and being driven in a Toyota disguised as a chariot, is another instance of the power of mythic metaphor in Indian politics.

Former Indian prime minister, P.V. Narasimha Rao, in his book, *The Insider* (1998), argues that Indian politics are essentially feudal. "Neither the democratic nor the federal principle had taken root to supplant the feudal ethos . . . [of] past centuries; the concept of kingship . . . was ingrained in the collective consciousness.... Democracy in action at best consisted of the question: Who should reign?" (quoted in Mishra 2000: 240)

If — to take this metaphor further — emperors and mandarins, albeit Communist, still rule in China, and divine monarchs rein in India through elections, what of the lands they govern? China is still called *Zhongguo* (the Middle Kingdom) in Chinese. The idea of a middle kingdom pertained not only to the centre of civilisation, surrounded by 'barbarians', but also to the country of equilibrium. As for India, its psycho-strategic dispositions are well revealed by the American specialist on South Asia, Stephen Cohen. Referring to the partition of post-independence India, he observed that it "broke up the strategic unity of the subcontinent that — albeit intermittently — goes back 2000 years to the first Mauryan Empire" (Cohen 1993). A united India would mean a geographic reach from the Persian Gulf to Southeast Asia and a diplomatic gravity to rival China's (*ibid.*). Add to continental unity, a maritime power projection across the Indian Ocean, and India could have been much greater than it is in the hierarchy of nations — perhaps second or third after the United States. K.M. Panikkar's seminal work, *India and the Indian Ocean,* first published in 1945, presents the case for control of the seas as follows:

> During its five thousand years of history, India like China has been conquered many time by invasions from the land side. But in the case of both, such conquests, though they led to temporary convulsions, only ended in the assimilation of the conqueror in the general pattern of the local civilisation.
>
> Control from the side of the sea is different. It operates as a stranglehold especially when, as in the case of India, as a result of geographical factors, the country's prosperity is dependent almost exclusively on sea trade. . . .
>
> . . . For sea trade no country is so centrally situated. . . . While to other countries, the Indian Ocean is only one of the important oceanic areas, to India it is the vital sea. Her life lines are concentrated in that area. (Panikkar 1962: 84-85)

With the 21st century underway, India as a great sea power has not come to pass. While not without progress, India's new naval doctrine which calls for 'blue water' capability by 2010, is judged overly ambitions to fund within such a short timeframe (International Institute for Strategic Studies, 2000b). Similarly,

India's August 1999 Draft Nuclear Doctrine would require, according to the International Institute for Strategic Studies (*ibid.*), "about $500 million annually over the next decade for even a minimal version" of the envisaged strategic force. India's ambitions, it seems, are out of reach of its capabilities. But ambition harnessed to a China-like determination to accomplish serious reform tasks, taps India's diversionary power. Shiva's dance does not have to lead to destruction — unless it is the destruction of petty political vanities. If China seeks its equilibrium between Heaven and Earth, *yin* and *yang, dharma* and *artha*; India is precariously balanced between the gods and the void. High-tech exit strategies from poverty present themselves on the one hand, the forces of 'partition' and 'demolition' menace on the other.

Chinese premier, Zhu Rongji, understood the condition well when he famously adhered to the view that China must crash or crash-through in implementing its reforms. 'Crash' could entail national fragmentation. This is no idle speculation for either China or India in view of the ease nowadays with which nations fall, fragment or force their entrenched leaderships from office. The weight of restive publics with heightened expectations needs to be borne through ever more enterprising and transmodern means. In other words it is a question of how to globalise in relation to the 'centre'.

How might this question be approached in *mandala* terms? Hall and Ames (1995) provide some guiding insights in their discussion of Chinese aesthetics:

> Among the Chinese, circles and squares have been dominated not by their peripheries but by their centres. It is not the bounded circle or the square one is apt to meet in Chinese art, literature, or philosophy, but the "radial" circle and the "nested" square which extend themselves ever outward from their centres. The Chinese claim that the world is but "the ten thousand things" bears little suggestion that it is a bounded or a boundable whole. Such a world is a set of foci from which relatedness to what at the moment is deemed "centre" may be negotiated. (Hall and Ames 1995: xxii)

China and India are great powers insofar as they concentrate on their civilisational centres — their historic regard for how to become human and thus enlightened — rather than their peripheries which can entrap them into narrow concerns for boundaries and borders. In any case, these are being outgrown. Happily, the 'borderless world' has become a cliché of our present digital age. New geopolitical *mandalas* of power are positioned to extend outwards into this borderless world from ancient centres of power. Rather than committing cultural suicide in order to survive the demands of globalisation and middle class/middle power values, these ancient centres of civilisation understand how to be great in the developed human sense. Their confidence should assist both their own people and the rest of the world to integrate the 21st century's diverse globalisation.

WORKS CITED

Chan, Wing-tsit (trans. and comp.) (1963), *A Source Book in Chinese Philosophy*, Princeton University Press, Princeton.

Cohen, Stephen (1993), 'The Regional Impact of a reforming India', in International Institute of Strategic Studies, *Adelphi Paper 276*, Brassy's, London.

Confucius (1988), *The Analects*, D.C. Lau (trans.), Penguin, Harmondsworth.

Dellios, Rosita (1989), *Modern Chinese Defence Strategy: Present Developments, Future Directions*, Macmillan, London.

—— (1997a), "How May the World be at Peace?": Idealism as Realism in Chinese Strategic Culture', in Valerie M. Hudson (ed.), *Culture and Foreign Policy*, Boulder, Lynne Rienner, Colorado, pp. 201-30.

—— (1997b), 'Reconceptualising Development as a Culture Mandala', conference paper, *4th International Conference on Development*, Institute for Malaysian and International Studies (IKMAS), Universiti Kebangsaan Malaysia, and the International Institute for Development Studies (IIDS), Calcutta, Universiti Kebangsaan Malaysia, Bangi, Malaysia.

—— (1999), 'China-United States Relations: The New Superpower Politics', *The Culture Mandala*, Vol. 3, No. 2, August, pp. 1-20, http://www.international-relations.com

—— (2000), 'Globalisation and the Mandala: Software for the Millennium', *The Culture Mandala*, Millennium Issue, Vol. 4, No. 1, December-January, pp. 1-10, http://www.international-relations.com

Dellios, Rosita and Heather Field (2002), 'China and the European Union: Potential Beneficiaries of Bush's Global Coalition'. *Australian Journal of International Affairs* Vol. 56, No. 1, April, pp. 83-98.

East Asia Analytical Unit (1996), *Asia's Global Powers: China-Japan Relations in the 21st Century,* Commonwealth of Australia, Canberra.

Hall, David L. and Roger T. Ames (1995), *Anticipating China: Thinking Through the Narratives of Chinese and Western Culture,* State University of New York Press, Albany.

Higham, Charles (1989), *The Archaeology of Mainland Southeast Asia,* Cambridge University Press, Cambridge.

International Institute of Strategic Studies (1999a), 'US Missile Defence: Strategy, Technology and Politics', *Strategic Comments* Vol. 5, No. 3, April.

—— (1999b), 'Sino-American Tensions: Bombs, Spies and Trade', *Strategic Comments,* 5(5), June.

—— (2000a), 'China's Ambitions in Myanmar: India Steps Up Countermoves', *Strategic Comments* Vol. 6, No. 6, July.

—— (2000b), 'India's Military Spending', *Strategic Comments* Vol. 6, No. 6, July.

Kissinger, Henry (1998), 'High-Minded Goals Require Realism', *Transitions* 5(11), Special Supplement, Nov. 1998, pp. 2-3.

Jones, W.T. (1968, 2nd edn), *A History of Western Philosophy: Hobbes to Hume,* Harcourt Brace Jovanovich, Inc., New York.

Kautilya (1967), *Arthasastra,* R. Shamasastry (trans.), Mysore Printing and Publishing House, Mysore.

Mabbett, I.W. (1978), 'Kingship at Angkor', *Journal of the Siam Society* Vol. 66, No. 2, pp. 1-58.

MacFarquhar, Roderick (2000), 'India: The Impact of Empire', in Robert B. Silvers and Barbara Epstein (eds), *India: A Mosaic,* NYREV Inc., New York, pp. 149-78.

Machiavelli, Niccolo (1981, 3rd edn), *The Prince,* George Bull (trans.), Penguin, London.

Mao, Zedong (1966), *Selected Military Writings of Mao Tse-tung,* Foreign Languages Press, Beijing.

Mishra, Panjak (2000), 'A New, Nuclear, India?', in Robert B. Silvers and Barbara Epstein (eds), *India: A Mosaic,* NYREV Inc., New York, pp. 227-73.

Richardson, Michael (1997), 'Diplomacy Defuses Fear of Beijing', *The Australian,* 11 January, p. 7.

Roy, Arundhati (2000), 'Introduction', in Robert B. Silvers and Barbara Epstein (eds), *India: A Mosaic,* NYREV Inc., New York, pp. xvii-xxxiv.

Ruggiero, Renato (1997), 'China and the World Trading System', *WTO News: 1995-1999 Speeches — Renato Ruggiero, Former DG,* World Trade Organisation, Geneva, http://www.wto.org/

Segal, Gerald (1999), 'Does China Matter?', *Foreign Affairs,* 78(5), September/October, pp. 24-36.

Sen, Amartya (2000), 'Tagore and His India', in Robert B. Silvers and Barbara Epstein (eds), *India: A Mosaic,* NYREV Inc., New York, pp. 55-106.

Sheridan, Greg (24 March 2000), 'Reluctant Passage to India', *The Australian,* p. 11.

Silvers, Robert B. and Barbara Epstein (eds) (2000), *India: A Mosaic,* NYREV Inc., New York.

Taiwan Security Research (13 November 2000), 'Weekly Report', http://www.taiwansecurity.org/

World Bank, 'Size of the Economy', *2000 World Development Indicators,* http://www.worldbank.org/

6

India, Multipolarity and Contested Globalisation

R. JAMES FERGUSON

1. Beyond a Stereotyped India

India's position in world affairs is often presented externally as that of a 'potential' great power which remains troubled by internal and regional problems. It is sometimes viewed as a state which only with difficulty is beginning to converge on the norms fostered in many international fora and promoted by dominant powers such as the US, EU and Japan.[1] In part, this image confuses the differences between a middle regional power (as India is within the South Asian context) and a power genuinely able to project power and influence global trends.[2]

More importantly, this stereotype of India as a troubled or 'failing' great power is based on a series of naive expectations that have been implicitly made of India.[3] As the world's second

1. Some of these negative images are outlined in Dixit, J.N., "External Threats and Challenges: An Overview of India's Foreign Policy", *World Affairs, 3 no. 1*, January-March 1999, p. 33.
2. See this conceptualisation in Hewitt, Vernon, *The New International Politics of South Asia*, Manchester, Manchester University Press, 1997, pp. 254-55.
3. For media stereotypes, sometimes perpetrated by both Western and Indian journalists, see Gautier, François, "A Stereotyped View", Indian Embassy in Washington Press File [Internet Access at http://www.indianembassy.org/new/NewDelhiPressFile/stereotyped_view.html].

most populous state and largest democracy, there has often been the expectation that India will naturally emerge as a great 'Asian' power alongside Japan and China.[4] Secondly, just as China and the tigers of Asia have been able to benefit from rapid industrialisation and an opening to export-reliant growth, it has been expected that from 1992 India might be able to repeat this type of performance. This has led to direct comparisons with Chinese economic performance,[5] often to India's detriment. In fact, such comparisons ignore the different timing of Chinese reforms (which were on track from 1978[6]), and the fact that India has begun to open more fully to the world economy at a different stage of globalisation. There is no automatic guarantee that the world economy will continue to reward more and more industrialised, labour-based manufacturing and export-directed nations.[7] Underlying this western expectation, of course, has been the hope of utilising the spending power of what has been touted as a growing middle-class with international tastes and expanding consumer power.[8]

---

4. Such expectations are also part of some Indian elite conceptions, as well an aspiration projected onto India by some regional commentators, *e.g.* in Pakistan and Bangladesh, see Hewitt, Vernon, *The New International Politics of South Asia,* Manchester, Manchester University Press, 1997, pp. 19, 25.

5. Arora, Guljit K., "Economic Development in China and India: A Comparative Study", *Strategic Analysis, 18 no. 11,* February 1996, pp. 1545-76; Halliday, Fred, "India and China: Challenges for a New Millennium", *Times of India,* 26 January 2000 [Internet Access].

6. See Arora, Guljit K., "Economic Development in China and India: A Comparative Study", *Strategic Analysis, 18 no. 11,* February 1996a, p. 1545.

7. Hewitt, Vernon, *The New International Politics of South Asia,* Manchester, Manchester University Press, 1997, p. 214.

8. There has been some controversy over the real size and significance of this middle class, even in economic terms, estimated in the early 1990s as anywhere between 12% and 40% of the population, 100 to 350 million, Dobbs-Higginson, Michael S., *Asia Pacific: Its Role in the New World Disorder,* Port Melbourne, William Heinemann, 1993, pp. 174, 178. In fact the 'consuming class' may comprise only 150 million, with only some 6 million with the sustained interest and

These expectations have placed an enormous burden on India as a developing state. In fact, a closer examination of the internal needs and regional environment of India suggests that such hopes gloss the real challenges that face government and society during the current period. Responsible policy-making within South Asia and by other countries toward the region may need to veer away from some of these inviting but dangerous stereotypes of being a 'great power'. Hence, the admonition by Brahma Chellany that 'India needs to remember that a major power is one that can withstand and inflict pain'[9] is totally insufficient in regional terms, ignores the reality of current globalisation trends, and underestimates the non-military forms of power that have become central to the international system. A 'major power' can no longer be defined in purely military terms.

India has also been seen as non-compliant to a number of norms and regimes that are strongly supported by the Western powers, Russia and to a lesser extent China. This includes a nuanced critique of the version of the CTBT proposed through 1995-1996,[10] a rebuttal of the NPT as a form of nuclear apartheid, a desire to become a permanent member of the UN Security Council (re-iterated in September 2000[11]), and an effort to

---

wealth for expensive foreign brand-named goods, see Tharoor, Shashi, *India: From Midnight to the Millennium*, N.Y., Harper Collins, 1998, pp. 280-82. For this as a neo-colonial desire to open Indian markets, see Rayan, Samuel, "India at the Millennium Crossroads", *Times of India*, 26 January 2000 [Internet Access].

9. Chellany, Brahma, "After the Tests: India's Options", *Survival, 40 no. 4*, Winter 1998-1999, p. 94.

10. For these concerns, including a 1988 effort by Rajiv Gandhi to initiate through the UN a 22-year programmed CTBT that would eventually eliminate all nuclear weapons, see Hewitt, Vernon, "Containing Shiva? India, Non-Proliferation, and the Comprehensive Test Ban Treaty", *Contemporary South Asia, 9 no. 1*, March 2000 [Internet Access via Proquest].

11. "India Seeks Permanent Security Council Seat", *Indolink News*, 20 September 2000 [Internet Access]. For the serious long-term implications that follow if India fails in this effort, see Hewitt, Vernon, *The New International Politics of South Asia*, Manchester, Manchester University Press, 1997, p. 116.

engage WTO processes in a way that buffers some of the impacts of globalisation.[12] Some Indians remain highly critical of dominant cultural norms in globalisation as little more than patterns of Westernisation and Americanisation, and have also begun to question the meaning of secular politics within India itself. Demands now being mediated through the WTO sometimes seem a 'one-way street of globalisation', where developed nations favour the wealth of multinational companies and elites rather than egalitarian development.[13] In the recent past disputes emerged between India and the U.S. over patent laws and the rate of phasing out of import restrictions in the Indian market.[14] More generally, there exists a real danger that the highly institutional and legalistic structure of the WTO may tend to undermine flexible approaches towards consensus on trade issues.[15] As such, recent Indian governments and wider Indian society are seen as highly critical of many aspects of the dominant patterns of globalisation ('globalisation-from-above'[16]), in spite of deeper engagement in world trade and WTO processes.

---

12. Thus from 1993 the BJP has been critical of the Indian accession to the GATT Uruguay round as abandoning the poor in India, Hewitt, Vernon, *The New International Politics of South Asia,* Manchester, Manchester University Press, 1997, p. 212. Currently, both India, Malaysia and other Asian nations are highly critical of too rapid a setting of a new WTO round, whose agenda needs serious consideration, "APEC Remains.Divided on How to Restart WTO Talks", *The Times of India,* 13 November 2000 [Internet Access].

13. Diwan, Ramesh, "WTO, MAI and National Interest", *Indolink Analysis,* 1997 [Internet Access]; Diwan, Ramesh, "Globalisation: Myth vs. Reality", *Indolink Analysis,* 1997 [Internet Access]. On the 'two-way street' and cultural fusion in the Asia-Pacific, see Mahbubani, Kishore, "The Pacific Way", *Foreign Affairs, 74 no. 1,* January/February 1995, pp. 100-11.

14. Kanth, D. Ravi, "US Seeks WTO Ruling to Accelerate India's Tariff Reform", *Asia Times,* 18 July 1997 [Internet Access].

15. Gordon, Prudence, "The World Trade Organisation — Throwing the Baby Out with the Bath Water?", *Australian Journal of International Relations, 50 no. 3,* November 1996, pp. 246, 251-58.

16. Roberts, Susan, "Geo-Governance in Trade and Finance and Political Geographies of Dissent", in Andrew Herod *et al.,* eds. *An Unruly*

Although there is some truth to these images, they run the risk of stereotyping India as a 'late comer' to the ruling club of 'advanced' international governance, of undermining the unique contributions that India can provide regionally and globally, and of dismissing key innovations in South Asian foreign policy. This paper will suggest that far from being 'out of step' with the global system, India has the opportunity to humanise and enrich globalisation processes that at present are contested, incomplete and in some cases destructive, especially to developing nations. To do this, however, India will need to engage widening circles of regional policy that will allow it to move beyond the grid-lock of conflict with Pakistan. In part this can be achieved through improving relations with China (in spite of any soft-alignment by the PRC with Pakistan), but more generally through an enhanced notion of multipolarity. Recently improved relations with the US are one step in the right direction, but need to move beyond diplomatic atmospherics or simple gains in bilateral trade and investment.

2. Widening Circles of Engagement: Beyond the Pakistan-China Nexus

On this basis, India can enhance its international profile in a number of ways. In part this is through continued engagement of India in several traditional circles of interest that extend from South Asia (via SAARC, the South Asian Association for Regional Cooperation),[17] into the wider Indian Ocean Region (enhancing IOR-ARC and weak South African and Australian linkages[18]), north and westwards into Central Asia and the Middle East,[19]

World?: Globalisation, Governance and Geography, London, Routledge, 1998, p. 117.

17. For prospects for SAARC, including movement from the SAPTA (South Asian Preferential Trade Agreement) process toward a Free Trade area, see Rodrigo, Nihal, "Attempts at Regional Cooperation in South Asia: An Interview", *World Affairs, 3 no. 1*, January-March 1999, pp. 12-13.
18. For past weakness in links with Australia, see Gordon, Sandy, *The Search for Substance: Australia-India Relations Into the Nineties and Beyond*, Canberra, ANU, 1993.
19. See Singh, Jasjit, "Growing South Asian Interests in the Persian Gulf Region: Problems and Opportunities", *Strategic Analysis, 23 no. 9*, December 1999, pp. 1419-34.

and eventually in a wider rapprochement with East Asia. At the global level, too, India, aside from its traditional involvement with the NAM movement,[20] also has a host of critical views which range from reform of the Security Council through to serious efforts to eradicate, rather than limit, nuclear weapons. In the end, however, India needs to develop a stronger dialogue with major powers, including the US, EU, Japan, Russia and China, in order to sustain influence on the global system.

In brief, strong opportunities exist for India within the Indian Ocean Rim Association for Regional Cooperation (IOR-ARC) setting, through continued dialogue with ASEAN through participation in the ASEAN Regional Forum, and via selective cooperation with middle powers such as South Africa and Australia.[21] It must be noted, however, that there needs to be continued momentum of both track I and track II process in IOR-ARC if this circle of engagement is to effectively benefit South Asia as a whole. The progress in 1999 membership, especially with the inclusion of Iran and Bangladesh, is extremely useful. Likewise, the addition of dialogue partners such as Japan and Egypt will also strengthen this organisation.[22] However, the formal membership of IOR-ARC needs to be seriously expanded to include more Middle Eastern states, and must eventually provide for full membership of Pakistan.[23] In the end, if Pakistan

20. For the new role of NAM in economic and ecological issues, see Hewitt, Vernon, *The New International Politics of South Asia,* Manchester, Manchester University Press, 1997, p. 118.

21. For earlier developments, see Ferguson, R. James, "Trading Cultures: Regional and Global Interactions in the Indo-Pacific Region", Paper prepared for *The Fourth International Conference on Development and Future Studies: Economic and Social Development Issues of the 21st Century,* Bangi, Malaysia, 2-4 September, 1997; Jayakumar, S., "ASEAN Committed to 'Partnership' with India: Post Ministerial Conference, 25 July 1996, Opening Statement", *Strategic Digest, 26 no. 10,* October 1996, pp. 1523-34; Naidu, G.V.C., "India and ASEAN", *Strategic Analysis, 19 no. 1,* April 1996, pp. 65-72.

22. Baruah, Amit, "IOR-ARC Rejects Pakistan's Message", *The Hindu,* 8 May 1999 [Internet Access].

23. See Jayanth, V., "Indian Ocean Rim Group to Take More members", *The Hindu,* 13 April 1999 [Internet Access].

is willing to accept the Charter principles of IOR-ARC, including the provisions for MFN trading status with other members including India, this would constitute a major diplomatic gain for South Asia as a whole. Although the IOR-ARC group may need to consolidate itself for some years, it should also proceed to accept more dialogue partners, including Britain, France and other European powers.

In engaging these regional 'circles', some major perceptual obstacles might need to be side-stepped. The first of these is the unfortunate dual-containment policy of the U.S. towards Iran and Iraq, which is counterproductive to wider regional stability and to Indian interests.[24] At present, the time is ripe for this policy to be moderated, first by allowing Iran to engage more fully with the world economy, and secondly through the easing of sanctions on Iraq which are having a disastrous effect on the health of the population of that country but are in no way forcing a change of leadership. The second obstacle that needs to be removed is the misperception that India and Pakistan cannot work together within international organisations. In fact these two countries have been able to engage in dialogue in some areas, including limited cooperation through SAARC, and limited function cooperation over water control of the Indus River and its tributaries.[25] Even in the more problematic area of strategic confrontation there have been efforts to limit the scale of conflict between the two countries. Thus after 1971, neither side has pushed into key territorial heartlands of the other, and both sides have tried to avoid attacking major population centres. Since that time, there have been several other agreements, 'not to attack each other's nuclear installations, reciprocal notification of key military exercises, and a hot line between the nations' army generals'.[26] Likewise, after the nuclear tests, in spite of

24. See Singh, Jasjit, "Growing South Asian Interests in the Persian Gulf Region: Problems and Opportunities", *Strategic Analysis, 23 no. 9*, December 1999, p. 1430.

25. For the difficult negotiations over the Indus River, see Newbill, Michael, "Indus Waters Treaty: A History", The Henry Stimson Centre [Internet Access at http://www.stimson.org/cbm/sa/indus.htm].

26. Ollapally, Deepa & Ramanna, Raja, "U.S.-India Tensions: Misperceptions on Nuclear Proliferations", *Foreign Affairs, 74*,

some intense negative rhetoric, talks were soon convened to reduce any immediate escalation of tensions between the two countries. The most positive statement of this aspiration to find accord between Pakistan and India as nuclear powers is found in the *Lahore Declaration* of February 1999,[27] though there is a considerable gap between the aspirations of this diplomacy and the reality of establishing a strategic balance in South Asia (see below).

These general steps, of course, need to be taken against the continued momentum of positive diplomacy in a number of multilateral fora, including NAM, the G15, the Commonwealth, and continued efforts by India to maintain its credibility for a future stronger role within the United Nations. In the end, however, any recognition that India is a major player in the international system with the ability (and moral prestige) required to help set norms, will need to be underpinned by enhanced relations with major global powers. India's long standing relationship with Russia is well-known, and though this has lagged with the economic 'down-sizing' of Moscow's influence from the late 1980s onward, there have been recent efforts to reinvigorate this 'friendship' through a summit between President Putin and Prime Minister Vajpayee. At that time, major weapons acquisitions from Russia were confirmed. In October 2000 the two countries signed 'a declaration on strategic partnership on greater defence and military-technical cooperation and joint effort to fight international terrorism, while giving a boost to the economic relationship between the two countries.'[28] Although the long-term benefits from this relationship can be debated, the term 'strategic partnership' in

Jan.-Feb. 1995, p. 16. See further Hewitt, Vernon, *The New International Politics of South Asia,* Manchester, Manchester University Press, 1997, p. 45; Dixit, J.N., "External Threats and Challenges: An Overview of India's Foreign Policy", *World Affairs, 3 no. 1,* January-March 1999, p. 35.

27. The text of this joint statement will be found at: http://www.indianembassy.org/South_Asia/Pakistan/lahoredeclaration.html

28. "India, Russia Sign Strategic Partnership, Nine Other Pacts", *Indolink,* 3 October, 2000 [Internet Access].

this context is highly significant,[29] since this is the same terminology used in the crucial Sino-Russian rapprochement since 1996. This terminology seems, at least from the Russian point-of-view, to be part of an emerging emphasis on developing greater multipolarity in the international system.[30]

Perhaps more crucial in the short to medium term has been the slowly normalising relationship between the U.S. and India. Tensions had existed over India's leadership in NAM (which opposed the hegemony of the 'North', Western nations), and then over India's perceived shift to what was viewed as 'soft' alignment with the Soviets. Furthermore, India did not agree with America's stance on the Nuclear Proliferation Treaty and the Comprehensive Test Ban Treaty. As India not only imported Soviet/Russian Weapons (since the Americans refused to supply them from 1962 onwards), but also developed its own missile technology, the U.S. came to view India's security stance as dangerously non-conformist. This negative U.S. view was reinforced by India's nuclear tests in 1998.

However, after the end of the Cold War, with the reduction of U.S. aid to Pakistan and with the economic reforms in India post-1992, U.S. policies began to change. There were several small signs of accommodation as early as 1984, with U.S. warship visits to Indian ports in the mid-1980s.[31] Joint naval exercises occurred for the first time in 1992.[32] In 1995, the then Defence Secretary William Perry and Commerce Secretary Ronald Brown visited India,[33] while in 1996 several trade delegations also tried to develop greater economic ties. For example, a U.S. business

29. Chengappa, Raj, "Sincerely Yours", *India Today,* 16 October 2000 [Internet Access].

30. Srivastava, Anupam, "India's Growing Missile Ambitions: Assessing the Technical and Strategic Dimensions", *Asian Survey, 40 no. 2,* March/April 2000, pp. 334-35.

31. Singh, Jasjit, "India Looks East: An Indian Perspective", Canberra, *India Looks East Workshop,* 5-6 December 1994, p. 20.

32. *Ibid.*, p. 21.

33. Wang, Hongyu, "Sino-Indian Relations", *Asian Survey, 35,* June 1995, p. 549.

delegation led by Ohio Governor George Vsinovich visited India in April 1996 to explore joint projects in high technology and 'environmentally friendly' areas,[34] while a delegation from Kentucky also discussed ventures to solve India's environmental problems.[35] Yet the U.S. government at that time responded 'rather passively to India's considerable efforts to improve relations'.[36] This was in part due to a strong anti-India lobby in the U.S., led by Indiana Republican Congressman Dan Burton. Congressman Burton hoped to reduce aid assistance to India, with his bills being defeated by 210 to 191 in 1995, and then 297 to 126 in 1996, indicating a thaw in U.S.-India relations. This is also seen in a large expansion of U.S. investment in India, which by the mid-1990s expanded 10 times to reach US$5 billion.[37] The U.S. Ambassador to India had stated that he expected investment to continue to increase.[38] In sum, India-U.S. relations then reached a level of practical accommodation in many areas, though they could not be described as 'warm'.

After a renewed chill in relations during 1998, it seems that the U.S. administration became willing to invest new efforts in its relationships with South Asia, including the possibility that the U.S. might accept the creation of a 'limited but credible deterrence' so long as India was willing to enter into some kind of international non-proliferation regime.[39] This shift was signalled by the March 2000 visit by President Clinton, in which India's importance to the region and the future of global politics

34. "U.S. Business Delegation to Visit India", *Indolink News from India*, 4 April 1996 [Internet Access].
35. "New Technologies from USA to Meet India's Environmental Challenges", *Indolink News from India*, 8 April 1996 [Internet Access].
36. Wang, Hongyu, "Sino-Indian Relations", *Asian Survey, 35*, June 1995, p. 549.
37. "Anti-India Bill Defeated in US Congress", *Indolink News from India*, 6 June 1996 [Internet Access].
38. "US Investment May Increase by 50% in India: Wisner", *India Journal*, 7 June 1996 [Internet Access].
39. Hewitt, Vernon, "Containing Shiva? India, Non-Proliferation, and the Comprehensive Test Ban Treaty", *Contemporary South Asia, 9 no. 1*, March 2000 [Internet Access via Proquest].

was explicitly recognised. President Clinton began to speak in terms of a 'new respectful partnership', of the two countries as 'natural allies', or of a 'true partnership of mutual respect'.[40] Among the most important outcomes of the meeting was the agreement to hold regular summit meetings, and regular meetings between ministerial and department heads. However, for India, the issue is whether this new diplomatic warmth will be translated in concrete economic and political benefits. At the least, however, the U.S. seems willing to engage more deeply with South Asia as a whole, and with India in particular.

Deeper engagement with Japan and the EU would also aid India's global influence. Aside from limited technological cooperation (since 1958), and growing aid and trade flows, tensions emerged with Japan over India's refusal to sign the NPT.[41] These tensions intensified with India's redefinition of its role as a nuclear power, with resulting Japanese 'measures' that reduced aid after the 1998 nuclear tests. In fact, circa 1998-1999 Japan undertook a strong diplomatic offensive in support of non-proliferation, and for a time tried to involve itself in resolving the India-Pakistan dispute. These efforts were not successful, and were not given strong support by the US or the other *status quo* nuclear powers.[42] Since Japan had committed 133 billion yen in loans and 3.5 billion yen in grants to India, with bilateral trade reaching US$4.56 billion in 1999, this was not a trivial issue.[43] For a short time, India-Japan relations were poor, with Japan temporarily withdrawing its minister and refusing to see

---

40. "Speech by the US President at the Banquet hosted by President K.R. Narayanan", *Strategic Digest, 30 no. 4,* April 2000, p. 392; "Address by the President of the United States of America to the Indian Joint Session of Parliament", *Strategic Digest, 30 no. 4,* April 2000, p. 393.
41. Hewitt, Vernon, *The New International Politics of South Asia,* Manchester, Manchester University Press, 1997, pp. 130-31.
42. See Limaye, Satu, "Tokyo's Dynamic Diplomacy: Japan and the Subcontinent's Nuclear Tests", *Contemporary Southeast Asia, 22 no. 2,* August 2000 [Internet Access via Infotrac].
43. *Ibid.*; "India, Japan Establish Global Partnership", *Xinhua News Agency,* 24 August 2000 [Internet Access via Infotrac].

an Indian special envoy.[44] However, with visits to Japan by the Indian Foreign Minister (December 1999) and Indian Defence Minister (January 2000) relations began to improve.[45] The visit by Japan's Prime Minister Mori Yoshiro in August 2000 signalled a serious effort to improve the relationship further, going so far as to speak of India and Japan as having become 'global partners'.[46] Once again, the issue is whether the long-term cooperation of the two countries can be sustained, outside of joint ventures in selected areas such as tourism and information technology.

India is also a major trading partner with many EU countries, and trade with Europe as a whole has grown rapidly so that the EU as a whole is India's largest trading partner.[47] However, there needs to be greater coordination between the EU and India on a number of political and strategic issues. There was a symbolic move in this direction from 1994 through dialogue conducted through a joint commission, by European Commission studies on the long-term relations with India, and through the development of an Indo-EC Economic Cross-Cultural Programme. By the year 2000, more serious proposals

44. Limaye, Satu, "Tokyo's Dynamic Diplomacy: Japan and the Subcontinent's Nuclear Tests", *Contemporary Southeast Asia, 22 no. 2,* August 2000 [Internet Access via Infotrac].

45. *Ibid.*

46. "India, Japan Establish Global Partnership", *Xinhua News Agency,* 24 August 2000 [Internet Access via Infotrac].

47. Summarised by the European Commissioner for trade policy as:

> Our bilateral trade has surged in the last twenty years: Indian exports to Europe were a paltry 1.8 billion ECUs in 1980, reached 4.8 billion in 1990 and in 1998 grew to 9.8 billion euro. Indian exports to Europe grew more quickly than to the rest of the world: since 1988, Indian exports in general grew at a rate of 11%, but exports to the EU were even more dynamic: 15% per year. The growth concerned not only traditional products such as textiles and agriculture but almost all product categories (including machinery, cars and chemicals). A parallel trend is noticeable for EU exports to India that from 2.4 billion ECUs grew to 6.4 billion in 1990 and reached 9.5 billion euro in 1998.

See Lamy, Pascal, "India-Europe Relations in the Age of Globalisation: the Challenges and Opportunities Ahead", Speech given at the Indian Institute

for cooperation between India and Europe had been mooted through the EU India Summit. As suggested by Pascal Lamy:

> Although there has recently been some progress, I am convinced that EU-India relations are far from realising their full potential. This is at least partially linked to the enormous information gap which exists in the EU about India and in India about the EU. And this despite the fact that we share several common features: a rich diversity of cultures, respect for democracy, and the commitment to economic progress, community values and social development.[48]

Key areas opened up for future cooperation with the EU include a more transparent WTO process which more readily meets the needs of developing countries (mooted by Pascal Lamy in March 2000).[49] Other areas of further collaboration could include development policies, environmental cooperation, and progress towards democratic governance in the global system. In the June 2000 Summit between EU and India efforts were outlined towards the building of a 'new strategic partnership' in which the 'EU and India are important partners in the shaping of the emerging multipolar world' of the 21st century.[50]

However, the most important area of political gain for India is in improving its relationship with the PRC. With the old geopolitics of Sino-Russian and U.S.-Soviet tensions now removed, the time is ripe for improved perceptions between India in China. The changing world context has greatly undermined the importance of Pakistan as a potential complication, and has meant that Beijing and New Delhi have

for Foreign Trade, New Delhi, 6 March 2000 [Internet Access at http://europa.eu.int/comm/trade/speeches_articles/spla15_en.htm].

48. *Ibid.*
49. Lamy, Pascal, "Strengthening the Multilateral Trade System: How Can the EU and India Cooperate?", Speech given to the Confederation of Indian Industries, New Delhi, 6 March 2000 [Internet Access at http://europa.eu.int/comm/trade/speeches_articles/spla16_en.htm].
50. "EU-India Summit Joint Declaration", 28 June 2000 [Internet access at http://europa.eu.int/external_relations/india/simmit_06_00/joint_declaration.htm].

more to gain from cooperation than competition.[51] It is suggested that such a direct approach toward cooperation should be engaged in, despite concerns over Chinese nuclear and missile capability, and worries over the transfer of technology to Pakistan.[52] Both these 'tactical' problems, in fact, emerge out of the earlier geopolitical linkages based on outdated bipolar global tensions.

Today, both India and the PRC are developing nations which are becoming major economic powers, and both have revisionist concerns over the structure of power and rule-creation in the international system. Put simply, rhetorical competition aside, in the current period 'China does not, in any direct sense, threaten India'.[53] Nor should Pakistan's importance to China be exaggerated.[54] Thus it is no longer productive to speak of China's 'containment' of India.[55] China's main current concerns are with modernisation, with the impact of American policies on East Asia, and with the hoped for unification with Taiwan.[56] India could elevate the threat it presents to China, but only at a risk of a return to geopolitical games that would isolate India from a stronger and wider international role. As suggested by Fred Halliday, the 'greatest challenge facing India is not its position relative to China, but that of ridding itself of the myth that its major challenge comes from China at all' and that India will waste its advantages 'by re-entering a world of strategic and

---

51. Halliday, Fred, "India and China: Challenges for a New Millennium", *Times of India*, 26 January 2000 [Internet Access].
52. Contra Chellany, Brahma, "After the Tests: India's Options", *Survival, 40 no. 4*, Winter 1998-1999, pp. 96-97.
53. Halliday, Fred, "India and China: Challenges for a New Millennium", *Times of India*, 26 January 2000 [Internet Access].
54. The parallel of US-Israel relations is misleading, contra Chellany, Brahma, "After the Tests: India's Options", *Survival, 40 no. 4*, Winter 1998-1999, p. 97.
55. *Ibid.*, p. 108.
56. See Srivastava, Anupam, "India's Growing Missile Ambitions: Assessing the Technical and Strategic Dimensions", *Asian Survey, 40 no. 2*, March/April 2000, p. 335.

nationalist competition from which its own history and qualitative strengths have the potential to free it.'[57]

Relations with China began to improve after 1988, with an agreement to settle border disputes peacefully, and the proposal that peace and tranquillity should be allowed to reign along the 'line of actual control' (LAC) until the matter could be fully resolved.[58] Dialogue between India and China was widened after the mutual signing of the Peace and Tranquillity Agreement (PTA) in 1993 through the use of Joint Working Groups.[59] Li Peng visited India in 1991, followed by a return visit by a visit by Narasimaha Rao in 1993. An important trip by Jiang Zemin in late 1996 suggested that China may have adopted a new positive view of South Asia as a whole, rather than aligning too narrowly with Pakistan.

This policy of mutual conciliation was somewhat set back by tensions after India's declared nuclear-weapon status in 1998, followed by a tense exchange of critical comments from both sides shortly after the tests.[60] Tough rhetoric by Defence Minister George Fernandes seemed to paint China in the role of 'enemy number one'.[61] However, within a year tensions began to reduce between China and India. Even when regional tensions

57. Halliday, Fred, "India and China: Challenges for a New Millennium", *Times of India*, 26 January 2000 [Internet Access].
58. Wang, Hongyu, "Sino-Indian Relations", *Asian Survey, 35*, June 1995, p. 547.
59. Srivastava, Anupam, "India's Growing Missile Ambitions: Assessing the Technical and Strategic Dimensions", *Asian Survey, 40 no. 2*, March/April 2000, p. 331.
60. See Malik, Mohan, "India Goes Nuclear: Rationale, Benefits, Costs and Implications", *Contemporary Southeast Asia, 20 no. 2*, August 1998, pp. 204-05; Srivastava, Anupam, "India's Growing Missile Ambitions: Assessing the Technical and Strategic Dimensions", *Asian Survey, 40 no. 2*, March/April 2000, pp. 315-16; Joshi, Manoj, "Sino-Indian Ties: The Big Sulk", *India Today*, 15 March 1999 [Internet Access].
61. Limaye, Satu, "Tokyo's Dynamic Diplomacy: Japan and the Subcontinent's Nuclear Tests", *Contemporary Southeast Asia, 22 no. 2*, August 2000 [Internet Access via Infotrac].

were heightened due to the conflict with Pakistan in the Kargil sector from May 1999, China promised that its own frontier with India would remain a 'cold border'.[62] Likewise, from mid-1999 China seemed keen to follow a policy of engagement, pursued through meetings between the foreign ministers of the two countries.[63]

Moreover, the Indian nuclear tests can be viewed as much more than a reaction to China's perceived strategic and nuclear superiority. In large measure, the nuclear tests were a challenge to the nuclear policies of all the other great powers, and a declaration of the covert capability that both India and Pakistan already had.[64] The wider political implications of the Indian tests has been summarised by Mohan Malik:

> . . . India's elite has long nursed a sense of grievance over the lack of respect accorded to India in view of its civilisational and cultural attributes, its population, and its potential, let alone its dominant position in South Asia. The nationalist Bharatiya Janata Party (BJP) wants India to be a nuclear, space and information technology (IT) power. The nuclear ambition, in particular, has always been part of the BJP's philosophy of negotiating with the outside world from a position of strength. Believing that it was a lack of advanced military technology by Asian powers like India, which led to their colonisation by European powers, nuclear weapons are seen as a currency of power by the military establishment, which had been urging successive

---

62. Srivastava, Anupam, "India's Growing Missile Ambitions: Assessing the Technical and Strategic Dimensions", *Asian Survey, 40 no. 2*, March/April 2000, pp. 331-32.
63. *Ibid.*, pp. 335-36. It also seems likely that Beijing is reluctant to support Pakistan without reservation, particularly if it is true that there has been some Pakistani support for insurrection in China's Xinjiang region, *Ibid.*, pp. 331-32, 335.
64. See Singh, Jasjit, "India's Nuclear Doctrine", in Singh, Jasjit (ed.), *Asian Strategic Review 1998-1999*, New Delhi, Institute for Defence and Strategic Studies, November 1999, pp. 9-23; Malik, Mohan, "India Goes Nuclear: Rationale, Benefits, Costs and Implications", *Contemporary Southeast Asia, 20 no. 2*, August 1998, pp. 191-215.

governments to cross the threshold from the very day that China did its first test.[65]

India has since moved to develop a declared nuclear doctrine designed to both legitimate its possession of nuclear weapons, but also avoid a sustained nuclear arms race in South Asia. The evolution of this doctrine has been controversial, and certain elements of the August 1999 *Draft Report of the National Security Advisory Board on Indian Nuclear Doctrine* (DND) led to a sustained debate on whether India could realistically move to a triad of launch platforms, and whether a 'minimal deterrence' could be combined with a strong second strike doctrine.[66] Nonetheless, the emerging outline of the doctrine does contain elements of restraint that need to be further calibrated. This is based on three core concepts,[67] including the development of a minimalist theory of deterrence, with the smallest degree of weaponisation and deployment combined with the real ability to launch a punitive counter-strike. India has also explicitly developing a doctrine of no-first use, with nuclear weapons not being deployed against states without nuclear weapons or nuclear-armed allies, and not deployed against non-nuclear threats.[68] India has also continued its support for an international campaign of complete disarmament, combined with efforts to persuade other powers, especially NATO and Russia, to return

---

65. Malik, Mohan, "India Goes Nuclear: Rationale, Benefits, Costs and Implications", *Contemporary Southeast Asia, 20 no. 2,* August 1998, p. 201.

66. See Srivastava, Anupam, "India's Growing Missile Ambitions: Assessing the Technical and Strategic Dimensions", *Asian Survey, 40 no. 2,* March/April 2000, pp. 311-41; Ghoshroy, Subrata, "Not a Catastrophe: Another Look at the South Asian Nuclear Tests", *Arms Control Today, 29 no. 8,* December 1999 [Internet Access via Proquest]. A copy of the report will be found on the Indian Embassy (Washington) Website at: http://www.indianembassy.org/policy/CTBT/nuclear_doctrine_aug_17_1999.html

67. See Singh, Jasjit, "India's Nuclear Doctrine", in Singh, Jasjit (ed), *Asian Strategic Review 1998-1999,* New Delhi, Institute for Defence and Strategic Studies, November 1999a, pp. 9-23.

68. *Ibid.*

to a non-first use doctrine.[69] In October it urged the development of bilateral or multilateral agreements enshrining the doctrine of 'no first use' for nuclear weapons,[70] a move not readily supported by the other nuclear powers.[71]

In the long run, it would not be surprising if India chooses to weaponise to the extent of developing a small, robust nuclear force capable of second strike capability.[72] It must be emphasised that such a force need not be based on numerical parity with China's nuclear force, but on the basis of creating a credible launch base, perhaps of between 132 and 350 warheads, including tactical weapons.[73] However, transition to the deployment of such a deterrent is fraught with problems, and there are serious theoretical and legal issues in such a transition.[74] Short term problems include an early stage before the development of second-strike abilities, when deployed weapons

69. *Ibid.*

70. "India Calls for Bilateral Or Multilateral Pacts On 'No First Use' of Nuke Arms", *Indolink*, 7 October 2000 [Internet Access].

71. Chellany, Brahma, "After the Tests: India's Options", *Survival, 40 no. 4*, Winter 1998-1999, p. 106.

72. It is estimated that between and .5 and 1% of India's GDP over a 10-15 period would be needed to create such a deterrent force, see Srivastava, Anupam, "India's Growing Missile Ambitions: Assessing the Technical and Strategic Dimensions", *Asian Survey, 40 no. 2*, March/April 2000, p. 313, footnote 2. This is possible for India, but would involve an overall rise in defence spending and related scientific research.

73. *Ibid.*, p. 318. In fact India might be able to base a workable deterrent of a 100 or less, see Chellany, Brahma, "After the Tests: India's Options", *Survival, 40 no. 4*, Winter 1998-1999, pp. 97, 107. From 1998, projected stockpiles of weapons-grade material suggested that by the year 2000 India might have enough material to produce approximately 86 nuclear weapons, and Pakistan up to 36 weapons, "India and Pakistan's Nuclear Tests", *Strategic Comments, 4 no. 5*, June 1998, p. 1.

74. See Friedberg, Aaron L., "Ripe for Rivalry: Prospects for Peace in Multipolar Asia", *International Security, 18 no. 3*, Winter 1993, pp. 5-33 [Internet Access via Infotrac], contra Chellany, Brahma, "After the Tests: India's Options", *Survival, 40 no. 4*, Winter 1998-1999, pp. 93-111.

will be potentially vulnerable to a first strike, the question of the evolution of nuclear doctrine in the triad of regional players (India-Pakistan-PRC), the maintenance of political command and control, and the fact that in the conventional theatre all sides have a culture of 'offensive defence'.[75] At the very least, India will have to recognise that China does not only face South. On the contrary, the PRC is still deeply concerned by its strategic lack of parity with the US, and even its conventional technological and military limitations in relation to Japan and Taiwan. Faced with the prospect of a new high altitude missile defence system that may be deployed in Japan, Korea and even Taiwan, along with the new Missile shield system that the U.S. is developing, China may well be encouraged to reconsider the effectiveness of its own nuclear deterrent.[76]

In such a setting, even a small nuclear arsenal in India combined with the new generation of Indian IRBMs[77] may have a much bigger ripple effect than intended by Indian planners. It must be remembered that 'misperceptions of the balance of power are most likely during radical shifts in the distribution of power' which challenge the *status quo* or expected trends in a complex setting such as East (and South) Asia.[78] Feeling itself underpowered in global terms, China might decide to bolster

75. Hewitt, Vernon, "Containing Shiva? India, Non-Proliferation, and the Comprehensive Test Ban Treaty", *Contemporary South Asia, 9 no. 1*, March 2000 [Internet Access via Proquest]. This is especially so bearing in the mind geographical realities of Pakistan, see Srivastava, Anupam, "India's Growing Missile Ambitions: Assessing the Technical and Strategic Dimensions", *Asian Survey, 40 no. 2*, March/April 2000, p. 330; Hewitt, Vernon, *The New International Politics of South Asia*, Manchester, Manchester University Press, 1997, p. 31.

76. See McGuire, Mitchell, *China's Nuclear Environment and the US Theatre Missile Defence Initiative*, The Centre for East-West Cultural and Economic Studies, Research Paper No. 6, May 1999.

77. For recent development of Indian capabilities, see Srivastava, Anupam, "India's Growing Missile Ambitions: Assessing the Technical and Strategic Dimensions", *Asian Survey, 40 no. 2*, March/April 2000, pp. 311-41.

78. Christensen, Thomas J., "Perceptions and Alliances in Europe, 1865-1940", *International Organisation, 51 no. 1*, Winter 1997, pp. 65-97 [Internet Access via Infotrac].

and modernise its own rather modest nuclear forces. In such a setting, India could find its own weaponising programme having the reverse effect of that intended. Instead of achieving a deterrence balance within South Asia, India could find itself facing a much stronger, and more modern, nuclear force within China. It must be stressed that such a reaction would not be based just on India's deployment of its deterrent, but on the changed balance of forces within Asia as a whole. Such a situation could lead to the escalation of Indian, Chinese and Pakistani nuclear programmes. There is no guarantee that India would win or benefit from such a race. To avoid such unintentional outcomes, India will need to diplomatically engage China and gain at least *de facto* acceptance that India is now a nuclear power with the moral right to a small but effective nuclear deterrent. The US has already given cautious signs of accepting this reality and is attempting to engage India in regimes controlling nuclear weapons and fissile resources, including negotiations on the proposed Fissile Material Cut-off Treaty (FMCT).[79]

Here nationalistic rhetoric boasting improved missiles and warheads having the reach to counterstrike targets deep in the Chinese heartland, including Shanghai and Beijing, may help justify Indian military budgets.[80] They may also gain some internal domestic support from some voters,[81] though 1999 elections did not suggest that due to its nuclear policies that the

79. See Ghoshroy, Subrata "Not a Catastrophe: Another Look at the South Asian Nuclear Tests", *Arms Control Today, 29 no. 8,* December 1999 [Internet Access via Proquest]. For U.S. 'benchmarks' in its parallel negotiations, see Srivastava, Anupam, "India's Growing Missile Ambitions: Assessing the Technical and Strategic Dimensions", *Asian Survey, 40 no. 2,* March/April 2000, p. 314.

80. Note the $3 billion shopping order placed with Russia in October 2000, including up to 150 Su-30 fighter-bombers, apparently in part to directly counter Chinese air-power capabilities. The Su-30s, along with India's small fleet of Mirage 2000s, are apparently able to act as a platform for India's nuclear weapons, Sheth, Ninad D., "The Upgrade Search", *India Today,* 16 October 2000 [Internet Access].

81. Hewitt, Vernon, "Containing Shiva? India, Non-Proliferation, and the Comprehensive Test Ban Treaty", *Contemporary South Asia, 9 no. 1,* March 2000 [Internet Access via Proquest].

BJP gained any extra electoral support in the lower house, where the BJP continues to lead to diverse coalition with a relatively narrow majority.[82] However, such threats are not only counterproductive but irresponsible. China, if its takes such rhetoric seriously, will be obliged to counter such planning and targeting.[83] Although PRC has long been aware of India's technical ability, the deployment of a serious deterrence (which is possible over a decade) would change the balance of nuclear forces in Asia as a whole. Stability can only emerge out of balanced patterns of transparent, mutual deterrence that are well understood as legitimate elements of nation defence, rather than as threats to the power aspirations of neighbouring states. In the medium term, India (and Pakistan), should be encouraged to joint some of kind of nuclear weapons control framework, even if one altered from existing *status quo* norms.[84] Likewise, though Indian missile programmes are not fully convergent with the details of the MTCR (Missile Technology Control Regime), India has developed and partly deployed these capabilities but has not yet become an exporter of such technology.[85]

82. Ghoshroy, Subrata, "Not a Catastrophe: Another Look at the South Asian Nuclear Tests", *Arms Control Today, 29 no. 8,* December 1999 [Internet Access via Proquest].
83. See Limaye, Satu, "Tokyo's Dynamic Diplomacy: Japan and the Subcontinent's Nuclear Tests", *Contemporary Southeast Asia, 22 no. 2,* August 2000 [Internet Access via Infotrac].
84. Extending the short time frame outlined in Hewitt, Vernon, "Containing Shiva? India, Non-Proliferation, and the Comprehensive Test Ban Treaty", *Contemporary South Asia, 9 no. 1,* March 2000 [Internet Access via Proquest]. It is possible that the BJP is hoping to build further domestic consensus before heading down the path of signing the CTBT, see Ghoshroy, Subrata, "Not a Catastrophe: Another Look at the South Asian Nuclear Tests", *Arms Control Today, 29 no. 8,* December 1999 [Internet Access via Proquest]. This is consistent with Prime Minister Vajpayee's statements that India would voluntarily forgo further nuclear tests, see "India-US Relations: A Vision for the 21st Century", *Strategic Digest, 30 no. 4,* April 2000, p. 414. See also Chellany, Brahma, "After the Tests: India's Options", *Survival, 40 no. 4,* Winter 1998-1999, pp. 102-03.
85. Srivastava, Anupam, "India's Growing Missile Ambitions: Assessing

A more balanced approach needs to set these tensions against the changing global environment:

> Additionally, the fear of a war between China and India can be dismissed because in the post-Cold War world, Sino-Indian economic and political interests are converging. Both countries are primarily interested in maintaining a peaceful environment to ensure unhindered economic growth which will allow them to exercise a greater degree of autonomy in international politics. The present trend of positive developments between China and India rather indicates that they are in a process of building up an Asian balance against the unilateral domination of the United States in Asian affairs. Although India's nuclear explosions of May 1998, avowedly for military purposes, and its defence minister's identification of China as the number one potential threat to India, slowed the Beijing-New Delhi rapprochement process, tensions seem to have subsided since both countries are emphasizing economic values more than military ones. Besides, strategic calculations suggest that a future war between China and India armed with nuclear weapons is most unlikely since both parties can lose much and gain nothing out of it. The slow but progressive trend in Sino-Indian relations suggests that the old parameters of military hostility, although unlikely to disappear totally, are gradually being replaced by the imperatives of political peace and diplomatic co-operation.[86]

Hence, India-China relations should not be based just on crude notions of international leverage, and this rapprochement policy

---

the Technical and Strategic Dimensions", *Asian Survey, 40 no. 2,* March/April 2000, pp. 337-39; Hewitt, Vernon, *The New International Politics of South Asia,* Manchester, Manchester University Press, 1997, p. 23.

86. Nuruzzaman, M.D., "SAARC and Subregional Co-operation: Domestic Politics and Foreign Policies in South Asia", *Contemporary South Asia, 8 no. 3,* November 1999, pp. 311-22 [Internet Access via Proquest]. A similar view will also be found in Srivastava, Anupam, "India's Growing Missile Ambitions: Assessing the Technical and Strategic Dimensions", *Asian Survey, 40 no. 2,* March/April 2000, pp. 334-35.

should not be interpreted as a form of appeasement.[87] Moreover, there are large areas of policy where India and China's policy are in accord:

> India insists that the post-Cold War world should not be a unipolar world; the strategic, economic, and political independence and self-determination of countries all over the world must be taken into account. India supports China's position on establishing a new international order, and therefore stresses that strengthening cooperation with China in this effort shall be very important to the peace and development of the region and of the world at large.[88]

These shared concerns remain today, and if anything are more pressing grounds for cooperation than before. While China-India relations began to thaw slightly from 1999 with some wider recognition of Indian concerns,[89] further concrete steps enhancing Indian military power without engaging China diplomatically could set Beijing and New Delhi on a mutually damaging collision course. Instead, India and China have more important global agendas on which they can cooperate. If countries such as China and India wish to be initiators and authors, rather than merely the objects, of current trends in globalisation, norm-setting, and new patterns of governance being explored through the UN and other international regimes, then close cooperation among 'middle-to-great' powers such as the European Union, Japan and China becomes extremely important. It is only with such international coordination, including liaison on some issues with countries such as France, Australia and South Africa, that India is likely to achieve many

87. Contra the crude threat assessments found in Chellany, Brahma, "After the Tests: India's Options", *Survival, 40 no. 4,* Winter 1998-1999, pp. 104-05, which show no understanding of China's wider foreign policy goals, for which see now Shih, Chih-yu, *Reform, Identity and Chinese Foreign Policy,* Taipei, Vanguard Institute for Policy Studies, 2000.

88. Wang, Hongyu, "Sino-Indian Relations", *Asian Survey, 35,* June 1995, pp. 546-554.

89. Joshi, Manoj, "Sino-Indian Ties: The Big Sulk", *India Today,* 15 March 1999 [Internet Access].

of its foreign policy goals and developmental needs. In part, this can be done through a re-examination of the concept of multipolarity.

3. The New Multi-Polarity

India can focus its international engagement through a serious restructuring of the concept of multipolarity. Rather than accept a bipolar or unipolar world system, key states including China, France, Russia and India have long argued that today several major centres of power need to be recognised within the world system.[90] On this basis, the possibility of sustained hegemonic dominance or preponderance of power by the remaining superpower seems unlikely, since such power soon generates 'countervailing forces', contesting the legitimacy of such a role.[91] Furthermore, the 'balance of power' model that was the basis of traditional realist models must be adapted in the light of the rise of geo-economic power, the influence of international institutions, and the impact of globalisation.[92] Hence, we need to consider not just 'poles' of power but levels and structures:

> No single hierarchy describes adequately a world politics with multiple structures. The distribution of power in world

---

90. See "France, India Share View on Multipolar World: Chirac", *Xinhua News Agency*, 18 April 2000 [Internet Access via Infotrac]; Dixit, J.N., "External Threats and Challenges: An Overview of India's Foreign Policy", *World Affairs, 3 no. 1*, January-March 1999, pp. 36-37.

91. See Guéhenno, Jean-Marie, "The Impact of Globalisation on Strategy", *Survival, 40 no. 4*, Winter 1998-1999, p. 16.

92. For empirical and theoretical problems with 'balance of power' and 'power balancing', see Vasquez, John A., "The Realist Paradigm and the Degenerative Versus Progressive Research Programmes: An Appraisal of Neotraditional Research on Waltz's Balancing Proposition", *American Political Science Review, 91 no. 4*, December 1997, pp. 899-912 [Internet Access via Infotrac]. At the very least, it may be necessary to include 'balance of threat' and 'balance of interests' to explain alliance behaviour, *Ibid.*, For the need to factor in decision-makers perceptions in order to arrive at theories that explain actual inter-state behaviour Christensen, Thomas J. and Snyder, Jack, "Progressive Research on Degenerative Alliances", *American Political Science Review, 91 no. 4*, December 1997, pp. 919-23.

> politics has become like a layer cake. The top military layer is largely unipolar, for there is no other military comparable to the United States. The economic middle layer is tripolar and has been for two decades. The bottom layer of transnational interdependence shows a diffusion of power.[93]

Multipolarity, of course, has been viewed by neo-realists as intrinsically less stable than bipolar systems, and that in general the fewer number of great powers in an international system the better.[94] However:

> The validity of this claim is by no means self-evident and, indeed, has been the object of a prolonged, heated, and ultimately inconclusive scholarly debate. Disagreement on the comparative merits is unresolvable on either deductive grounds (clever arguments can be made on both sides of the question) or, because of the relative rarity of bipolar systems, on the basis of historical evidence. In any case, with the sudden collapse of the old bipolar order, a new and more pressing issue has begun to assert itself: What may account for differences in the functioning of systems of similar structure? And, specifically, why is it that some multipolar systems have proven more stable (in terms both of their duration and of the level of conflict within them) than others?[95]

While the dangers of multipolarity are recognised, including the possibility of competition and alliance politics among these key powers (now expressed through the concepts of 'strategic partnerships' and 'special relationships'), a constructive, cooperative multipolarity can also be envisaged. In particular, it is necessary to move beyond the simple concept of power-

93. Harkavy, Robert E., "Images of the Coming International System", *Orbis, 41 no. 4*, Fall 1997, pp. 569-90 [Internet Access via Infotrac], following Nye, Joseph, "What New World Order?", *Foreign Affairs*, Spring 1992, p. 88.
94. Friedberg, Aaron L., "Ripe for Rivalry: Prospects for Peace in Multipolar Asia", *International Security, 18 no. 3*, Winter 1993, pp. 5-33 [Internet Access via Infotrac].
95. *Ibid.*

balancing among several discrete national powers, where complexity, lack of quickness in seeking balance, the role of revisionist powers, strategic miscalculation or misperceptions,[96] and irrational alliance building can undermine any sense of security offered by the system.[97] In the current global system, power is also nested within regional systems, within global patterns of trade and financial flows, partly arbitrated through international institutions which radically alter the nature of both the system and the poles of power at play. A range of diverse institutional actors must be added as sources of power, including institutions ranging from the WTO and UNESCO through to International NGOs. Likewise, cooperation in regional and international organisations has improved the relations among nations[98] as well as deepened their interdependence economically. Power is dispersed in complex ways, suggesting that in spite of US dominance at the national level, we in fact see a large number of institutional actors influencing norms and generating constraints on national policies.

For the current period, various models of world order have been proposed as valid descriptions, ranging from anarchic national tribalisms, 'clash of civilisations', 'zones of peace' versus 'zones of turmoil', through to bipolar-redux (with the rise of another power, perhaps China, to challenge the U.S.), or power preponderance models.[99] Multipolarity, on the other hand, envisages several major powers coming together to shape the

---

96. Christensen, Thomas J., "Perceptions and Alliances in Europe, 1865-1940", *International Organisation, 51 no. 1,* Winter 1997, pp. 65-97 [Internet Access via Infotrac].

97. See Harkavy, Robert E., "Images of the Coming International System", *Orbis, 41 no. 4,* Fall 1997, pp. 569-90 [Internet Access via Infotrac]; Friedberg, Aaron L., "Ripe for Rivalry: Prospects for Peace in Multipolar Asia", *International Security, 18 no. 3,* Winter 1993, pp. 5-33 [Internet Access via Infotrac].

98. Friedberg, Aaron L., "Ripe for Rivalry: Prospects for Peace in Multipolar Asia", *International Security, 18 no. 3,* Winter 1993, pp. 5-33 [Internet Access via Infotrac].

99. Harkavy, Robert E., "Images of the Coming International System", *Orbis, 41 no. 4,* Fall 1997, pp. 569-90 [Internet Access via Infotrac].

international system, both through cooperative and competitive frameworks. This can be seen as a possible model only if the wider dimensions of economics, culture, regionalisation and institution-building are added. On this basis, the US cannot ignore the current economic power of Japan or the regional interests of the EU, APEC and ASEAN, or the future potentials of China and India. Models of a 'new trilateralism' have also been proposed to suggest a burden sharing approach towards interconnected global challenges.[100] Equally importantly, a number of older great powers (Russia, France, Germany) and prospective new powers (China, Japan, the ASEAN grouping, South Africa, Brazil and Argentina) have not been entirely willing to accept a minor role as mere adjuncts to a US led global system.

In the long term, there are real problems with the U.S. utilising a straightforward power-preponderance strategy. Even if this might work in control of the Persian Gulf, for instance, it was clear that even against Iraq and Yugoslavia the U.S. needed allies; diplomatically, militarily (in terms of ground troops), and financially to help pay for operations. Thus one of the 'strengths' of the NATO-led Kosovo operation has been the strong supportive role played by British, French and German forces. On this basis, at the very least, the US cannot by itself structure the global international system. It needs allies, mainly voluntary ones, but sometimes coerced ones as well. Other problems for US global-leadership are those traditionally related to hegemons, even if only at the economic and diplomatic level. Hegemons are subject to the challenge of 'spoilers', weaker states who may nonetheless impose costs and challenge the will and legitimacy of strong states (North Korea, Iraq and Iran have been cast in such roles), as well the rise of new or potential powers that can upset the real power or incite fears in the old power (a role often foisted onto the PRC in the coming 20-50 year period). Likewise, Pakistan is sometimes cast in this role regionally through its ability to inhibit India's dominance

100. Ferguson, R. James, "Shaping New Relationships: Asia, Europe and the New Trilateralism", *International Politics, 4,* January 1998, pp. 1-21.

within South Asia.[101] Furthermore, in terms of economic interdependence, even dominant powers are subject to 'reflection' and competitive effects from trading partners (such as China and Japan for the US), while serious downturns in consumer economies can reduce the hegemon's growth and confidence. In the long run, it may be too politically risky, economically too expensive and resource-draining for America to maintain unipolar dominance for any length of time.[102]

At present, the global system has not so much developed a 'simple multipolarity' of roughly equal great powers, but rather a regional multipolarity of several regional subsystems (sometimes terms 'multi-multipolarity').[103] In such a setting, India can greatly increase its regional and global profile through conscious employment of a new model of multipolarity, combined with a circles of engagement approach.

4. Institutional Engagement in a Period of Emergent Globalisation

One of the basic problems with 'balance-of-power' in application is that is it very easy to misjudge power equations during periods of rapid change. Furthermore, simple power enhancement does not necessarily make a nation more secure:

> On the other hand, rapid national economic growth, and the shared feelings of power and entitlement that tend to go with it, may be at least as important a cause of expansionism as the efforts of embattled elites to maintain domestic power.[104]

---

101. See Ayoob, Mohammed, "From Regional System to Regional Society: Exploring Key Variables in Regional Order", *Australian Journal of International Relations, 53 no. 3*, 1999, pp. 247-60; Hewitt, Vernon, *The New International Politics of South Asia*, Manchester, Manchester University Press, 1997, p. 257.

102. Harkavy, Robert E., "Images of the Coming International System", *Orbis, 41 no. 4*, Fall 1997, pp. 569-90 [Internet Access via Infotrac].

103. Friedberg, Aaron L., "Ripe for Rivalry: Prospects for Peace in Multipolar Asia", *International Security, 18 no. 3*, Winter 1993, pp. 5-33 [Internet Access via Infotrac].

104. *Ibid.*

In the current period, the dominant challenge is not so much a geo-political contest with other nations, but a geo-economic interaction with the forces of a new international political economy which places new burdens and opportunities before societies. On this basis notions of 'greatness' and relative power have a totally transformed context:

> What is the meaning of balance of power if 'powers' are no longer sovereign actors, but interdependent players caught in a network of transnational interactions? What is the meaning of hegemony if the dominant power of our time, the US, is itself a 'reluctant sheriff', whose power, even if it is backed by the traditional instruments of military might, often seems to depend more on 'soft power', and on the autonomous decisions of non-state actors who project American economic and cultural influence?[105]

Here, India can pursue several parallel strategies. The first of these is the buffering of globalisation effects and international influence through regional engagement, strengthening both the SAARC and IOR-ARC grouping, but also through continued dialogue with ASEAN and the ARF. More directly, India has begun to strengthen its role within the WTO and UN, though it has not yet been able to proactively set norms in truly global fora. Lastly, India needs to take a very active role on global issues through 'issue-specific frameworks'.[106] This include a stronger debate in specific agenda and regimes which have set norms, or attempted to set such norms, in areas ranging from green-house gas emissions to nuclear testing. In the long run India cannot afford to stand outside of such arrangements, nor can it be forever seen as the non-conformist dissenter. Rather, India, as a great power in a diplomatic sense, needs to begin to engage in serious and concerted dialogue with the international community in making and shaping these rules and regimes, forming appropriate coalitions with other countries, organisations, or even INGOs on specific issues.

---

105. Guéhenno, Jean-Marie, "The Impact of Globalisation on Strategy", *Survival, 40 no. 4,* Winter 1998-1999, p. 6.

106. For this formulation, see *Ibid.*, p. 8.

There is a real cost, of course, in such engagement. It requires a boosting of economic resources in related areas (including research, policy and foreign affairs areas), a willingness to develop transparent policies which are promoted overseas and sustained through engagement in international fora, and the need to heighten India's current reputation as a global leader. Old liabilities such as an obsession with countering Pakistan or competition with China could not be sustained without damaging such a global role for India. However, India has many credentials that may prepare it for such a path: its commitment to NAM, its desire for a nuclear weapons-free world, its understanding of the problems facing the developing countries, its highly educated academic and bureaucratic elites, its national use of the *de facto* global language (English), its open and active news media, and its skills in computing and communications capabilities[107] that will help it keep up with the new media-oriented diplomacy. For example, India seems to have little hesitation in opening up to the World Wide Web, and through its Sankhyavahini project is keen to open up a window to the world with very 'high bandwidth'.[108] This is in contrast to countries like the PRC, which though keen to develop computer expertise, are hesitant about the 'cultural pollution' and political content that might then become available through a totally open Internet system. Here, too, India's diverse religious, cultural and ethnic resources can be a benefit in forging personal and social links to numerous civil communities. Likewise, its overseas Indians, or Non-Resident Indians (NRIs) as they are sometimes called, are also a key resource providing a network of understanding in many countries overseas.[109] But these 'circles

107. See Natarajan, R., "Emergence of India as Knowledge Superpower: Some Issues", *India Network Economic News*, 3 May 2000.

108. *Ibid.*

109. In modern times, India, like China, was the source of a diaspora of traders and immigrants who spread out into the Indo-Pacific and the world. 'Overseas Indians' are found in Malaysia (comprising 8-9% of the population), Singapore (comprising 7%), Burma, Hong Kong, and as far afield as Fiji, Australia, east Africa and South Africa, with small groups found in Indonesia and Thailand. A small but active Indian population is also found in the United States, see Gordon, Sandy,

of engagement' also need a deep content whereby India can provide key diplomatic and cultural resources for the diverse communities with which it engages. This contribution can explored through a return to a progressive foreign policy in which it leads (in conjunction with others) rather than follows international norms.

5. Civilising Non-Reciprocity

'Multipolarity' can be re-interpreted to indicate different phases of activity that move beyond the tradition roles of military, economic and diplomatic power. On this basis there are a large number of poles of activity that can allow a civilising engagement of the forces of globalisation. In the case of India, this includes a conscious use of its cultural and religious diversity (countering many current images in the news market place), the development and utilisation of its scientific, legal and educational infrastructure, and the extension of key concepts such as the first principle of non-reciprocity as found in the Gujral doctrine (now only applied to South Asia).

Within SAARC, the South Asian Association for Regional Cooperation, India has been able to advance positive relations with most of its members in spite of continued tensions with Pakistan.[110] In part, this has been due to the general success of the Gujral Doctrine, enunciated in 1996 by I.K. Gujral (first as foreign minister and for a time as Prime Minister). This doctrine was based on five principles:

These principles are: first, with neighbours like Bangladesh,

---

The Search for Substance: Australia-India Relations Into the Nineties and Beyond, Canberra, ANU, 1993, pp. 98-99. Most of these groups, of course, like the Chinese diaspora, are second, third or fourth generation residents, and wish to view themselves as nationals of Malaysia or Singapore etc., Suryanarayan, V., "Overseas Chinese and Overseas Indians in Southeast Asia: A Comparative Study", *Strategic Analysis, 18 no. 9*, December 1995, p. 1207). See further Tharoor, Shashi, *India: From Midnight to the Millennium*, N.Y., Harper Collins, 1998, pp. 143-58.

110. Ayoob, Mohammed, "From Regional System to Regional Society: Exploring Key Variables in Regional Order", *Australian Journal of International Relations, 53 no. 3*, 1999, pp. 247-60.

> Bhutan, Maldives, Nepal and Sri Lanka, India does not ask for reciprocity, but gives and accommodates what it can in good faith and trust; second, no South Asian country should allow its territory to be used against the interests of another; third, no country should interfere in the internal affairs of another; fourth, all South Asian countries must respect each other's territorial integrity and sovereignty; and, finally, they should settle their disputes through peaceful bilateral negotiations.[111]

This policy has also been followed in general by the later BJP government, and has been generally positive in affecting the way India's smaller neighbours have viewed her regional role. However, Pakistan has been critical of the doctrine as helping develop a kind of Indian regional 'hegemony', ruling out both the internationalisation of issues and changes to what Pakistan sees as an unfair *status quo*.[112] This concern of covert 'Indian expansionism' has also generated Pakistan and Sri Lankan resistance to accepting subregional cooperation processes within SAARC (designed to create a 'growth circle' among Bangladesh, Bhutan, Nepal and north-eastern India), as well as engendering fierce debates within Bangladesh and Nepal on this issue.[113] This idea of subregional cooperation had received strong support from then Indian Foreign Minister I.K. Gujral.[114]

From a critical viewpoint, the Gujral doctrine might be interpreted as simply a more sophisticated version of the old

---

111. Murthy, Padmaja, "The Gujral Doctrine and Beyond", *Strategic Analysis, 23 no. 4,* July 1999, pp. 639-40.

112. See *Ibid.*, pp. 639-52. For the way that Indian policy can sometimes fuel anti-Indian sentiment, *e.g.* in Sri Lanka, see Hewitt, Vernon, *The New International Politics of South Asia,* Manchester, Manchester University Press, 1997, pp. 66-68. For a rebuttal of any hegemonic pretensions in Indian foreign policy, see Dixit, J.N., "External Threats and Challenges: An Overview of India's Foreign Policy", *World Affairs, 3 no. 1,* January-March 1999, pp. 28-39.

113. See Nuruzzaman, M.D., "SAARC and Subregional Co-operation: Domestic Politics and Foreign Policies in South Asia", *Contemporary South Asia, 8 no. 3,* November 1999, pp. 311-22 [Internet Access via Proquest].

114. *Ibid.*

'India Doctrine' aimed at keeping India paramount within a South Asia free from the engagement of outside power.[115] However, if taken seriously, this need not exhaust the content of the non-reciprocal aspect of the Gujral concept. To some extent, this extension of the Gujral doctrine could be viewed as a pragmatic use of the idea of 'other-regarding' behaviour in international relations as one of the best ways of reducing threat and enhancing a shared sense of security.[116] At its core, the doctrine 'rests on the premise that India recognises that it is only when the benefits of regional interaction are equitably shared that South Asia would prosper.'[117]

On this basis, the principle of non-reciprocity can begin to be applied to a wider setting than South Asia. Within the realistic means at the disposal of India, it might be possible for begin to diffuse tensions with China by unilateral actions that build confidence and move towards a fruitful future. This need not involve large trade-offs in territory, nor should conventional security along the border with Pakistan be ignored. Here, the rubric of 'reasonable compromises on points of difference' might be a starting point.[118] However, by engaging in unilateral moves that underline India's serious effort to step outside of competition with its neighbours, India can cease being driven by the regional insecurities of a weak Pakistan, and by the global insecurities of its major global peer, China. Such moves would need to based on a careful calibration of shared interests. Although political instability within Pakistan may make this problematic bilaterally in the short term, the current leadership

---

115. Fears noted in *Ibid.*

116. See Vasquez, John A., "The Realist Paradigm and the Degenerative Versus Progressive Research Programmes: An Appraisal of Neotraditional Research on Waltz's Balancing Proposition", *American Political Science Review, 91 no. 4,* December 1997, pp. 899-912 [Internet Access via Infotrac].

117. Rodrigo, Nihal, "Attempts at Regional Cooperation in South Asia: An Interview", *World Affairs, 3 no. 1,* January-March 1999, p. 18.

118. See Dixit, J.N., "External Threats and Challenges: An Overview of India's Foreign Policy", *World Affairs, 3 no. 1,* January-March 1999, p. 38.

of China seems ready to entertain a more cooperative agenda. Areas of possible confidence building could include preparation for Pakistan's entry into IOR-ARC, deepened information technology collaboration with China, and trilateral track II efforts at developing a regionally transparent system of nuclear deterrence.

Likewise, India can draw on its own huge resource of cultural, religious and intellectual tools to assert itself as a virtual 'civilisational superpower'. To do this convincingly, the internal issue of religious pluralism and cultural diversity may need to be addressed in a more positive, constructive light, rather than being viewed mainly as a threat to Indian domestic stability. Amartya Sen, perhaps with some exaggeration, has suggested that "Secularism as it is practised in India . . . reflects the sum of collective feelings of intolerance of the different communities and is not based on combining their respective capacities for tolerance."[119]

This issue is not just a pluralism-versus-fundamentalism debate.[120] With its '19 national languages, over 250 primary dialects, and 6 major religions', India presents a picture of great cultural complexity.[121] It must be remembered that approximately 20% of the population comprise 2,000 'ethnic groups, castes, tribals, and so on'.[122] Keeping a balance between regional and national interests, between different religions, classes and castes[123] must be the first priority of any government.

---

119. In Tharoor, Shashi, *India: From Midnight to the Millennium*, N.Y., Harper Collins, 1998, p. 121. For the limits of secularism in the current 'transmodern' period, see Cleveland, Harlan & Luyckx, Marc "Governance and Religions: The Role of Religion in Public Policy", *World Affairs, 3 no. 1*, January-March 1999, pp. 62-74.

120. See Tharoor, Shashi, *India: From Midnight to the Millennium*, N.Y., Harper Collins, 1998, pp. 4-5.

121. See Hewitt, Vernon, *The New International Politics of South Asia*, Manchester, Manchester University Press, 1997, p. 10.

122. Arora, Guljit K., "Economic Development in China and India: A Comparative Study", *Strategic Analysis, 18 no. 11*, February 1996a, p. 1550.

123. The complex 'caste' system of India, though counter-balanced by

Furthermore, these divisions are exacerbated by the growing gap between expectations and the delivery by governments of an improved quality of life to sectors of the population, especially among the young.[124] The Indian government, then, needs to attend to economic growth and social justice. Key developmental needs, including improved health services, infrastructure development, increased energy production,[125] the creation of more jobs and continued food security are the core national needs of India. From this viewpoint, 'India's primary strategic objective is the socio-economic growth and betterment of the quality of life of its . . . people'.[126] Unless this is done, India is

---

government efforts to engage positive policies towards the 'Dalits', has meant that India retains a complex status system, based only in part on the traditional four *varnas* and overlaid by subgroups or *jati* related to occupational affiliation, see Milner, Murray Jr., *Status and Sacredness: A General Theory of Status Relations and an Analysis of Indian Culture*, Oxford, OUP, 1994, pp. 46-62.

124. Singh, Jasjit, "India Looks East: An Indian Perspective", Canberra, *India Looks East Workshop*, 5-6 December 1994.

125. For a sample of the growing demand on Indian resources in these areas, see Tharoor, Shashi, *India: From Midnight to the Millennium*, N.Y., Harper Collins, 1998, p. 190.

126. Singh, Jasjit, "India Looks East: An Indian Perspective", Canberra, *India Looks East Workshop*, 5-6 December 1994, p. 11. Although World Bank figures suggest that poverty has declined from 55% to 39% between 1975 and 1989, Hewitt, Vernon, *The New International Politics of South Asia*, Manchester, Manchester University Press, 1997, pp. 10, 240, the problem remains critical for India. One of the main aims of Indian policy has always been not just to increase GDP and GNP, but also to ensure through various welfare policies that economic growth lifts the everyday quality of life of Indians from sub-human conditions, Arora, Guljit K., "Economic Development in China and India: A Comparative Study", *Strategic Analysis, 18 no. 11*, February 1996a, pp. 1546-47. Though overall poverty may have dropped towards 35% by 1997, rural poverty still remains a real challenge, see "Fighting Poverty in South Asia: South Asia Poverty Brief", World Bank Report, April 2000 [Internet Access]. On the crucial need for development as a key security concern, see also Hewitt, Vernon, *The New International Politics of South Asia*, Manchester, Manchester University Press, 1997, p. 142.

unlikely to survive as a unified, democratic state that can play an important role in world affairs.

Such diversity does impose enormous challenges for India, and can help seed security problems and centrifugal forces that could threaten to undermine the unity of the Indian state. However, neither a passive secularism, nor an identity based on one creed, is likely to provide the social adhesion needed for a dynamic but stable society. It can be suggested that:

> In a pluralistic society such as ours the State cannot afford to either favour or marginalise any one or other religion. Nor can it dispense with religion altogether because it is a major force in the life of the people. The State must therefore be equidistant from all religions and at the same time be equally supportive of all of them.[127]

Such religious diversity can also provide certain intellectual and cultural resources that have roles in foreign policy. Alongside cultural connections with Southeast Asia (especially Thailand, Malaysia and Indonesia), India can also be viewed as the world's second most populous Muslim state. On this basis it has the intellectual resources not only to understand Islam and the Middle East, but also could be accorded observer status in a number of Islamic organisations.[128] Likewise, its Christian communities, for example, have provided a number of excellent education institutions that are used by Indians of all religious outlooks.[129] Sikhs, Jains, Buddhists, Parsis and other religious

---

127. Rayan, Samuel, "India at the Millennium Crossroads", *Times of India*, 26 January 2000 [Internet Access]. See also Mahapragya, Acharya, "The Excesses of This Century Will Climax Only to Inspire a Return to Spirituality", *Times of India*, 26 January 2000 [Internet Access].

128. See Singh, Jasjit, "Growing South Asian Interests in the Persian Gulf Region: Problems and Opportunities", *Strategic Analysis, 23 no. 9*, December 1999, pp. 1419-34. For example, to the Organisation of the Islamic Conference, bearing in mind that Thailand has Observer status there.

129. Tharoor, Shashi, *India: From Midnight to the Millennium*, N.Y., Harper Collins, 1998, pp. 93, 135. See in general Pye-Smith, Charlie, *Rebels and Outcasts: A Journey Through Christian India*, Harmondsworth, Penguin, 1998.

denominations either originated within India or have found long-standing homes on the subcontinent. Further, Hinduism, when detached from any political urge to assert a particular view of Indian identity for the purposes of mass mobilisation,[130] can be a pluralistic, open religion that has deep reservoirs of tolerance.[131] With its emphasis on an overarching divine unity embracing millions of different forms of expression, Hinduism should also be intellectually equipped for genuine dialogue with other religions, in spite of the misuse of Hinduism in local ethnic and 'caste' conflicts. On this basis, an open Indian culture can help provide a 'common civilisational space' for Indians of diverse creeds.[132] It is possible to argue that 'India's strength is that it is a conglomeration of minorities using democratic means to ascertain majority opinion on the crucial questions of the day.'[133] This vision, of course, is largely compatible with Nehru's vision of a diverse, pluralistic, tolerant and yet united India.[134]

---

130. See Van Der Veer, Peter, "Gender and Nation in Hindu Nationalism", in Tonnesson, Stein & Antlöv, Hans (eds), *Asian Forms of the Nation*, Surrey, Curzon, 1996, pp. 131-50; Ruud, Arild Engelsen, "Contradictions and Ambivalence in the Hindu Nationalist Discourse in West Bengal", in Tonnesson, Stein & Antlöv, Hans (eds), *Asian Forms of the Nation*, Surrey, Curzon, 1996, pp. 151-80; Tharoor, Shashi, *India: From Midnight to the Millennium*, N.Y., Harper Collins, 1998, pp. 119-20. For the late evolution of the term 'Hinduism', developed largely in contrast to Muslim and Western thought, see Smith, Wilfred Cantwell, *The Meaning and End of Religion*, London, SPCK, 1978, pp. 63-65.

131. See Tharoor, Shashi, *India: From Midnight to the Millennium*, N.Y., Harper Collins, 1998, pp. 54-59, 128-30; Frawley, David, "One Truth, Different Paths", *Times of India*, 26 January 2000 [Internet Access]. For the diversity and relative tolerance found in Kerala in this context, see Tharoor, Shashi, *India: From Midnight to the Millennium*, N.Y., Harper Collins, 1998, pp. 68-70.

132. Tharoor, Shashi, *India: From Midnight to the Millennium*, N.Y., Harper Collins, 1998, p. 134.

133. *Ibid.*, p. 78.

134. See Saksena, K.P., *Cooperation in Development: Problems and Prospects for India and ASEAN*, New Delhi, Sage Publications, 1986, p. 47; Tharoor, Shashi, *India: From Midnight to the Millennium*, N.Y., Harper Collins, 1998, p. 127.

Furthermore, this long civilisational legacy can be more actively utilised within the current age of globalising knowledge, constituting a new cognitive basis of the social world:

> The new generation of Indians should take up this task of world-making as their goal. The new world order of the computer and the information revolution offers the country a situation quite favourable to its unique spiritual and intellectual talents. . . . Such a new India would combine science and spirituality in a global perspective, adding the intuitive insights of the ancient rishis to the critical acumen of modern scientists.[135]

On this basis, India cannot only extend its prestige, but also begin to break out of debilitating geopolitical tensions with Pakistan and China, as well as gaining a better normative balance with Europe and the United States. Such policies would need to be sustained consistently over a number of years to gain leverage on the international system. Internal tensions and foreign policy hedging could easily undermine the emergence of such a coherent world strategy. However, maintenance of 'multipolar' policies operating through selective 'engagement circles' could indeed sustain India as a great power, in the true sense of the term, during the coming decades.

WORKS CITED

Anand, Vinod, "India's Military Response to the Kargil Aggression", *Strategic Analysis, 13 no. 7,* October 1999, pp. 1053-70.

Arora, Guljit K., "Economic Development in China and India: A Comparative Study", *Strategic Analysis, 18 no. 11,* February 1996a, pp. 1545-76.

Arora, Vasantha "Controversy of Pak's Deploying of Chinese M-11 Missiles", *India West,* 21 June 1996b [Internet Access].

——, "U.S. Is Against India Deploying Missiles, Even In Self-Defense", *India West,* 21 June 1996c [Internet Access].

Ayoob, Mohammed, "From Regional System to Regional Society: Exploring

135. Frawley, David, "One Truth, Different Paths", *Times of India,* 26 January 2000 [Internet Access]. This view is also supported in Mahapragya, Acharya, "The Excesses of This Century Will Climax Only to Inspire a Return to Spirituality", *Times of India,* 26 January 2000 [Internet Access].

Key Variables in Regional Order", *Australian Journal of International Relations, 53 no. 3*, 1999, pp. 247-60.

Bakshian, Douglas, "Bhutto Praises Clinton for Arms Transfer Approval", *Indolink News from India*, 16 April 1996 [Internet Access].

——, "Fresh Talks Likely Between India-Pakistan", *Indolink News from India*, 10 June 1996 [Internet Access].

Baruah, Amit, "IOR-ARC Rejects Pakistan's Message", *The Hindu*, 8 May 1999 [Internet Access].

Chellany, Brahma, "Nuclear Weapons and India in Asia", Paper presented at the *India Looks East Workshop*, Australian National University, December 5-6, 1994.

Chellany, Brahma, "After the Tests: India's Options", *Survival, 40 no. 4*, Winter 1998-1999, pp. 93-111.

Chengappa, Bidanda M., "Pakistan's Compulsions for the Kargil Misadventure", *Strategic Analysis, 13 no. 7*, October 1999, pp. 1071-82.

Chengappa, Raj, "Sincerely Yours", *India Today*, 16 October 2000 [Internet Access].

Christensen, Thomas J., "Perceptions and Alliances in Europe, 1865-1940", *International Organisation, 51 no. 1*, Winter 1997, pp. 65-97 [Internet Access via Infotrac].

—— & Snyder, Jack, "Progressive Research on Degenerative Alliances", *American Political Science Review, 91 no. 4*, December 1997, pp. 919-23.

Cleveland, Harlan & Luyckx, Marc, "Governance and Religions: The Role of Religion in Public Policy", *World Affairs, 3 no. 1*, January-March 1999, pp. 62-74.

Dhaliwal, Rav, "India Keen to Promote New Destinations to Singaporeans", *Straits Times*, 26 June 1996 [Interactive Internet Access].

Datta-Ray, Sunanda K., "The Task for India Is to Invest in the Quality of Its Schools", *International Herald Tribune*, 19 November 1998, p. 11.

Dellios, Rosita & Ferguson, R. James, "Australia and ASEAN: Submission to the Foreign Affairs Subcommittee", in JOINT STANDING COMMITTEE ON FOREIGN AFFAIRS, DEFENCE AND TRADE, *Asean Enquiry*, Canberra, AGPS, 1997, vol. I, pp. 95-121.

Diwan, Ramesh, "Globalisation: Myth vs. Reality", *Indolink Analysis*, 1997 [Internet Access].

——, "WTO, MAI and National Interest", *Indolink Analysis*, 1997 [Internet Access].

Dixit, Aabha, "Indian Navy: Working Out of a Financial and Operational Crisis?", *Asia Pacific Defence Reporter*, March-April 1996, pp. 19-20.

——, "India's Defence Policy and Production — Challenges and Opportunities", *Asia-Pacific Defence Reporter*, Jan-Feb. 1996, pp. 8-9.

Dixit, J.N., "External Threats and Challenges: An Overview of India's Foreign Policy", *World Affairs, 3 no. 1*, January-March 1999, pp. 28-39.

Dobbs-Higginson, Michael S., *Asia Pacific: Its Role in the New World Disorder*, Port Melbourne, William Heinemann, 1993.

Drudge, Michael, "Russian Foreign Minister in India to Revive Ties", *Indolink News from India*, 30 March 1996 [Internet Access].

Ferguson, R. James, "Shaping New Relationships: Asia, Europe and the New Trilateralism", *International Politics, 4*, January 1998, pp. 1-21.

——, "Trading Cultures: Regional and Global Interactions in the Indo-Pacific Region", Paper prepared for *The Fourth International Conference on Development and Future Studies: Economic and Social Development Issues of the 21st Century*, Bangi, Malaysia, 2-4 September 1997.

Frawley, David, "One Truth, Different Paths", *Times of India*, 26 January 2000 [Internet Access].

Friedberg, Aaron L., "Ripe for Rivalry: Prospects for Peace in Multipolar Asia", *International Security, 18 no. 3*, Winter 1993, pp. 5-33 [Internet Access via Infotrac].

Gautier, François, "A Stereotyped View", Indian Embassy in Washington Press File [Internet Access at http://www.indianembassy.org/new/NewDelhiPressFile/stereotyped_view.htm].

Guéhenno, Jean-Marie, "The Impact of Globalisation on Strategy", *Survival, 40 no. 4*, Winter 1998-1999, pp. 5-19.

Ghoshroy, Subrata, "Not a Catastrophe: Another Look at the South Asian Nuclear Tests", *Arms Control Today, 29 no. 8*, December 1999 [Internet Access via Proquest].

Gordon, Sandy, *The Search for Substance: Australia-India Relations Into the Nineties and Beyond*, Canberra, ANU, 1993.

——, "India and Southeast Asia: A Renaissance in Relations", Canberra, *India Looks East Workshop*, 5-6 December 1994.

——, "Economic Growth Dissipated On Regional Arms Race", *Asia-Pacific Defence Reporter*, December 1994-January 1995, pp. 46-49.

Gupta, Shekhar, *India Redefines its Role*, Adelphi Paper 293, London, IISS, 1995.

Halliday, Fred, "India and China: Challenges for a New Millennium", *Times of India*, 26 January 2000 [Internet Access].

Harkavy, Robert E., "Images of the Coming International System", *Orbis, 41 no. 4*, Fall 1997, pp. 569-90 [Internet Access via Infotrac].

Heisbourg, Francois, "The Prospects for Nuclear Stability Between India and Pakistan", *Survival, 40 no. 4*, Winter 1998-1999, pp. 77-92.

Herod, Andrew, Tuathail, Gearóid & Roberts, Susan M. (eds), *An Unruly World?: Globalisation, Governance and Geography*, London, Routledge, 1998.

Hewitt, Vernon, "Containing Shiva? India, Non-Proliferation, and the Comprehensive Test Ban Treaty", *Contemporary South Asia, 9 no. 1*, March 2000 [Internet Access via Proquest].

——, *The New International Politics of South Asia*, Manchester, Manchester University Press, 1997.

Jayakumar, S., "ASEAN Committed to 'Partnership' with India: Post Ministerial Conference, 25 July 1996, Opening Statement", *Strategic Digest, 26 no. 10*, October 1996, pp. 1523-34.

Jayanth, V., "Indian Ocean Rim Group to Take More members", *The Hindu*, 13 April 1999 [Internet Access].

Jha, Ganganath, "India's Vietnam Policy in Regional Perspective", *Strategic Analysis, 18 no. 10*, January 1996, pp. 1423-32.

Joshi, Manoj, "Sino-Indian Ties: The Big Sulk", *India Today*, 15 March 1999 [Internet Access].

Kanth, D. Ravi, "Gujral Plans Road Trip to Ease Wary ASEAN Investors' Fears", *Asia Times*, 15 July 1997 [Internet Access].

——, "US Seeks WTO Ruling to Accelerate India's Tariff Reform", *Asia Times*, 18 July 1997 [Internet Access].

Kremmer, Christopher, "Australia Joins Tariff War Against New Delhi", *Sydney Morning Herald*, 17 July 1997b [Internet Access].

Lamy, Pascal, "Strengthening the Multilateral Trade System: How Can the EU and India Cooperate?", Speech given to the Confederation of Indian Industries, New Delhi, 6 March 2000 [Internet Access at http://europa.eu.int/comm/trade/speeches_articles/spla16_en.htm].

——, "India-Europe Relations in the Age of Globalisation: the Challenges and Opportunities Ahead", Speech given at the Indian Institute for Foreign Trade, New Delhi, 6 March 2000 [Internet Access at http://europa.eu.int/comm/trade/speeches_articles/spla15_en.htm].

Limaye, Satu, "Tokyo's Dynamic Diplomacy: Japan and the Subcontinent's Nuclear Tests", *Contemporary Southeast Asia, 22 no. 2*, August 2000 [Internet Access via Infotrac].

Mahapragya, Acharya, "The Excesses of This Century Will Climax Only to Inspire a Return to Spirituality", *Times of India*, 26 January 2000 [Internet Access].

Mahbubani, Kishore, "The Pacific Way", *Foreign Affairs, 74 no. 1*, January/February 1995, pp. 100-11.

Malik, Mohan, "Sino-Indian Relations and India's Eastern Strategy", Paper presented at the *India Looks East Workshop*, Australian National University, December 5-6, 1994.

——, "India Goes Nuclear: Rationale, Benefits, Costs and Implications", *Contemporary Southeast Asia, 20 no. 2*, August 1998, pp. 191-215.

——, "The Future of Asian Geopolitics: An Indonesian-China-India Axis?", *Asia-Pacific Defence Reporter*, February/March 2000, pp. 19-20.

McGuire, Mitchell, *China's Nuclear Environment and the US Theatre Missile Defence Initiative*, The Centre for East-West Cultural and Economic Studies, Research Paper No. 6, May 1999.

Miglani, Sanjeev, "Malaysia and India Share a Vision", *Asia Times*, 18 December 1996 [Internet Access].

Milner, Murray Jr., *Status and Sacredness: A General Theory of Status Relations and an Analysis of Indian Culture*, Oxford, OUP, 1994.

Morrow, Jennifer, "India Refuses to Sign Nuclear Treaty", *Indolink News from India*, 20 June 1996 [Internet Access].

Murthy, Padmaja, "The Gujral Doctrine and Beyond", *Strategic Analysis, 23 no. 4*, July 1999, pp. 639-52.

Nag, Arindam, "Gowda Addresses Foreign Investment to Play Vital Role In PM's Plans", *India West*, 21 June 1996 [Internet Access].

Naidu, G.V.C., "India and ASEAN", *Strategic Analysis, 19 no. 1*, April 1996, pp. 65-72.

Natarajan, R., "Emergence of India as Knowledge Superpower: Some Issues", *India Network Economic News*, 3 May 2000.

Nuruzzaman, M.D., "SAARC and Subregional Co-operation: Domestic Politics and Foreign Policies in South Asia", *Contemporary South Asia, 8 no. 3*, November 1999, pp. 311-22 [Internet Access via Proquest].

Ollapally, Deepa & Ramanna, Raja, "U.S.-India Tensions: Misperceptions on Nuclear Proliferations", *Foreign Affairs, 74*, Jan.-Feb. 1995, pp. 13-18.

Panikkar, K.M., *India and the Indian Ocean: An Essay on the Influence of Sea Power on Indian History*, 3rd ed., London, George Allen & Unwin, 1962.

Pye-Smith, Charlie, *Rebels and Outcasts: A Journey Through Christian India*, Harmondsworth, Penguin, 1998.

"President Clinton's Visit to India", *Strategic Digest, 30 no. 4*, April 2000, pp. 389-418.

Rayan, Samuel, "India at the Millennium Crossroads", *Times of India*, 26 January 2000 [Internet Access].

Roberts, Susan, "Geo-Governance in Trade and Finance and Political

Geographies of Dissent", in Andrew Herod *et al.*, eds. *An Unruly World?: Globalisation, Governance and Geography*, London: Routledge, 1998, pp. 116-34.

Rodrigo, Nihal, "Attempts at Regional Cooperation in South Asia: An Interview", *World Affairs, 3 no. 1*, January-March 1999, pp. 12-13.

Ruud, Arild Engelsen, "Contradictions and Ambivalence in the Hindu Nationalist Discourse in West Bengal", in Tonnesson, Stein & Antlöv, Hans (eds), *Asian Forms of the Nation*, Surrey, Curzon, 1996, pp. 151-80.

Saksena, K.P., *Cooperation in Development: Problems and Prospects for India and ASEAN*, New Delhi, Sage Publications, 1986.

Sheth, Ninad D., "The Upgade Search", *India Today*, 16 October 2000 [Internet Access].

Shih, Chih-yu, *Reform, Identity and Chinese Foreign Policy*, Taipei, Vanguard Institute for Policy Studies, 2000.

Singh, Jasjit, "Growing South Asian Interests in the Persian Gulf Region: Problems and Opportunities", *Strategic Analysis, 23 no. 9*, December 1999, pp. 1419-34.

——, "India Looks East: An Indian Perspective", Canberra, *India Looks East Workshop*, 5-6 December 1994.

——, "India's Nuclear Doctrine", in Singh, Jasjit (ed), *Asian Strategic Review 1998-1999*, New Delhi, Institute for Defence and Strategic Studies, November 1999, pp. 9-23.

——, "Trends in Defence Expenditure", in Singh, Jasjit (ed), *Asian Strategic Review 1998-1999*, New Delhi, Institute for Defence and Strategic Studies, November 1999, pp. 24-127.

Smith, Wilfred Cantwell, *The Meaning and End of Religion*, London, SPCK, 1978.

Srivastava, Anupam, "India's Growing Missile Ambitions: Assessing the Technical and Strategic Dimensions", *Asian Survey, 40 no. 2*, March/April 2000, pp. 311-41.

Suryanarayan, V., "Overseas Chinese and Overseas Indians in Southeast Asia: A Comparative Study", *Strategic Analysis, 18 no. 9*, December 1995, pp. 1207-24.

Tharoor, Shashi, *India: From Midnight to the Millennium*, N.Y., Harper Collins, 1998.

Van Der Veer, Peter, "Gender and Nation in Hindu Nationalism", in Tonnesson, Stein & Antlöv, Hans (eds), *Asian Forms of the Nation*, Surrey, Curzon, 1996, pp. 131-50.

Vasquez, John A., "The Realist Paradigm and the Degenerative Versus

Progressive Research Programmes: An Appraisal of Neotraditional Research on Waltz's Balancing Proposition", *American Political Science Review, 91 no. 4*, December 1997, pp. 899-912 [Internet Access via Infotrac].

Wang, Hongyu, "Sino-Indian Relations", *Asian Survey, 35*, June 1995, pp. 546-54.

Yahya, Faizal, "Singapore-India: A Confluence of National Interests", *Asian Studies Review, 19 no. 2*, November 1995, pp. 25-37.

7

Environmental Globalism — South-North Relationship

DHULASI BIRUNDHA VARADARAJAN

1.1 Sustainable development refers to creating a style of economic development which is sustainable within the context of the planet's eco-system and human society. It has been formulated largely as an initiative of the United Nations through a series of reports and conferences to provide an answer to the world's environmental and economic malaise. Acid rain, the greenhouse effect, the growing hole in the ozone layer and other serious environmental problems have thrown doubt on the planet to absorb the spill over effects of economic development.

1.2 While economic growth is the dominant social paradigm there is a significant body of dissent that calls for solutions other than GNP. The dissidents claim is that continuous growth in the industrial nations will not only mortgage the future but will place a disproportionate burden on the less developed nations by encouraging them to export their natural capital and forcing them to bear the burnt of global environmental deterioration. The concept of sustainable development as a goal presumes that "development policies" can no longer solely be applied to the third world but have also be applied to the whole world. It is in this sense that we speak of "International Development Policy" or as Erusts U.V. Weizsacker puts it "earth policy".

2.1 The new emphasis on International rules with a concern for global environment issues and international co-operation is a marked change from earlier OECD attitudes to environmental problems. Three global treaties *viz.*, 1987 Montreal Protocol on CFCs, 1975 Convention on International Trade in Endangered Species of Wild Fauna and Flora (CITES) and 1989 Basel Convention on the Control of Transboundary movements of hazardous wastes and their disposal, have contained provision for enforcement that conflict with older economic treaties.

2.2 Global concerns about accelerating environmental deterioration and uncontrolled exploitation of renewable and finite resources evolved into the concept of sustainable development. The problem with Environmental Externalities whether they impinge on local or global common property resources is that there is no self-correcting mechanism for private consumers and firms engaged in the use and production of traded goods and services to take account of such externalities and compensate the affected parties for the damage and welfare losses that are inflicted. Hence free trade has the potential to degrade the environment and contributes to market failure independently of domestic sources of market failure (Choudhury and Islam 1995).

As Pearce (1993: 55) argues, trade liberalization is likely to give rise to negative environmental externalities, but also to some environmental gains. Moreover open economies have greater opportunities to acquire the most modern environmentally friendly production technologies and research intensive low cost environmental clean-up technologies from the developing countries (Rondinelli 1994).

2.3 Tighten end Environmental regulation in the developed countries has had direct repercussion on south Asia as firms in the former seek out countries where environmental safeguards are either weak or poorly enforced in order to transfer production or dump toxic waste (Lucas et al. 1992). A study by low and yeasts (1992) of the period 1965-88 found that the share of pollution intensive industries in the world trade had declined, while the share of these industries in developing countries exports had been rising. Other studies Leonard, 1988; Grossman and Krueger 1991 suggest that the "pollution haven" effect does not have a significant effect in motivating trade or investment flows (Faes 1994). Export oriented service sectors would appear to present more significant opportunities, but relatively pollution intensive manufacturing industries will still account for the bulk of new investment in south Asia.

2.4 It is argued that environmental standards can only be gradually enhanced at the same rate as competitor countries. Some argued that South Asian countries cannot afford the luxury of having the same degree of environmental controls as the richer countries and that in earlier stages of development the developed countries had even weaker environmental regulations.

3.1 The complex linkages between trade and environment constitute challenges in the pursuit of sustainable development as well as potential areas of conflict. The debate on the interface between environmental and trade policies has resulted in increased awareness of the importance of these linkages in both developed and developing countries.

3.2 In 1991 the OECD established joint committee on trade and environment which produced a set of procedural guidelines regarding

- Transparency and consultation will be allowed in the development and implementation of trade and environment policies.
- Promotion of International Co-operation on Environmental matters consistent with UNCED Agenda 21 and the Rio Declaration.
- Ecological interdependence on a global scale should be taken into account in trade policy formulation.

3.3. The 1970's forums focused on the trade effects of environmental measures such as the influence of environmental policies on global trade flows and the international competitiveness of countries implementing environmental protection measures. The 1990s debate, however, emphasis the opposite question, *viz.* the effects of free trade on the environment (GATT 1992: 19-47; Low 1992).

3.4 The World Trade Organisation (WTO) which was opened in January 1995 is now embroiled with the issue of incorporating environmental clauses. Central to this issue is the specification of environmental floor on which free trade should occur. This was in response to fears expressed by environmental groups over unregulated trade; largely to block the pursuit of short term interests that can destroy environmental standards.

3.5 The WTO aims to keep international trade open and impose a minimum standard of discipline on contracting parties. If included within its jurisdiction, the WTO, interlaid may also manage trade conflicts related to environmental standards. On environmental controls, it is expected to impose process standard on trade. There have already been efforts to integrate these standards in the General Agreement on Trade and Tariffs (GATT), Agreement on Technical Barriers to Trade and the widespread application of eco-labels in developing economics at least to it (Wiemann, 1994).

3.6 The stipulated environmental clauses are regarded the minimum permissible ground to ensure that trade is undertaken fairly, *i.e.* the competition will be based on efficiency rather than cut-throat price wars at the expense of the environment calls to include these conditions which was intimated by the United States and strongly backed by France, has created confusion and anxiety amongst several nations especially developing economies.

3.7 The European, position appears to have been shaped by a combination of genuine interest to safeguard the environment globally as well as protectionism. Officiates from developing economics question the sincerity of developed nations, governments in calling for harmony in environmental standards. There are also many who believe that development has to precede the establishment of common environmental standards globally. Indeed some feel that the environmental conditions included in the WTO agenda are Euro centre and that they are hardly the most pressing concerns of developing economies.

3.8 Tying of environmental clauses to trade sanctions may undermine their foreign exchange earnings potential which can bring misery for many. Development assistance to developing economies is a major alternative suggested by developed economies. Several feel that the developed economies with their financial and innovative muscle, can assist the transference of safer process technologies to developing economies. Sympathisers of developing economies argue that the developed world being the prime innovator and producer of toxic chemicals should take the lead in their removal. As a Gatekeeper the WTO acting on the complaints of ILO and UNCED or a more specialised environmental body, can advise trading nations to penalize offending firms. As blanket sanctions over the whole economy will be unfair and more importantly harmful, some feel that penalties should be meted out to violating firms only.

3.9 The European Union's (EU) current position on Environment Related Trade Measures (ERTMs) can be characterises as strongly favouring the principle of multilateralism against unilateralism (*eg* USA). Quite recently, the idea of compensation was carried into the EU discussions (Rajah Rasiah 1995). The compensation principle would require that unilateral measures that do not fulfil the conditions of multilateralism and Article XXb are to be combined with the duty to compensate the exporting country in a financial and technical manner in order to enable the countries concerned to implement the standards in question. In June 1994, the EU Commission tabled proposals to the EU Council and European Parliament for a new GSP System starting on January 1st, 1995. This clause discussed whether products manufactured from tropical wood should be the subject of additional tariff reduction, if they originate from countries applying International Tropical Timber Organisation (ITTO) standards which is regarded positive discrimination. This clause could be the beginning of a broader EU trade policy that integrate production methods into the GSP System and beyond.

3.10 Such clauses are currently mainly advocated by France and most Southern European countries, whereas they are opposed by Denmark and Britain, Germany and Netherlands belong to those countries that do not fundamentally disagree with the conclusion of environmentally motivated positive discrimination attributes in the GSP. Since such a stand is not very practical, they feel that developing countries should be given enough time to adjust to such standards.

4.1 The World Watch Institute has suggested in its 1997 state of the World Report that Eight Nations — the E8 — will disproportionately shape global environmental trends (World Bank, 1998), Brazil, China, Germany, India, Indonesia, Japan, Russia and the United States together they account for more than half of the world's population, its economic output, its carbon emission and its forests (Table 1).

TABLE 1

Eight Environmentally Important Countries

	Share of world population	Share of gross world produce	Share of world carbon emissions	Share of world forest area	Share of flowering plant species
	1996	1994	1995	1990	1990 (a)
United States	5	26	23	6	8
Russian Federation	3	2	7	21	9
Japan	2	17	5	0.7	2
Germany	1	8	4	0.3	1
China	21	2	13	4	12
India	17	1	4	2	6
Indonesia	4	0.7	1	3	8
Brazil	3	2	1	16	22
Total	56	59	59	53	—

Source: The World in 2020 — Towards a New Global Age, Oxford, 1998.

4.2 The South regions contribution to the Greenhouse gas effect and other international environmental problems is far below that associated with the United States and Japan (Fesharaki and Wu 1992). Even so, the developing countries are under greater pressure to take action on this issue following the United Nations Conference on Environment and Development held in Rio de Janeiro in 1992.

4.3 Another problem noted is the import of toxic wastes to South Asia from the industrialised countries — some times under the guise of recycling in order to take advantage of weaker environment rules and correspondingly lower costs, for the disposal of hazardous waste. Despite the ratification by many countries of the 1989 Basel Convention of Transboundary movements of hazardous wastes and their disposal and the subsequent tightening of the convention in 1994 in order to check. Waste exports for recycling large amount of toxic wastes are imported into the countries of South Asia. India, for example, imported almost 8000 tons of plastic waste and 26,800 tons of tin waste from the United States in 1993 and 106000 tons of ferrous waste from Canada in 1992 (Bidwai 1996). A large part of these wastes is not recyclable and is processed in small units which routinely violate safety and environmental laws and which use inexpensive but inefficient processes (Moazzam Hossain 1999).

4.4 The overall costs of sustainable policies have been shown to be large in absolute numbers, but small in relative terms. The World Bank estimates that developing countries need to expand 2 per cent to 3 per cent of GDP per year to achieve greater sustainability (Carton Brandon et al. 1993). In Asia, this translates to about $38 bullion per year by 2000, two-thirds of which is in East Asia (Table 2). Several issues arise concerning the financing of their investments. First to what degree can they be made financially viable? The most financially viable environment related investments are those that are good for both economic development and the environment. Second to what degree do investments under consideration address environmental problems with cross-border or global impacts, such as global warming ozone depletion, biodiversity and pollution of the seas.

4.5 In these cases, strong arguments exist for international cost-starting to help finance the investment costs. Such payments should not be thought of as development assistance, but as economically efficient allocations of costs and sharing of benefits. These concepts are recognised in the GEF and the Montreal protocol.

TABLE 2

Estimates of Additional Investment Required for the Environment in Asia by 2000

	East Asia	South Asia	Total
	US $ billions per year		
1. Water Supply and Sanitation	7.0	5.4	12.4
2. Reducing Emission from Energy generation	2.0	0.7	2.7
3. Changing to unleaded fuel control on vehicle pollution	3.9	0.9	3.8
4. Reducing Industrial pollution	3.6	1.2	4.8
5. Soil Conservation and Afforestation	5.0	3.6	8.6
6. Additions Resources for Agriculture and Forestry Research	1.4	1.0	2.4
7. Family Planning	1.4	1.0	2.4
8. Primary and Secondary education for girls	0.7	0.2	0.9
Total	24.0	14.0	38.0

Source: World Banks and Asians Development Bank Estimates.

4.6 The global environmental facility was established in 1990 with $ 1.3 billion to provide grants and concessional funds over a three year pilot phase. The facility assists developing countries address four global environmental areas: Global warming, Loss of biological diversity, pollution of International waters and depletion of stratospheric ozone. The GEF draws collaboratively on the experience and expertise of the UNEP, UNDP and the World Bank. Since 1990, $ 24 million (33 per cent of the total) have been directed towards Asia through investment project, technical assistance and research (Table 3). Under the Montreal protocol for protection of the ozone layer five projects have been prepared in Asia, of which four have been approved (Table 4).

5.1 To conclude first of all, industrial countries should keep in mind that the major responsibility for environmental protection lies within their own territory. Trade measures can by no means substitute for an effective and efficient national policy of external cost internalisation.

TABLE 3

G.E.F. Funding

Country	GEF Funding	Project Cost US $ Millions	GEF Funding US $ Millions	Banks Funding US $ Millions
1. Bhutan	Trust fund for conservation	20.0	10.0	—
2. China	Ship waste Disposal	64.0	30.0	15.0
3. Philippines	Integrated Protected Areas	301.0	20.0	224.0
4. Philippines	Leyte Geo-Thermal	1300.0	30.0	365.0
5. India	Non-conventional Energy project	—	30.0	120.0
6. Thailand	Promotion of Elector Energy Systems	—	15.5	30.0
7. Indonesia	Bio-Diversity Conservation	—	12.0	22.0
8. China	Sichuan Gas Transmission	—	10.0	300.0
9 India	Cost Effective options for Limiting Green House Gas Emissions TA	—	1.5	—

Source: Toward on Environmental Strategy for Asia, The World Bank Publishers, 1993.

TABLE 4

Funding under Montreal Protocol

Country	Project	Cost US $ Millions
Philippines	ODS Phase-out Engineering	0.18
Thailand	ODS Phase-out Engineering	0.40
China	ODS Phase-out Engineering	1.50
Indonesia	ODS Phase-out Engineering	0.25
Malaysia	Halons and MAC Recycling	1.63

Source: Towards an Environmental Strategy for Asia, The World Bank Publications, 1993.

5.2 Secondly international relations should be based on the principle of national sovereignty. However, the concept of national sovereignty reaches its limits when the activities of one country harm another country in a considerable manner.

5.3 On the issue of transboundary pollution, co-operation should take precedence over confrontation. Global treaties intended to coerce countries into adopting particular environmental policies and standards are unlikely to achieve the desired goals. The most, immediate environmental problems facing developing countries are unsafe water, inadequate sanitation, soil depletion indoor smoke from cooling fires and outdoor smoke from coal burning are different from and more immediately life threatening than those associated with the affluence of rich countries such as carbon-di-oxide emissions, depletion of stratospheric ozone, photo chemical smog's, acid rain and hazardous wastes.

5.4 The capacity of developing countries to enjoy sustained income growth will depend on industrial countries economic policies, improved access to trade and capital markets, policies to increase savings and lower world interest rates and policies that promote robust, environmentally responsible growth in industrial countries. Some of the benefits from environmental policies in developing countries — the protection of tropical forests and of bio-diversity, for example — accrue to rich countries, which ought therefore to bear an equivalent part of the costs.

WORKS CITED

Bidwai, P. (1996), "Toxic Waste Disposal" in *The Hindu*, Survey of the Environment, 96, New Delhi.

Carter Brandon and Ramesh Ramankutty (1993), "Towards an Environmental Strategy for Asia," World Bank Discussion Papers No. 224.

Choudhury, A. and Islam (1993), "The Newly Industrialising Economics of East Asia", London and New York, Routledge.

Fesharaki and Wu, K. (1992), "Energy Policies in Asian-Pacific Developing Countries", *Asian-Pacific Economic Literature*, 6, 2: 11-49.

Fries, S. (1994), "Trade and the Environment" in N. Kirmani et al.,

International Trade Policies: The Uruguay Round and Beyond it, Background Papers, Washington DC: International Monetary Fund.

GATT (1992), "Trade and the Environment", in *GATT, International Trade 90-91*, Vol. I, Geneva, pp. 19-47.

Grossman, G.M. and Krueger, A. (1991), "Environmental Impacts of a North America Free Trade Agreement", National Bureau of Economic Research Working Paper, No. 3914, Cambridge M.A., National Bureau of Economic Research.

Leonard, J. (1988), "Pollution and the Struggle for the World Product", New York: Cambridge University Press.

Low P., ed. (1992), "International Trade and the Environment", World Bank Discussion Paper 159, Washington, D.C.

Lucas, R.E., Wheeler, D. and Hellige, H. (1992), "Economic Development, Environmental Regulation and the International Migration of Toxic Industrial Pollution: 1960-80" in P. Low (ed), *International Trade and the Environment Discussion* Paper No. 159, Washington D.C., World Bank.

Peare, D. (1993), "Can GATT Survive the Environmental Challenge?" The Green Globe Year Book, Oxford, Oxford University Press.

Rajah Rasiah and Norbert Von Hofmann (1995), "Social and Environmental Clauses and Free Trade: Europe and South East Asia", Friedrich Ebert Stifling, Germany.

Moazzam Hossain, Iyanatul Islam and Reza Kibria (1999), "South Asian Economic Development, Transformation, Opportunities and Challenges", Routledge, London.

Wiemann J. (1994), "International Trade and Environment", Paper presented at Eurokolleg EU — Trade Policy: Between Liberalisation and a Global Social and Environmental Policy, Brussels 21-22, September in Rasiah (ed.), *Ibid.*

8

SOME ASPECTS OF TRADE RELATIONS BETWEEN AUSTRALIA AND INDIA

M.A.B. SIDDIQUE

The Objective of the Study

The objective of this paper is to analyse the patterns and trends of trade between Australia and India since the signing of the Trade Agreement in 1976 and draw out implications for further enhancement of trade between these two countries. It will specifically investigate the relative competitive position of the two countries in the world market as well as in the market of each other in order to determine the future scope for increase in trade. The study has obvious policy implications for both Australia and India.

Structural Changes in Australia's Trade

Primary products have always accounted for the bulk of Australia's exports, although their share in the total declined from 67.3 per cent in 1980 to 43.4 per cent in 1999. The share of unprocessed products in total exports declined more rapidly (from 46.6 per cent to 28.8 per cent) as opposed to that of processed primary products (from 20.7 per cent to 14.6 per cent) during this period.

In contrast, the share of manufactured goods in total export earnings of Australia remarkably increased from 19.2 per cent in 1980 to 32.5 per cent in 1999. The main contribution came from the increase in the share of elaborately transformed manufactures (ETMs), which increased from 10.8 per cent to

23.3 per cent. The share of simply transformed manufactures (STMs) remained steady during this period with some fluctuations.

Australia achieved these desirable changes in her export structures through movements in cost and price competitiveness; export oriented industry specific policies; and changes in business culture and attitude. International factor such as the acceleration in the growth of world ETM imports, also favoured Australia.[1] Australia also implemented a series of macroeconomic reforms from the beginning of the 1980s. Gradual removal of protection against exports, large efforts to build bilateral relations with the dynamic regions of the world,[2] and the introduction of a number of microeconomic reforms significantly improved Australia's relative competitive position over the years.

Direction of Trade

While Australia's share of exports to EU[3] (EEA)[4] and NAFTA[5] declined between 1980 and 2000, the Asian countries have become increasingly important as the market for Australia's exports (as well as the most important sources of Australia's imports). For example, between 1980 and 2000, the share of the Asia-Pacific region (APEC)[6] in Australia's exports has increased from 64.1 per cent to 73.2 per cent most of which was contributed by an increase in the share of ASEAN (from 7.5 per cent to 13.2 per cent). The share of SAARC[7] countries in Australia's

1. Sheehan, P.J. et al. (1994), p. ix.
2. Changes in Australia's bilateral trade relations with its important trading partners is discussed later.
3. European Union: Austria, Bulgaria, Czech Republic, Hungary, Poland, Romania, Slovak Republic, USSR (former), and Yugoslavia (former).
4. European Economic Areas: *EU*, Iceland, Norway.
5. North America Free Trade Agreement: Canada, Mexico, and USA (including Puerto Rico and US Virgin island).
6. Asia Pacific Economic Co-operation: NAFTA, ASEAN 6 (Brunei, Indonesia, Malaysia, the Philippines, Singapore and Thailand), China, Chile, Hong Kong, Japan, Korea and Taiwan.
7. South Asia Association for Regional Cooperation: Bangladesh, Bhutan, India, Maldives, Nepal, Pakistan and Sri Lanka.

exports increased (from 2.1 per cent to 2.7 per cent) during the same period.

The relative importance of OECD (or industrially developed countries) as Australia's export destinations has been gradually declining over the years. Almost 50 per cent of Australia's exports are now (2000) directed to the developing countries.

The Table 1 shows Australia's merchandise trade balance with some major trading partners.

Australia's trade balances with its top 20 trading partners demonstrate that Australia has enjoyed prolonged bilateral trade surplus with Japan, Korea, Indonesia, Malaysia and India. In particular the surplus with India has increased remarkably — from $53,348,000 in 1980 to $876,377,000 in 2000.

TABLE 1

Australia's Merchandise Trade Balance with Some of Its Top Twenty Trading Partners: 1980-2000* (A$'000)

Country[a]	1980	1985	1990	1995	2000
1. Japan	2,542,289	1,378,060	2,908,878	3,505,018	4,671,754
2. United States of America	-1,554,132	-2,968,144	-6,946,178	-11,400,829	-13,559,933
3. Korea, Republic of	267,308	683,853	1,446,637	3,221,169	3,305,061
4. New Zealand	302,162	437,358	443,028	1,237,222	2,365,139
5. China	645,545	686433	-69,912	-685,110	-2,549,439
6. Singapore	-66,323	70,160	771,902	1,397,648	498,611
7. Taiwan	-117,478	-205,843	-124,460	532,547	1,443,486
8. United Kingdom	-698,721	-1,038,626	-1,619,328	-163,990	-2,198,261
9. Hong Kong	-99,839	182,553	495,076	1,709,114	1,930,745
10. Indonesia[b]	48,534	67,968	588,690	915,301	-294,205
11. Malaysia	217,868	285,421	267,224	612,329	-1,627,972
12. Thailand	87,030	44,559	111,775	590,184	-719,028
13. India	53,348	69,042	309,333	446,613	876,377
14. Italy	7,583	-300,771	-596,810	-775,779	-1,468,382
15. Netherlands	43,509	106,547	522,747	-5,491	387,936
16. Saudi Arabia	-407,592	-169,166	-389,021	-473,134	333,143
17. Philippines	77,293	80,583	319,914	580,417	847,035
18. Germany[c]	-508,943	-1,076,612	-2,193,802	-3,778,429	-4,545,828
19. Canada	-107,436	-307,957	-468,007	-127,868	-681,564
20. Belgium-Luxembourg	79,941	535	48,207	-220,147	349,883

Source: DFAT, (2000b), pp. 62- 65.

*For Australian fiscal years which run from 01 July to 30 June.

[a] Ranked by DFAT in order exports in 1999-00.

[b] Includes Timor.

[c] Includes Federal Republic of Germany and Democratic Republic of Germany.

Trade Intensities

The Trade intensity index measures the share of one country's trade with its counterpart as a proportion of the reporting country's share of the world trade.[8] It provides a useful analytical tool for measuring the relative importance of the bilateral trading relationship of a country with its trading partners.

The intensity indices of Australian exports exhibit that outside Asia, Australia trades most intensively with New Zealand. Within Asia, Australia's export indices with Korea, Taiwan, China, Indonesia and India and South Africa have been high and have increased since 1990. Although Australia's export indices with Japan have been high, they have been declining consistently since 1985. Intensity indices of Australia's exports with the USA, UK, Germany, Italy and Canada have been quite low and have declined with some fluctuations.

Australia's import trade intensity indices also confirm that it trades most intensively with New Zealand. Its import trade intensity indices with respect to India have increased between 1985 and 1996 (from 0.95 to 1.16). Australia's import trade index with respect to the USA has been lower than Japan except for 1985, indicating that Japan is still an important source of Australian imports. Australia's import trade intensity with respect to Korea, China, Malaysia, and Indonesia, have also been quite high with some fluctuations over the years.

Growth of Australian Exports

Average annual growth rates of Australian exports by various economic areas fluctuated over the years. The rate of growth of Australia's total exports has declined over the years. It is interesting to note that the rate of growth of exports to South-East Asia has been the highest (23.6 per cent) and well above the average of total exports of Australia (10.1 per cent) during 1980-2000. The rate of growth exports to EEA and OECD has been lower than the average of total exports.

---

8. For details on trade intensity indices see, Brown (1949), Kojima (1964), Drysdale and Gaurnaut (1982).

TABLE 2

Intensity Indices of Australia's Exports to Its Top 20 Export Partners: 1980-2000*

Country[a]	1980	1985	1990	1995	1999	2000
1. Japan	3.93	3.98	3.87	3.48	3.45	3.48
2. United States of America	0.93	0.53	0.74	0.42	0.33	0.52
3. Korea, Republic of	1.92	2.29	2.82	3.17	3.46	3.24
4. New Zealand	16.65	14.74	18.16	26.63	17.60	27.62
5. China	3.56	1.68	1.58	1.66	1.62	1.59
6. Singapore	1.96	1.95	2.64	2.18	2.41	2.62
7. Taiwan	—	2.87	2.22	2.24	—	—
8. United Kingdom	0.79	0.59	0.56	0.67	0.77	0.61
9. Hong Kong	1.29	1.59	1.08	1.04	1.09	0.95
10. Indonesia[b]	2.98	2.58	4.21	4.14	4.38	4.52
11. Malaysia	4.11	2.60	2.21	2.02	1.94	1.63
12. Thailand	1.51	1.09	1.18	1.73	1.77	2.05
13. India	1.19	1.31	1.82	2.26	2.26	2.17
14. Italy	0.40	0.43	0.36	0.45	0.42	0.47
15. Netherlands	0.32	0.36	0.53	0.30	0.31	0.50
16. Saudi Arabia	0.81	1.52	0.84	0.96	2.34	3.73
17. Philippines	2.02	2.11	2.41	2.50	2.53	2.06
18. Germany[c]	0.26	0.30	0.22	0.18	0.18	0.16
19. Canada	0.67	0.26	0.44	0.47	0.40	0.36
20. Belgium-Luxembourg	0.26	0.23	0.29	0.25	0.47	—

Sources: Estimated from: International Monetary Fund (various issues).

* For calendar years.

[a] Ranked by DFAT in order of exports in 1999-00.

[b] Includes Timor.

[c] Includes Federal Republic of Germany and Democratic Republic of Germany.

It is not therefore surprising to note that developing countries have emerged as important destinations for Australia's exports as opposed to the OECD[9] or industrialised countries.

The OECD countries (12.1 per cent) and the average rate of growth of total exports from Australia throughout the entire period.

The most recent (1998-00) average annual growth rates of Australian exports by various geographic regions reveal that

9. Organisation for Economic Co-operation and Development: EU, Australia, Canada, Czech Republic, Hungary, Iceland, Japan, Republic of Korea, Mexico, India, Norway, Poland, Switzerland, Turkey and USA.

North Asia and South-East Asia have lost their relative importance as Australia's export destinations and Sub-Saharan Africa (12.1 per cent), Middle-East and North Africa (10.7 per cent) and Oceania (12.1 per cent) have emerged as Australia's dominant trading partners (Table 3). Growth rates of Australia's exports to these regions have been much higher than the average growth rate of Australia's total exports (7.9 per cent) for this period.

TABLE 3

Average Annual Rates of Growth of Australia's Merchandise Exports to Country Groups: 1980-2000*

	1980-2000	1985-2000	1990-2000	19995-2000
Geographic Regions				
North Asia	9.7	8.0	6.4	4.3
South-East Asia	13.5	14.0	8.4	1.8
South Asia	12.2	12.3	13.3	14.4
Middle East & North Africa	4.5	4.7	9.7	23.3
Sub-Saharan Africa	11.5	15.4	22.6	14.6
Oceania	10.0	9.9	9.6	4.5
Economic Areas				
APEC, of which	10.0	8.8	7.0	5.1
- ASEAN	13.6	14.0	8.4	1.8
- North-East Asia	9.7	8.0	6.4	4.3
- NAFTA	7.4	5.7	5.2	14.8
- Australasia	10.2	9.9	9.7	4.2
EEA, of which	7.7	6.0	6.0	10.7
- SAARC	12.2	12.3	13.3	14.4
Industrialised and developing				
OECD	8.5	6.9	5.5	6.8
Developing Countries	11.4	10.9	9.8	6.5

Source: Department of Foreign Affairs and Trade, (2000b), p. 26.

*For Australian fiscal years which run from 01 July to 30 June.

Significant inter-country variations are also noticed in the growth rates of Australia's exports to its important trading partners (Table 4). The average rate of growth of Australia's total rate of growth of exports to developing countries (13.7 per

TABLE 4

Rates of Growth of Australia's Merchandise Exports to its Top 20 Trading Partners 1980-2000*

Country[a]	1980 to 2000	1985 to 2000	1990 to 2000	1995 to 2000
1. Japan	7.2	5.2	2.9	2.5
2. United States of America	7.0	5.2	5.1	17.4
3. Korea, Republic of	15.9	14.0	10.8	4.7
4. New Zealand	11.5	11.3	11.2	5.1
5. China	11.1	10.8	15.4	8.3
6. Singapore	14.1	13.2	5.3	4.1
7. Taiwan	14.3	11.7	9.6	8.3
8. United Kingdom	8.7	9.1	8.8	14.2
9. Hong Kong	14.2	10.3	9.1	3.8
10. Indonesia[b]	13.7	14.4	8.6	-0.5
11. Malaysia	10.7	11.6	9.6	-1.3
12. Thailand	16.7	17.7	10.1	-1.9
13. India	13.5	12.9	12.6	12.0
14. Italy	7.8	5.9	6.6	5.9
15. Netherlands	7.7	3.9	0.0	13.2
16. Saudi Arabia	4.3	6.5	16.8	35.4
17. Philippines	13.0	14.7	13.0	7.4
18. Germany[c]	4.7	2.1	1.6	4.3
19. Canada	8.6	8.2	5.0	0.6
20. Belgium-Luxembourg	11.1	10.7	10.3	18.4

Source: DFAT, (2000b), p. 24.

*For Australian fiscal years which run from 01 July to 30 June.

[a]Ranked by DFAT in order of exports in 1999-00.

[b]Includes Timor.

[c]Includes Federal Republic of Germany and Democratic Republic of Germany.

cent) has been higher than that of the merchandise exports during 1979-2000 has been 11.4 per cent. Exports to Republic of Korea, Taiwan, Singapore, Hong Kong, Indonesia, Malaysia, India and the Philippines have grown at higher rate than the average rate of growth of total exports during this period. Particularly, the average annual growth rate of Australian merchandise exports to most of its South-East and North Asian countries such as Thailand (30.4 per cent), Republic of Korea (20.5 per cent), Singapore (42.2 per cent), has been well above the average rate of growth of total exports. The average rate of growth of Australia's export to India has been –13 per cent. By contrast, exports to Japan (Australia's largest export destination), the USA, UK, Italy, Canada and Germany have grown at a lower rate.

5. India as a Destination for Australia's Exports

During 1980, Australia-India's trade was of the order of A$290.91 million. Since then the bilateral trade has increased steadily. Australian-India trade for 2000 was A$2.56 billion.

Historically, Australia's imports of merchandise have fallen far short of its exports to India. Thus, the balance of trade has always been in favour of Australia during the period under review (except in 1983-84 and 1993-94).

Composition of Australian Exports

TABLE 5

Change in Composition of Australia's Merchandise Exports to India Based on Trade Exports Classification (TREC) 1980-1999*

TREC Description	Distribution of Exports (per cent)				
	1980	1985	1990	1995	1999
Primary Products	*53.1*	*78.5*	*33.1*	*71.4*	*68.7*
11 Unprocessed	33.9	68.3	26.7	70.5	66.0
12 Processed	19.1	10.3	6.5	0.8	2.7
Manufactured Products	*45.7*	*19.9*	*16.0*	*26.2*	*17.9*
23 Simply Transformed Manufactures (STM)	27.3	15.6	9.5	6.3	5.5
24 Elaborately Transformed Manufactures (ETM)	18.3	4.3	6.5	19.9	12.4
Miscellaneous Products (NES)	*1.3*	*1.6*	*50.9*	*7.5*	*13.3*
Total Exports	100.0	100.0	100.0	100.0	100.0

Source: Estimated from: DFAT (1998), pp. 46-47 and DFAT (2000a), pp. 54-55.

* For calendar years.

Exports of Primary Products

India has become an important destination for Australia's primary products. While the contribution of primary products to Australia's total export earnings declined over the years, this group of goods constituted 43.4 per cent of Australia's exports to India in 1999. Exports of Australia's primary products to India increased from A$94.359 million in 1980 to A$1,043.77 million in 1999.[10] Again, while Australia's earnings from exports of unprocessed primary products declined from 46.6 per cent in 1980 to 28.8 per cent in 1999, an opposite trend is noticed with respect to Australia's exports of primary products to India. The contribution to these products of Australia's total export earnings from India increased from 53.1 per cent in 1980 to 68.7 per cent in 1999.

The trend in Australia's exports of processed products to India is in line with changes in composition in the structure of Australia's exports over the years. The contribution of processed products of Australia's total export earnings declined from 20.7 per cent in 1980 to 14.6 per cent in 1999. The contribution of this class of products to total export earnings of Australia from India also decreased from 19.1 per cent in 1980 to 2.7 in 1999.

Exports of Manufactured Products

Although exports of Australia's manufactured products to India increased from A$81.192 million in 1980 to A$788.253 million in 1999,[11] India has not emerged as one of the major destinations for exports of Australia's manufactured products. The share of manufactured products in Australia's total exports to India declined from 45.7 per cent in 1980 to 17.9 per cent in 1999 with wide fluctuations in the share of ETMs. The share of STM also gradually declined throughout the entire period.

Trade Intensities and Share of Trade with India

We have already seen that Australia's export intensity and

10. DFAT, *Exports of Major Commodities Time Series 1980 to 1997*, Canberra: Commonwealth of Australia, 1998, p. 47 and DFAT *Exports of Major Commodities Times Series 1982 to 1999*, Canberra: Commonwealth of Australia, 2000, p. 47.
11. DFAT (1998), p. 46 and DFAT (2000a), p. 45.

import trade indices with respect to India have increased steadily since 1985. The bilateral share of India of Australia's exports has increased from 0.84 per cent to 1.11 per cent during 1980-00 (fiscal years). In contrast, Australia's share of imports from India has decreased from 0.70 per cent in 1979-80 to 0.6 per cent in 1999-00.

The bilateral share of Australia's imports from India has remained below 1 per cent and has steadily declined between 1979 and 1999 (fiscal years) with some minor fluctuations. However total merchandise trade has been following an increasing trend over the same period. As mentioned earlier, the balance of trade has always been heavily in favour of Australia.

Intra-industry Trade between Australia and India

TABLE 6

Australia and India Intra-Industry Trade Index*

SITC	1980	1985	1990	1995	2000
0	6.43	41.75	69.98	51.11	71.49
1	78.60	19.31	32.89	—	—
2	14.49	18.76	39.93	22.02	10.79
5	59.89	70.32	82.91	94.94	61.84
67	13.93	0.38	78.62	84.17	73.97
6	88.54	50.89	53.95	60.44	58.58
74	92.86	69.33	65.68	74.76	89.34
7	96.13	86.42	90.18	73.97	94.73
8	7.05	30.11	27.83	0.07	45.63
988	—	—	—	19.99	24.80
9	81.47	83.05	1.56	—	—

Source: For data between 1980 and 1990, IIT index estimated from ABS, *Foreign Trade Australia: Comparative and Summary Tables*, Catalog. No. 5410.0, various issues. For data between 1995 and 2000, IIT index estimated from DFAT, *Composition of Trade Australia*, various issues.

*For Australian Fiscal years which run from 01 July to 30 June.

It has been noted above that Australia has experienced a remarkable shift in its export trade — the dominance of primary sector has been declining while the manufacturing sector has been increasing. Consequently, intra-industry trade (the value of exports of a group of industrial products in exchange for imports of similar products from the trading partner of a particular country) flows between Australia and India for a number of industrial products has increased over the years. The change in intra-industry flows can be measured with the help of intra-industry index that was developed by Grubel and Lloyd (1975).

It is derived by using the following formula

$$\text{Intra-Industry Trade Index} = [1-(\text{abs}(X_{ij}-M_{ij}))/(X_{ij}+M_{ij})] \times 100$$

where

X_{ij} = Country i's exports of product j to its trading partner;

M_{ij} = Country j's imports of product j from the same trading partner.

The index will have a range between 0 and 100. It becomes zero if product j is only exported to or imported from the trading partner of country i; It becomes 100 when the value of exports of product j of country i becomes exactly equal to the value of imports of product j from the same trading partner.

Australia's intra-industry trade indices of a number of commodity groups (SITC0, SITC2, SITC5, SITC7 and SITC8) have considerably increased between 1980-2000. These are quite high too. The intra-industry index of machinery and transport equipment (SITC7) has been close to 100 in 2000, indicating that the value of exports of this group of products from Australia to India is almost equal to the value of imports of similar products from India.

From the intra-industry index with respect to number of commodity groups (such as SITC0, SITC5, SITC67, and SITC74), it can be concluded that Australian markets have been gradually opened to the goods produced in India.

The average annual growth rate of Australia's exports of primary products to the world has been 5.8 per cent in contrast to 10.9 per cent to India. Similarly, the growth rate of exports of unprocessed primary products to the world has been 6.5 per cent in comparison to 10.3 per cent to India. Processed primary products recorded growth rates of 4.4 per cent and 41.5 per cent for the World and India respectively.

During the period between 1998 and 2000, Australia's exports to India declined by 13.4 per cent. However exports to India had been growing at an average annual growth rate of 12.0 per cent per annum during 1994-99. India was the 13th most important export destination for Australia during 1999.[12] Exports to India have grown at a much higher rate at 15.7 per cent, than the rate of growth of Australia's total exports (6.5 per cent) throughout the period between 1994 and 1999.

TABLE 7

Average Annual Growth Rates of Australian Merchandise Exports Based on TREC: 1994-1999*

TREC Description	Percentage Distribution of exports to:	
	World	India
Primary Products(a)	5.8	10.9
11 Unprocessed	6.5	10.3
12 Processed	4.4	41.5
Manufactured Products(b)	6.2	4.8
23 Simply Transformed Manufactures (STM)	4.8	8.5
24 Elaborately Transformed Manufactures (ETM)	6.7	3.3
30 Miscellaneous Products, nes	8.4	103.3
Total Exports	6.5	15.7

Source: DFAT, (2000a), pp. 23 and 47.

*For calendar years.

Notes: (a) Excludes commodities subject to a confidentiality restriction.
(b) Includes commodities subject to a confidentiality restriction.

12. DFAT (2000b), p. 20.

Australia's imports from India have grown at 10.8 per cent between the period 1980 to 2000.[13] Growth rate of Australia's imports from India accelerated during 1990 to 2000 (11.8 per cent). India was the 26th largest importing nation of Australia during 2000 fiscal year.[14] However, the annual growth rate of imports from India have been lower than the average rate of growth of total imports of Australia during 1980 to 2000 (fiscal years).

Aspects of International Competitiveness of Australia and India

Revealed Comparative Advantage Index (RCAI)

To measure the international competitiveness of a country, usually the revealed comparative advantage index (RCAI) for that country is estimated. RCAI for a country can be measured with the help of the net export ratio, the export performance ratio and the export specialization ratio.[15] The most common measure of RCAI is the export specialization ratio. It involves three steps: (i) measuring the share of a particular commodity group in a country's total exports; (ii) measuring the share of that commodity group in the world exports; (iii) divide (i) by (ii).

Symbolically,

$$RCAI = \{X_{ij}/X_i\}/(W_j/W)$$

where

X_{ij} = country i's export of product j;

X_i = country i's total merchandise exports;

W_j = world exports of product j; and

W = world total merchandise exports.

If the RCAI of a particular commodity group is greater than unity, the export share of the commodity group in a country exceeds the world average export share of that commodity group, implying that the country tends to have relatively high

13. DFAT (2000b), p. 50.

14. *Ibid.*, p. 46.

15. For details, see, Mohammed Ariff (1991: 78-86).

comparative advantage in that commodity group. On the contrary, an RCAI of less than unity indicates that the country has a lower comparative advantage in that commodity group than the world average level.

The RCAI has been calculated for Australia and India for a number of commodity groups Tables 8 and 9. It is revealed that Australia has comparative advantages in a number of food and mineral products as well as in some manufactured

TABLE 8

Australia: Revealed Comparative Advantage Index (RCAI): 1980-1997*

	1980	1985	1990	1995	1996	1997
Food & Live Animals, Beverages & Tobacco	3.36	2.58	2.10	2.34	2.61	2.74
Crude materials, excluding fuels	4.50	5.22	3.69	3.99	4.12	4.35
Mineral Fuels etc.	0.46	1.41	1.62	2.23	2.00	2.27
Animal and vegetable oil, fat	0.96	0.65	0.30	0.69	0.67	0.66
Chemicals, related products (nes)	0.31	0.21	0.25	0.42	0.41	0.39
Iron & Steel	0.81	0.51	0.57	0.82	0.79	0.74
Non-ferrous Metals	2.30	3.33	3.51	3.43	3.11	2.78
Machines and transport equipment	0.21	0.11	0.16	0.33	0.33	0.34
Basic & Miscellaneous manufacturing Goods	0.55	0.48	0.47	0.62	0.59	0.56

Estimated from: UN (1999), pp. 30-35 and various other issues.

Note: Figure for 1998 onwards were not available at the time of calculation (Oct. 2001).

*For calendar years.

products (Table 8). It has strong comparative advantages in producing food and live animals, beverages and tobacco, crude materials, mineral fuels and non-ferrous metals. Its comparative advantage over mineral fuels has increased over the years; an opposite average annual is also noticed with respect to animal, vegetable oil, and fat. It should be noted here that Australia's higher comparative advantage still lies in primary and resource based commodities.

TABLE 9

India: Revealed Comparative Advantage Index (RCAI): 1980-1996*

	1980	1985	1990	1994	1995	1996
Food & Live Animals, Beverages and Tobacco	2.72	2.67	1.73	1.73	2.13	2.11
Crude materials, excluding fuels	1.99	1.90	2.08	0.98	1.02	1.36
Mineral fuels etc.	0.02	0.32	0.27	0.24	0.22	0.18
Animal & vegetable oil, fat	0.80	0.68	0.67	1.20	1.56	1.24
Chemicals, related products (nes)	0.59	0.46	0.84	0.88	0.86	0.96
Iron & Steel	0.30	0.14	0.50	1.01	1.04	1.13
Non-ferrous Metals	0.10	0.21	0.26	0.36	0.24	0.35
Machines & Transport equipment	0.32	0.21	0.21	0.19	0.20	0.21
Basic & Miscellaneous Manufacturing Goods	1.93	1.99	1.96	2.12	2.02	1.97

Estimated from: UN (1999) and UN (1996), various issues.

Note: Figures for 1997 onwards were not available at the time of calculation (Oct. 2001).

*For calendar years.

India has a strong comparative advantage in basic and miscellaneous manufactured goods. Its comparative advantage has also fluctuated over the years (Table 9). Its comparative advantage in food and live animals, beverages, tobacco and crude materials has decreased since 1980. On the contrary, its comparative advantage over basic and miscellaneous goods increased during 1980-1994.

Australia has relatively high comparative advantages in food, live animals, beverages, tobacco and crude materials. RCAI of India indicates that it has relatively high comparative advantage in basic miscellaneous products, iron and steel, and animal and vegetable fat.

Thus, there are a number of commodities in which Australia has comparative advantage over India and *vice versa*. Therefore, there is significant scope for increasing trade of these commodities between the two countries. Australia and India can possibly develop a common marketing strategy (without violating the WTO regulations) in areas where these two countries have relatively high comparative advantages.

Constant Market Share (CMS) Analysis

India and Australia's bilateral trade performance, relative to their competitors can be evaluated using the constant market share analysis (CMS). The methodology used for this analysis is based on the methodology used by Tyers and Phillips (1984).

Export growth is decomposed into 3 components; the standard growth effect, the commodity composition effect and the competitiveness residual.[16]

The 'Standard Growth' term indicates the general growth of imports in the destination country and reflects the export growth performance of the focus country's competitors. The standard growth term is the 'standard' for which the exporter can compare its export performance with. A high standard growth term relative to their export growth indicates that the focus country is not as competitive as their competitors.

In our analysis, the focus country's competitors will be the world, thus standard growth is measured as the growth of world imports in the destination country.

The 'commodity composition' component measures the

16. The market distribution effect does not enter into our analysis.

amount of export growth that was attributable to the exports of commodities that had strong demand in the exporting destination. If a country demands a particular commodity, than naturally it is expected that the focus exporter should perform well with that commodity. A positive commodity composition term will mean that the exporter's composition of exports consist mainly of those goods that have achieved strong import in the focus destination. A large commodity composition effect implies that export growth is reliant on the demand for certain commodities in the export destination.

Finally, the 'competitiveness residual' component is the net gain in market share by the focus exporter in the export destination. A positive term implies that the focus exporter is a strong competitor in terms of relative prices. Caution should be used when interpreting this term since the residual does not take into account trade barriers and trade is measured in values rather than volume.

The CMS analysis was applied to Australia and India for the period 1988-1997. In total, six CMS analyses were conducted (i) Australia as the focus exporting country and India as the destination country (results in Table 10) and (ii) India as the focus exporting country and Australia as the destination country (results in Table 11). The data were also divided into three intervals in which CMS analyses were conducted, 1988-91, 1992-94 and 1995-97.

From the Tables, we can compare each county's export growth rate (to each others market) to the standard growth rate to see how well Australia and India performed against their competitors (the world). Australia seemed to perform well in India's market, as her export growth rate was higher than the standard growth rate in two of the three periods analysed. On the other hand, India's exports to Australia only performed better than the standard growth rate in one of the three periods.

In 1992-94 Australia's export growth to India can be explained largely by the commodity composition effect, which was relatively high in 1992-94 (46.1%). The commodity groups that had the largest share of Australian exports to India were

Coal, Coke and Briquettes (55.6 per cent) and Wool (10.7 per cent) in 1994. As expected, Indian imports of Coal, Coke and Briquettes and Wool grew by 28.9 and 4.6 per cent respectively in the period 1995-97, thus resulting in a larger commodity composition effect.

TABLE 10

CMS Analysis of Australian Exports to India: 1988-97*
(Percentage)

	Growth of Australia's exports to India	Growth of India's imports from the rest of the world	Commodity composition effect	Competi-tiveness Residual
1988-91	14.91	0.82	12.42	1.67
1992-94	4.03	18.79	46.15	-60.92
1995-97	53.67	11.68	10.68	31.31

*For calendar years.

TABLE 11

CMS Analysis of Indian Exports to Australia: 1988-97*
(Percentage)

	Growth of India's exports to Australia	Growth of Australia's imports from the rest of the world	Commodity composition effect	Competi-tiveness Residual
1988-91	7.31	26.79	35.85	-55.33
1992-94	48.19	10.96	61.56	-24.33
1995-97	15.05	18.30	12.16	-15.42

*For calendar years.

In the other two periods, 1988-91 and 1995-97, Australia experienced positive competitiveness residuals. This implies that on average Australia's export market share had increased for that period.

The performance of India's exports into Australia in terms of 'competitiveness' has been poor for the entire period of 1988-97 with negative residual components for each of the three periods analysed. These negative terms indicate that on average, India had lost its export market share in Australia.

Future Trade Prospects

Merchandise Trade

The composition of Australia's exports to India has been changing. While commodities, mainly coking coal, wool and pulses, still account for the bulk of exports, and will do so for many years to come, the most rapidly growing area of exports is in ETMs.

India is emerging as a major market. One of the most striking features of the market is the sheer number of consumers, which is of direct interest to countries selling consumer goods. The size of the consumer market is between 100 and 300 million people depending on the type of the product.[17]

From Australia's point of view, the major opportunities in the Indian markets arise from its massive development needs in the fields of power, energy and mineral resources, telecommunications, infrastructure (roads and ports), food processing and services. India's need to rapidly expand the power and steel industries presents opportunities for a significant expansion in exports of both coking and thermal coal. There are also opportunities to supply ETMs as the demand for capital goods, components and other manufacturing inputs rises.[18]

Services

With the relaxation of foreign exchange controls, opportunities are likely to emerge in the tourism and education industries. About two million Indians travel abroad annually.

---

17. DFAT (1994), p. 30

18. *Ibid.*

About 30% of these passengers are travelling to jobs in the Middle East. The remaining 1.4 million passengers travel to other destinations (primarily the USA and UK) for tourism, business, migration or studies. There are a growing number of Indians who can afford to travel abroad. Approximately 20 million people fall into the upper-middle and upper income brackets with the capacity to travel to long haul destinations such as Australia. Visa international estimates that there are 40 million Indians living with annual household incomes over $US30.000.[19]

Thus the outbound travel market holds considerable promise for growth. There is considerable potential for the expansion of tourism to Australia.[20]

With considerable growth in the size of middle and upper middle class of people in India, demand for overseas education has increased over the years and is expected to continue to grow in the future. Australian education providers should take these opportunities.

Conclusion

Bilateral trade relations between two countries do not solely depend on economic factors. Other factors to be taken into consideration are: domestic political demands; regional security and global strategic pressure; ideological considerations, people-to-people contacts; geographical proximity; and affinity between leaders.[21] In the past bilateral trade between Australia and India has never reached its optimum level as India has not been taken seriously by Australian governments for various reasons, despite effective trade relations with a number of North and South-East Asian countries. It has been shown that in recent years the average annual rate of growth of Australia's merchandise exports to North and South-East Asian regions has slowed down. The impact of the Asian economic crisis on these regions has not yet been fully realised.

19. DFAT (1995), *op.cit.*, p. 33.

20. Currently, approximately, 14,000 passengers or less than 1% of the Indian outbound market travels to Australia each year (DFAT 1995: 32).

21. Gurry, Meg in Vicziany, M. (1993), p. 11.

It can, therefore, be argued that demand for Australia's exports in these regions will continue to decline. By contrast, the rate of growth of Australia's exports to SAARC countries and particularly to India has increased considerably in recent years. Most of the SAARC countries, including India, have not been seriously affected by the Asian economic crisis. It is, therefore, expected that the demand for Australian products in this region will continue to grow. Australia can no longer afford to neglect India as a strategic trading partner.

WORKS CITED

ABS (1981), Foreign Trade Australia: Comparative and Summary Tables 1969-70 to 1979-80, *Catalogue No. 5410.0.*

—— (1987), Foreign Trade Australia Part 2: Comparative and Summary Tables 1984-85 and 1985-86, *Catalogue No. 5410.0.*

—— (1991), Foreign Trade Australia: Comparative and Summary Tables 1989-90, *Catalogue No. 5410.0* .

Ariff, M. (1991), pp. 78-86.

Bhagwati, J. (1996), "India: Retrospect and Prospect", *ANU Public Lecture Series,* K.R. Narayanan Oration.

Balassa, B. (1965), "Trade Liberalisation and Revealed Comparative Advantage", *Manchester School of Economics and Social Studies,* Vol. 33, No. 2.

Barratt, Paul (1992), "Winning Asian Markets in the Eighties: A Model for the Nineties", *Australian Quarterly,* Vol. 84, No. 4, pp. 379-410.

Brown (1949).

Department of Foreign Affairs and Trade (DFAT) (2000a), *Exports of Major Commodities Times Series 1982 to 1999,* Canberra: Commonwealth of Australia.

—— (1998), *Exports of Major Commodities Time Series 1980 to 1997,* Canberra: Commonwealth of Australia.

—— (2000b), *Direction of Trade Time Series 1979-1980 to 1999-2000,* Canberra: Commonwealth of Australia.

—— (1998), *Direction of Trade Time Series 1977 — 1997,* Canberra: Commonwealth of Australia.

—— (2000), *Composition of Trade Australia 1999/2000,* (October 2000), Canberra: Commonwealth of Australia.

—— (2000), *Composition of Trade Australia 1998/1999,* (March 2000), Canberra: Commonwealth of Australia.

—— (1996), *Integrated Country Promotion — Australia-India and New Horizons*, Canberra: Commonwealth of Australia.

—— (1994), *India's Economy at the Midnight Hour: Australia's India Strategy*, Canberra: Commonwealth of Australia.

—— (1990), *Agreement Between the Government of Australia and the Government of the Republic of India on Development Co-operation*, (25 October 1990, Canberra), Australian Treaty Series, 190, No. 38.

—— (1976), *Trade Agreement Between the Government of Australia and the Government of India* (2 August 1976, Canberra), Australian Treaty Series, No. 2.

Drysdale, P. and Garnaut, R. (1982), "Trade Intensities and the Analysis of Bilateral Trade Flows in Many-Country World: A Survey", *Hitotsubashi Journal of Economics*, Vol. 22, No. 2.

Frank, W.T. and Ghosh, R.N. (1981), "Some Aspects of Economic Relations Between Australia and South and Southeast Asia" in A. Kerr (ed.), *The Indian Ocean Region: Resources and Development*, Western Australia: University of Western Australia Press.

Garnaut, Ross (1991), "Australia Revolutionises: the New Trade Commitments", *International Economic Insights*, Vol. 2, No. 4, pp. 2-5.

Grubel, H.G. and Lloyd, P.J. (1975), *Inter-industry Trade: The Theory and Measurement of International Trade in Differentiated Products*, London: Macmillan.

International Monetary Fund (IMF) (1992), *Direction of Trade Statistics Yearbook*, Washington, D.C: International Monetary Fund.

—— (1987), *Direction of Trade Statistics Yearbook*, Washington, D.C: International Monetary Fund.

—— (2000), *Direction of Trade Statistics Yearbook*, Washington, D.C: International Monetary Fund.

—— (2001), *Direction of Trade Statistics Quarterly*, (June 2001), Washington, D.C: International Monetary Fund.

Kojima (1964).

Shand, Ric and Kalirajan, K.P. (1996), *From Crisis to Consensus: Economic Reforms in India.*

Sheenhan, P.J., Pappas, N. and Cheng, E. (1994), *The rebirth of Australian industry : Australian trade in elaborately transformed manufactures, 1979-1993.* Melbourne, Vic.: Centre for Strategic Economic Studies, Victoria University of Technology.

Tyers, R. and P. Phillips (1984), "AESA Merchandise Trade with the Pacific Basin: Factor Composition and Performance", *Pacific Economic*

Papers, No. 116. Australia-Japan Research Centre, Australian National University.

United Nations (UN) (1999), *International Trade Statistics Yearbook,* New York : United Nations, Vol. I.

Various Issues of International Trade Statistics Yearbook, New York, United Nations.

9

South Africa and Australia: Possibilities of Economic Co-operation

R.N. GHOSH AND M.A.B. SIDDIQUE

1. Country Profile: South Africa

South Africa has a population of 40.6 million (1997). The rate of growth of population since 1990 has been 2.2 per cent per annum. More than 50 per cent of the people live in urban areas.

Manufacturing and government services are two of the largest employers in the economy each employing about 19 per cent of the total working population. About 12 per cent of the total working population are engaged in each of the agriculture and trade, catering & hospitality sectors of the economy. Historically, the importance of agriculture has declined in terms of its contribution to employment (from 17.5 per cent in 1970 to 11.0 per cent in 1995).

In 1997, South Africa's per capita gross national product (GNP) amounted to US$3,210, which places South Africa in the World Bank's category of middle income economies. Life expectancy in South Africa during the same year was similar to the 65 years average in other middle income countries. However, other social indicators (in 1997), such as adult female literacy (16.8 per cent), infant mortality rate (48 per cent); sanitation in 1994 (53 per cent with access); and female labour force (37.6 per cent) show that South Africa is relatively behind other middle income economies.

Per capita income in South Africa does not in itself reflect the wide income disparities between the four principal ethnic groups in the country: blacks (76.3 per cent), whites (13.7 per cent), Asians (2.5 per cent) and coloured people (8.5 per cent). According to one estimate made in 1991, per capita income of the white population was R20,600 compared with R2,400 of the blacks, R5,900 of the coloured and R8,100 of the Asians. While there were 307,000 vacancies in white schools, 2,000,000 blacks were not able to obtain places in schools. Two per cent of the whites lived below the poverty line in 1990, as compared to 53 per cent of the blacks. About 2 million black households were housed in appalling conditions during the same year. The disparity between the whites and the blacks is pronounced in almost every aspect of life. Out of 6,564 persons employed in senior public services only 195 or 2.84 per cent were blacks; moreover, compared to 180,000 whites in managerial positions, only 3,000 or 1.6 per cent were blacks.

During the period of 1985-1996 South African real gross domestic product (GDP) increased at an average annual rate of only 1.21 per cent with negative growth rates in 1985, 1991 and 1992. The recession of the early 1990s is mainly attributed to high inflation, low productivity of labour accompanied by high average wage increases, excessive governmental intervention in order to protect the inefficient industries, foreign exchange control and political uncertainty. In 1993, GDP growth rate became positive (1.29 per cent) and since then the economy has been making a slow recovery. The growth rate in the current fiscal year (1997-98) is estimated at just over 2 per cent.

The service sector, which produced approximately 56.9 per cent of GDP in 1997, makes the largest contribution to the economy of South Africa. Between 1980 and 1997 the contribution of this sector ranged from 43.2 per cent to 56.9 per cent. During the same period South Africa witnessed a gradual decline in its industry and manufacturing sectors. The overall contribution of the industrial sector to GDP declined from 50.0 per cent in 1980 to 38.5 per cent in 1997. Similarly, the contribution of the manufacturing sector declined from 22.5 per cent in 1980 to 20.7 per cent in 1995. The decline of these two sectors has been quite significant since 1989. The services sector, on the other hand, expanded remarkably during this period. The contribution of this sector to GDP increased from 40.6 per cent in 1974 to 54.5 per cent in 1995. Agriculture's contribution to GDP centred around 6.0 per cent between 1974 and 1994.

South Africa's record of savings and investment has been very disappointing since 1990. In the 1970s and 1980s, the ratio of gross domestic savings to GDP ranged from 26 to 36 per cent. However, since 1990 this ratio has been sharply declining to its current low level of 19.1 per cent (1997).

South Africa's peaceful transition from "apartheid" to democracy in 1994 made it possible for her renewed access to the world's financial markets and to multilateral institutions such as the World Bank and the IMF, and it opened the doors for trade missions and visits by foreign investors. Since the government came to power after the first democratic elections in South Africa in 1994, it has introduced two important policy measures in order to achieve a fundamental transformation of the economy. One of its challenges was to reduce the socio-economic gap between white and black people. After the new government came to power in May 1994 it introduced the RDP, and two years later, in June 1996, the GEAR document was launched to indicate the broad framework of the national government's social and economic objectives.

The fundamental objective of RDP is well documented in the preamble of this integrated and coherent socio-economic policy document of President Nelson Mandela: "At the heart of the Government of National Unity is a commitment to effectively address the problems of poverty and the gross inequality evident in almost all aspects of South African society. This can only be possible if the South African economy can be firmly placed on the path of high and sustainable growth."

RDP seeks to mobilise the resources and population of South Africa to create a strong, dynamic, democratic, non-racial and non-sexist society in order to eliminate poverty, low wages, and extreme inequalities. The five key programmes which are envisaged in RDP Base Document are: meeting basic needs;

developing human resources; building the economy; democratising the state and society; and implementing the RDP. The Office of the RDP (under the RDP Ministry in the Office of the President) was mainly responsible for coordinating reprioritisation and largely dealt with the poverty oriented and developmental strategies. It also promoted policy and co-ordinated and strengthened developmental planning at a national level as well as in the newly established nine provinces. An RDP fund, through which an increasing share of the national budget was allocated to RDP projects, facilitated expenditure reprioritisation and the initiation of several new major development programmes such as Primary School Nutrition, the Culture of Learning, Clinic Building, School Building and so on Unfortunately, most of the RDP funded projects experienced very slow progress as they required rigorous planning. As well they faced the problem of cumbersome tender procedures, a lack of experience in private-public partnerships and insufficient communications. Recognising these shortcomings, the government closed the RDP Office in mid-1996, when it was about to publish its first major macroeconomic strategy for growth, employment and redistribution.

The strategy for rebuilding and restructuring the economy in line with the goals of RDP was further developed in the GEAR document, which aims at achieving:

(a) a competitive fast-growing economy which creates sufficient jobs for all workers;

(b) a redistribution of income and opportunities in favour of the poor;

(c) a society in which sound health, education and other services are available to all; and

(d) an environment in which homes are secure and places of work are productive.

Until 1992 the ANC — the major party in the ruling Coalition — was committed to what is now branded as African socialism. The GEAR document marks a turn-around in the ANC policy in favour of an open competitive economy. This document proposes to introduce a structural adjustment programme in the South African economy to make it subject to market discipline. The document is therefore in keeping with the basic objectives of IMF and the World Bank which require the member countries to open up their economies and to liberalise the market. There is no doubt that the highly protected South African economy, during the apartheid era, had become isolated from the economy of the rest of the world. There is therefore an urgent need to make the South African economy more globally competitive by introducing liberal economic reform.

A market can function only in an environment of political stability. Within the short period since it came to power in 1994, the new South African government has achieved some remarkable success: it has achieved political stability, brought inflation under control, and completed the long process of political transition. However, both social and economic transitions of the South African economy are yet to begin in a significant manner. The crime and law and order situation is a matter of grave concern. Historically, income, wealth and unemployment inequalities have always been and still are at unacceptably high levels. To reduce unemployment and to remove the injustice and inequalities of the present society, the South African economy has to grow rapidly in the next few decades. But with the current level of domestic savings (16.5 per cent of GDP in 1996) it is highly unlikely that the economy would achieve a 6 per cent annual GDP growth rate by the year 2000, as envisaged in the GEAR document. Yet with a 6 per cent growth in GDP, South Africa would just be able to absorb the annual addition to the labour force due to the demographic factors. If the objective is to reduce the level of unemployment below its current unacceptably high level, it is necessary to aim at a much higher growth rate of, say, 9 or 10 per cent. To achieve this the level of gross investment has to be significantly accelerated from its current level of 17 or 18 per cent to 27 or 30 per cent.

Successful policies to achieve high growth rates would largely depend upon two circumstances:

(a) A new partnership between private capital and the national government in which the responsibility of the latter is to provide the "enabling environment" for the former. Unfortunately the perception of investors in South Africa seems to be that the national government is pro-labour and pro-union.

(b) Co-operation from other countries, more especially from the OECD countries including Australia, which can provide both direct investment and equity funds to South Africa, is also needed. The process of globalisation of the South African economy can be successful only with support from the major economies of the world.

1.1 *Industrial Policy*

The key goals of the industrial strategy adopted by the current government are to substantially increase net national investment, especially in manufacturing; to create jobs; and to meet the basic needs of society. Manufactured goods constitute about 70 per cent of South African exports. Earnings from exports of gold constituted about 25.5 per cent in 1994 as compared to 51.4 per cent in 1980. The rest of the export earnings came from the export of primary and intermediate commodities.

In the RDP White Paper, the following objectives of the industrial policy are identified: employment generation, increased investment, improved trade performance; and enhanced productivity. The implementation of such an ambitious industrial policy will be a challenging task, as it "will require a commitment from the entire nation, including tripartite decision-making which draws contribution from government, labour and business." The White Paper emphasises priorities for investments in electricity, health, housing, education, telecommunications and information infrastructure, transport, and public works such as roads, water and sanitation. Investment in these areas will be encouraged in order to guarantee the provision of basic needs and infrastructure. The RDP aims to design products and processes for marketing in Africa, Asia, Eastern Europe, the Pacific Rim and South America. South Africa has already been successful in exporting products designed for community telecommunication facilities and in electrification. The government does not wish to leave the private sector without any guidance, rather it wants to support the sectors which will respond to RDP investment and growth areas. This support will be in the form of training, research and development, design, technology acquisition and export marketing. The sectoral policies of the RDP are designed to achieve the following objectives:

(a) To extend the international competitive edge of selected industries;

(b) To support the light manufacturing sub-sectors which have the potential to thrive without protection which is currently provided;

(c) To encourage establishment of forward linkages between primary commodity industries and manufacturing industries;

(d) To support agro-manufacturing sectors which are less capital intensive and more labour intensive; and

(e) To raise productivity through human resource development and technological development.

Given that the domestic industrial sectors enjoyed high protection during the sanction era, RDP intends to pursue a competition policy designed to reform those market structures that underpin high prices and complacency, and that constitute major entry barriers to small and medium scale enterprise.

1.2 *Trade and Investment Policy*

In the RDP White Paper the government clearly recognises the need for reforms in the historically followed protective trade policy of South Africa. Trade policy reform, including improving productivity and competitiveness, was integrated into the overall restructuring of the country's economy. Fortunately, the end of apartheid and the installation of a democratic government in South Africa witnessed the opening up of a number of new markets for goods and services produced in South Africa via the Generalised System of Preferences (GSP) and granting of the status of MFN. The post-apartheid trade policy is designed to increase the export of manufactured goods from South Africa. The government is eager to reduce protection but wishes to advance cautiously with gradual reduction and steady liberalisation of trade as espoused by the WTO. However, the government intends to continue protecting "sensitive industries" in order to assist them to overcome the stronger international competition. There is a safeguard in the new government policy against unfair foreign trade practices, and the government will introduce anti-dumping measures and other countervailing strategies to protect manufacturers. To assist new enterprises, especially black-owned businesses, the new trade policy of the government also includes programmes designed to realise the exporting potential of small and medium sized enterprises, which tend to be more labour-absorbing.

Foreign investment is welcome in accordance with the objectives of growth with creation of employment. The government is committed to creating an enabling environment for encouraging domestic and overseas private investment by establishing a climate of political stability, economic growth, and transparent, stable and consistent policies. In the RDP White Paper it is stated that no distinction will be made between domestic and foreign investors in terms of treatment. Subject to regulations administered by the South African Reserve Bank, foreign investors will have access to foreign exchange for the purpose of remitting after tax profits and debt service, or approved loans; purchasing inputs and repatriating proceeds on the sale of assets.

The government initiated a number of reforms relating to trade and investment in South Africa. Since the end of sanctions against this economy, a number of bilateral trade agreements and treaties have been signed between South Africa and a number of other countries (such as Australia, Britain, India, Japan, and the USA) with the aim of enhancing trade and investment. South Africa was able to attract a number of large grants and loans from international donors and lenders. In October 1994 an agreement was signed between the European Union (EU) and South Africa, making available more than R1,000 million in potential loans. About 4,000 foreign business people representing 50 countries attended the South Africa International Trade Exhibition (SAITEX '94) which was organised in

Johannesburg in November 1994. The country also participates in activities of the World Trade Organisation (WTO).

Since the government came to power in 1994, there has been competition between the USA and the UK for becoming South Africa's main trading partner. Between January and October of 1994, the UK overtook the US as South Africa's main trading partner. Trade with the UK amounted to R4,875 million as opposed to $3,509 million with the USA. Japan became third with a trade of R3,489 million with South Africa during the same period. Australia's trade with South Africa has remarkably increased since 1991. Between 1991 and 1996, Australia's total trade with South Africa increased from A$0.3 billion to A$1.4 billion recording a trend growth rate of 35 per cent per annum.

South Africa wants to enhance its technological capacity in order to increase its competitiveness in the production of manufactured goods. The pro-manufacturing industrial policy has been followed by a corresponding policy for exports of manufactured goods. In general, the government is supportive of the internationally competitive industries, which have strong international linkages. Attempt has also been made to strengthen relations with neighbouring countries in Southern Africa which import about 20 per cent of South African exports.

1.3 *South Africa's International Economic Relations*

1.3.1 *South Africa and SADC*

With the inclusion of the Republic of Congo and the Republic of the Seychelles, the SADC has a total membership of 14. South Africa acceded to the SADC Treaty in August 1994 and participates in its activities through the offices of the Department of Foreign Affairs.

South Africa is like the economic locomotive of the entire southern African region. Using electricity generation in a country as an indicator of its relative economic strength, South Africa generates 86 per cent of the total electricity output in the SADC region. South Africa's smaller neighbours are of course sometimes suspicious of the economic giant's motives in the region. But Mandela's leadership is widely respected, and the past fear of South Africa does not seem to sour the present relationship in the region any more.

Within SADC, South Africa is responsible for coordinating the finance and investment sector. The Finance and Investment Sector Coordinating Unit (FISCU), which is located within the South African Department of Finance, reports to a Committee of SADC Ministers responsible for finance and investment. More generally, South Africa has both the capacity and expertise to open up the SADC region to trade, investment and mining. South Africa is also sometimes called upon to help when some countries of SADC do not have their own institutions to solve a fiscal, or a financial problem. For example, South Africa offered technical help to Zaire to set up a unified monetary system.

Furthermore, South Africa often provides financial assistance for various developmental projects for the SADC countries. The policymakers of South Africa clearly recognise the integrated development needs of the Southern African region as a whole. Most of the SADC countries suffer from poverty, unemployment, and hunger. With the establishment of a black majority government in South Africa, it has become almost impossible to stop the inflow of economic migrants from its neighbouring countries. South Africa has its own problems of poverty and unemployment amongst black people, therefore the newly arrived blacks from other regions of Southern Africa find it impossible to get jobs, and consequently many of them tend to engage in criminal activities. There is the growing belief in South Africa that the criminal activities of these outsiders are mainly responsible for the deterioration of the law and order situation. It is believed that South Africa has a major role to play to improve the standard of living of the people in the southern African region. It is under this spirit that the Development Bank of Southern Africa, which is the major specialised bank engaged in developmental activities in South Africa has now formally extended its role beyond the boundaries of South Africa to include all 14 SADC countries.

By setting up a base for operation from South Africa, Australian companies could possibly supplement South Africa's interests to the countries of SADC.

1.3.2 *The Southern African Customs Union (SACU)*

South Africa is also a member of the Southern African Customs Union (SACU). SACU recently agreed to revise the 1969 Customs Union Agreement, which was quite rigid and undemocratic. SACU comprises South Africa, Botswana, Lesotho, Namibia, and Swaziland. To initiate the process of democratisation of SACU a Customs Unions Task Team (CUTT) was formed in 1994 consisting of three working groups, namely, an institutional working group, a trade policy working group and a technical working group. The task of the first group is to develop a new and democratic institutional framework for the SACU. The second is responsible for investigating relevant policy issues; and the third is assigned to develop a new revenue-sharing formula that would be fair, sustainable and pro-development.

Although SACU is still in the process of development, the South African economy has already been well integrated into the customs union. Of the countries which form the SACU, Botswana has been a great economic success – thanks to diamond mining and tourism.

Like Australia, the SACU members are major producers of minerals for the world market. However, Australia cannot join SACU to formulate a common strategy for mineral exports because of WTO restrictions on such strategy for member countries. But it is possible for Australia to achieve economic co-operation with the SACU in non-tariff areas.

1.3.3 *Indian Ocean Rim-Association for Regional Co-operation (IOR-ARC)*

The group, with 14 founding members, was established in March 1997 at a ministerial meeting in Mauritius and includes countries from both the southern and northern hemispheres. It is formally known as the Indian Ocean Rim–Association for Regional Co-operation (IOR-ARC). It is another regional organisation with aims to promote economic, political and cultural co-operation.

The 14 founding members are Australia, India, Indonesia, Kenya, Madagascar, Malaysia, Mauritius, Mozambique, Oman,

Singapore, South Africa, Sri Lanka, Tanzania and Yemen. In aggregate, these countries have nearly one quarter of the world's population, including the second and fourth most populous countries in the world, namely India and Indonesia. Australia, India and South Africa are the major players in the IOR-ARC group in terms of their economic strength in the region.

The membership, as it stands, spreads over three continents. Previously all these countries were colonies or protectorates of European powers except Northern Yemen which, following amalgamation with Southern Yemen, became Republic of Yemen in 1990. However, although Australia has been a British colony in a technical sense, it has for practical purposes remained independent since the formation of Federation in 1901. Ten of these 14 countries are members of the Commonwealth.

Economically, following the classification of the OECD, only two (Australia and Singapore) of the 14 countries fall in the developed country category. Three of the countries (Malaysia, Mauritius and Oman) are classified as upper middle-income country, *i.e.* per capita annual income between US$2,696 and US$8,355. Four of these countries (India, Indonesia, Kenya and Sri Lanka) are considered as low income countries, *i.e.* per capita annual income is less that US$675. Madagascar, Mozambique, Tanzania and Yemen are considered least developed countries, *i.e.* in addition to an annual per capita income of less that US$675, the overall living standard is well below other low income countries. South Africa is considered a low income country if the living standard of the minority white population is excluded.

The member nations of IOR-ARC have agreed to organise the association along similar lines to APEC, but will not involve a formal treaty or binding agreement between members. Although its charter has not yet been finalised and unlikely to be agreed upon before the next ministerial meeting, it is expected to focus on a declaration of support for trade liberalisation from the countries bounding the Indian Ocean. Whilst economic co-operation remains the major focus of the Association, there are additional spin-off objectives as well — cultural and educational co-operation are to mention a few. The focus of the organisation is multi-sectoral with particular emphasis on economic, trade and security issues. Economists and the business community are already estimating the co-operation between these 14 countries will generate trade worth Aus$1.5 trillion.

One important feature of this co-operative approach is that the initiative in specific areas is not taken by governments, but by sectoral groups. For example, the Centre for Maritime Policy at the University of Wollongong in Australia recently organised a seminar to discuss security in the Indian Ocean Region attended by representatives from India and other countries. It is interesting to note that the organisers described the seminar as an "...important step in building a sense of regional community in the Indian Ocean Region...". Similarly, a number of other institutions have already commenced work to facilitate bonding between the member countries on various aspects of economic development and co-operation. The recent paper by John Wood and Ms Gosselink of the University of Notre Dame identifying 70 international agreements and agencies which have significant implications for this group, is an example. The Centre for Migration and Development Studies at the University of Western Australia has also been actively involved in the second-tier (research) track of IOR-ARC and the Centre will be represented at a seminar in New Delhi in November 1997.

The precise relationship between this group and other regional groups is not yet clear. A particular issue, which needs to be carefully looked at, is the role and responsibilities of individual member countries when there is a conflict of interest between organisations with some countries having dual membership. For example, India and Sri Lanka are members of SAARC, Malaysia and Indonesia are members of ASEAN, and Australia, along with some ASEAN countries, is a member of APEC.

In a comparatively recent paper (Kalirajan and Shand, 1996), the authors have made an econometric analysis of the scope for economic co-operation between Australia and the Indian Ocean group of countries, and a detailed analysis of the future of trade within these countries by estimating what is known as the export intensity indices. Unfortunately, the estimated indices do not go beyond 1992.

The following table reproduced from the study is interesting, as it tends to indicate the direction of future trade. Amongst Indian Ocean grouping (IOG) countries, India is a major single country destination for Australia's exports. Amongst regional groups within IOG, the Indian Ocean Islands, SAARC and Southeast Asia also absorb significant volumes of Australia's exports. South Africa does not appear prominently in the table mainly because of apartheid, which had led to a rapid decline in trade between Australia and South Africa. It is only after 1990, as the figures in the table indicate, that trade between the two countries began to pick up.

TABLE 1

Australia's Bilateral Export Intensities with Respect to Trading Partners in the Indian Ocean: 1965-92

Year	India	Indian Ocean Islands	North and East Africa	South Africa	SAARC	South East Asian	West Asia
1965-69	1.29	2.68	0.66	0.99	1.42	2.07	0.82
1970-74	1.52	2.78	0.87	1.57	1.80	2.51	1.56
1975-79	1.56	3.36	0.60	1.03	1.85	2.47	1.27
1980-84	1.26	2.76	0.52	0.57	1.31	1.93	1.40
1985	1.40	2.10	0.52	0.42	1.58	1.87	1.96
1986	1.67	2.29	0.79	0.60	1.49	1.81	1.93
1987	1.63	1.76	0.37	0.52	1.33	1.85	1.86
1988	2.12	1.70	0.43	0.70	1.81	2.00	1.81
1989	1.71	2.12	0.32	0.82	1.83	2.03	2.15
1990	1.93	1.53	0.30	0.71	1.82	2.20	2.40
1991	2.44	1.84	0.36	1.06	2.09	2.02	1.39
1992	2.39	2.02	0.54	1.15	1.99	1.98	1.06

Source: Kalirajan, K.P. and R.T. Shand (1996), Table 1.

The main conclusion emerging is that there is considerable scope for future expansion of Australia's trade with the Indian Ocean group of countries, in particular with South Africa and India.

It should be noted that the main objectives of the Indian Ocean rim initiative have been identified as follows:

(a) promote the welfare of the peoples of the participating countries through carefully-designed programmes to improve their standards of living and quality of life;

(b) promote the sustained growth and balanced development of the region and of the member-states;

(c) formulate and implement programmes for economic co-operation, including expansion of trade, tourism, direct investment, scientific and technological exchanges and human resource development;

(d) reduce impediments and lower barriers towards freer and enhanced flow of goods, services, investment and technology within the region;

(e) encourage close interaction of trade and industry, academic institutions scholars and the peoples of the member countries;

(f) strengthen co-operation and dialogue among countries on global economic issues; and

(g) promote co-operation in development of human resources, through closer linkages among training institutions, universities and other specialised institutions.

The value of Australia's total merchandise exports to South Africa has grown from US$95.6 million in 1990 to US$301.6 million in 1994, a trend growth rate of 35.06 per cent per annum. The major commodities which Australia exported to the world market during 1994 included food and live animals, crude materials, inedible excluding fuels, mineral fuels etc., and manufactured goods. The structural changes which have taken place in the exports sectors of Australia since 1970. While the relative importance of food and live animals (0), and crude materials, inedible excluding fuels have declined over the years, the manufactured goods gained more importance in exports during the same period. The commodity group mineral fuels etc. was Australia's second largest export earner during 1994. However, its importance reached its peak (26.3 per cent) in the mid-1980s. During 1994, manufactured goods earned about 19 per cent (the highest of all) of total exports earnings by Australia from merchandise exports as opposed to 15 per cent in 1970. Australia has achieved these structural changes through a number of trade and macroeconomic reforms since the beginning of the 1980s. Gradual removal of protection against imports, large efforts to build bilateral relations with the dynamic countries of the Indian Ocean region such as India and South Africa, and the introduction of a number of microeconomic reforms have significantly improved Australia's economic performance.

It is likely that Australia's future need for expansion of exports will be in manufactured goods and South Africa may become an important trading partner in this respect. Manufactured goods comprised about 31.42 per cent of Australian total exports to South Africa during 1994. Products from food and live animals made up 20.31 per cent of Australian exports to South Africa during the same year. According to one estimate, exports of ETMs from Australia have grown at a trend rate of 42 per cent between 1991 and 1996, making South Africa the fastest growing market for Australia's ETMs, which again highlights the importance of South Africa as a future trading partner.

Australian merchandise imports from South Africa have increased at a trend rate of about 26 per cent since 1991. In absolute value they increased from US$76.4 million in 1991 to US$214.3 million in 1994. However, the share of total merchandise imports from South Africa to total Australian imports declined from 0.6 per cent in 1980 to its lowest level (0.19 per cent) in 1991. Since then it has been increasing having reached 0.41 per cent in 1994. Historically, the commodity group machines and transport equipment has been the largest commodity group of imports into Australia ranging from 36 per cent to 47 per cent of total Australian imports between 1970 and 1994. The other major commodity groups imported by Australia are basic manufactured goods, chemical and related products, and mineral fuels. Australia imports a number of these commodities from South Africa.

Manufactured goods made up about 45 per cent of Australia's imports from South Africa during 1994. Chemical related products constituted about 21 per cent of Australia's imports from South Africa during the same year. The other important commodities imported by Australia from South Africa include iron and steel, machines and transport, non-ferrous metals, and food and live animals.

There exists significant scope for further expansion of trade between Australia and South Africa in a number of areas, for example, in basic manufacture, chemical related products, iron and steel, machinery and transport equipment, non-ferrous metals, and food and lives animals, there should be room for considerable expansion.

Consideration of Revealed Comparative Advantage Index (RCAI) for both Australia and South Africa would shed further light on the international competitiveness of exporting industries.[1] It is interesting to note that for a number of commodity groups such as crude materials excluding fuels and non-ferrous metals, RCAI for both Australia and South Africa is greater than one, indicating thereby that these two countries have comparative advantage in these commodity groups. However, the RCAI of these commodity groups for Australia is much higher than that of South Africa, which confirms that Australia has relatively higher comparative advantage in these commodity groups as compared to South Africa. The RCAI of

1 . The RCAI is determined by calculating the share of a particular commodity group in an economy's total exports and then dividing by that commodity group's share of world exports.
Symbolically, RCAI = {Xij/Xj}/(Wi/W)
where i = commodity, j = country and W = world.
If the RCAI of a particular commodity group is greater than unity, the export share of the commodity group in a country exceeds the world average export share of that commodity group implying that the country tends to have relatively high comparative advantage in that commodity group. On the contrary, a RCAI of less than unity indicates that the country has a lower comparative advantage in that commodity group than the world average level. We intend to calculate the RCAI for a selection of South Africa's and Australia's industries for the period 1991-96.

commodity groups food & live animals and beverages & tobacco for Australia is significantly greater than 1.

It is interesting to note that this index for South Africa is less than 1. This implies that for these commodity groups Australia has a relatively higher comparative advantage than South Africa.

Similarly, RCAI of mineral fuels for Australia is greater than 1, while that of South Africa is less than 1. Thus, Australia has relatively higher comparative advantage in this commodity group and South Africa does not. In iron and steel South Africa has relatively higher comparative advantage than Australia, as RCAI of this commodity group for South Africa is much higher than 1 and for Australia it is less than 1. In a group of commodities such as animal and vegetable oil, and fat and machines and transport equipment neither Australia nor South Africa has any comparative advantage.

It appears from the above that Australia and South Africa can develop a common marketing strategy for trading the commodities in which they have relatively high comparative advantages.

South Africa has also taken a number of initiatives to expand its exports to Australia. As mentioned earlier, between 1991 and 1994 South Africa's total exports to Australia increased at the rate of about 26 per cent per annum. "Of South Africa's top 20 export markets, seven are in southern Africa. Five of those are among South Africa's top 10 markets. Many South African companies have extensive commercial networks in place in southern Africa covering a broad range of sectors including food and beverage distribution and retailing, infrastructure engineering, energy systems, and telecommunications. Strategic partnering with these companies will offer significant opportunities for Australian companies to expand into southern Africa."

2.1 *Development Assistance*

As stated earlier, the South African government has launched an ambitious development strategy, which is generally known as the strategy of GEAR. The importance of achieving growth with redistribution of income does not need to be emphasised.

The historical forces which resulted in appalling socio-economic disparities between the white and the black people of South Africa will of course not disappear overnight. Time and long term efforts will be needed by way of improving the employability of the black population. The Australian government could play a significant role to enhance the socio-economic status of the huge black population by offering assistance in certain key sectors and crucial areas such as education, housing and health. There is no doubt that a significant number of the black population are poorly housed, fed, educated and led a very unhealthy life. If they are provided with better education, health facilities and housing facilities, they will be better prepared to obtain jobs, which the current government is committed to achieve under the strategy of GEAR.

Development assistance should assist the government of South Africa in its effort to develop human resources in order to guarantee the supply of skilled manpower for future development of the country. Currently, a large number of skilled people (mainly whites) are leaving the country. Many of them even do not bother to register as emigrants with the Department of Immigration. Hence the official statistics may be heavily downward biased. But the shortage of skilled labour is a major problem faced by both the public and private sectors in South Africa. The attempt by the current government to fill many high level positions by blacks through its redundancy programme (for whites) has essentially backfired. Many of the newly recruited blacks do not have the necessary skills, expertise, and experience to perform their respective duties. Some of them have also deserted their jobs.

As a result, whites that went for voluntary retirement with lucrative financial incentives are now being re-employed by the government as consultants at a high rate of remuneration.

It is, therefore, necessary to make every effort to reduce the skill gap in South Africa. What is important is to draw up comprehensive manpower planning, to forecast the medium to long-term demand for labour at different levels of skills, and then to orient public policies accordingly.

Australia and South Africa have a more or less similar educational system. Given the geographical dispersion, distance education is a big necessity for educating the people who live in remote areas. South Africa can significantly gain from the Australian experience. Similarly, Australian educational institutions can develop academic links with their counterparts in South Africa for providing educational training to the huge number of black South Africans. Further research is needed in this area.

We can envisage a positive role for AusAID to fill up the gap in our knowledge of the manpower needs for southern Africa in the coming decade.

2.2 *Areas of Future Co-operation*

The Parliamentary Joint Standing Committee on Foreign Affairs, Defence and Trade published a major report (November 1996) on Australia's Relations with Southern Africa. The Committee was appointed with the following terms of reference:

> "To investigate and report on Australia's political, security and trade interests in Southern Africa in the post-apartheid era...."

The wide-ranging report of the Joint Standing Committee covered the entire region of SADC, with particular reference to South Africa. A very detailed study was made of security issues, trade and investment opportunities and Australia's overseas development assistance programme. Special issues such as health, education and training, housing, women's and workers' rights, and environment, were also examined in some detail, with reference to southern Africa, comprising SADC. The report contained 42 specific recommendations.

Subsequent to this report, the first Australia-South Africa Joint Ministerial Commission held its meeting in Pretoria on July 9-10, 1997. At the end of the meeting the Ministerial Commission issued a communiqué in which the main areas of future economic co-operation between Australia and South Africa were identified as follows:

(i) To develop new sectors for trade, new fields for investment, and new areas for co-operative work;

(ii) To maintain the momentum in growth of bilateral trade;

(iii) To encourage reciprocal investments between Australia and South Africa; and

(iv) To assist Australian and South African business firms in using each other's countries as a base for trading into the wider regions of Asia and Africa respectively.

The Ministers noted how these working groups formed by business representatives (processed food and food processing, automotive parts, and mining equipment and technology) had been working on the possibilities of effective exchanges and contacts. There was also a services (working) group, which included business representatives, drawn from a wide variety of industries and product lines.

Some observers take the view that Australia and South Africa are competitors in the world markets, and that therefore there is little room for co-operation between these two major economies in the Indian Ocean region. As stated earlier, it is indeed true that Australia and South Africa have relative strength in mining and minerals, and in agricultural produce and agro-based industries. The two countries produce gold, diamonds, iron ore, coal and many other non-ferrous metals for export in the international market. Similarly, the two countries have developed enormous expertise in the processed food and food-processing and winemaking industries. Superficially, therefore, the two countries are competitors, as these two economies do not seem to be complementary.

In a real sense, however, Australia and South Africa are not competitors. The myth that Australia and South Africa are competitors grew during the apartheid years. Some South Africans were of the view that the only reason why Australia was supporting sanctions against South Africa was to stop her from competing with Australia. That view was of course completely untrue, because as soon as the sanctions were lifted, trade between Australia and South Africa increased dramatically. Indeed, Australia's opposition to apartheid had an economic cost. However, in the post-apartheid period, Australia is likely to reap the benefit from a general feeling of euphoria in South

Africa and the extremely favourable attitude of the South African government towards Australia.

It is important to remember that, historically and traditionally, South African export markets have been in Europe, especially in Germany. Australia, on the other hand, historically depended upon the UK market, and over the past three decades, Japan has emerged as Australia's biggest trading partner. In a real sense, therefore, there is not much competition between Australia and South Africa for the same limited world markets. There is, on the other hand, enormous opportunity for co-operation and collaboration in the areas of transfer of technology, investments and trade, agriculture and mining, tourism and in the services sector. The possible areas of future co-operation are examined in greater detail in the next few sections of this paper.

2.2.1 *Infrastructure Projects*

South Africa has very well developed infrastructure in terms of roads, railways and telecommunications between the major cities. However, the remote areas in South Africa still do not have good infrastructures for trade and industrial development. South Africa's immediate neighbours such as Swaziland, Namibia, Mozambique, Zimbabwe and Lesotho have poor infrastructure facilities. For that matter, there is a great need for systematic development of infrastructure in the entire SADC region.

For the SADC region as a whole, a number of initiatives known as Spatial Development Initiatives (SDI) are now either under consideration or in actual progress (Fig. 1). The most famous of the SDI projects is the Maputo Development Corridor (MDC) which is intended to provide a major road link between Johannesburg (South Africa) and Maputo (Mozambique). The Maputo Corridor is expected to encourage trade and industrial development in the Gauteng and Mpumalanga provinces of South Africa and in the Maputo province of Mozambique. Development in these areas is expected to stem the flow of illegal migrants to South Africa from Mozambique and other northern neighbours. MDC will be eventually extended westwards to link Johannesburg with Botswana and Namibia to Walvis Bay in the Atlantic Ocean. This western extension of MDC will be known as the Trans-Kalahari Transport Corridor.

Other major infrastructure development projects, some of which are still in the planning stage, are:

(i) Tazara Development Corridor to link Dar-es-Salaam and Lusaka;

(ii) The Benguela Development Corridor from Benguela in Angola to Lusaka;

(iii) The Nacala Development Corridor in Malawi and Mozambique;

(iv) The Beira Development Corridor between Mozambique and Zimbabwe; and

(v) The Kwa-Zulu Natal SDI and the Algoa-Kei SDI in South Africa.

Fig. 1: Possible Development Corridors and SDI's in the SADC Region.

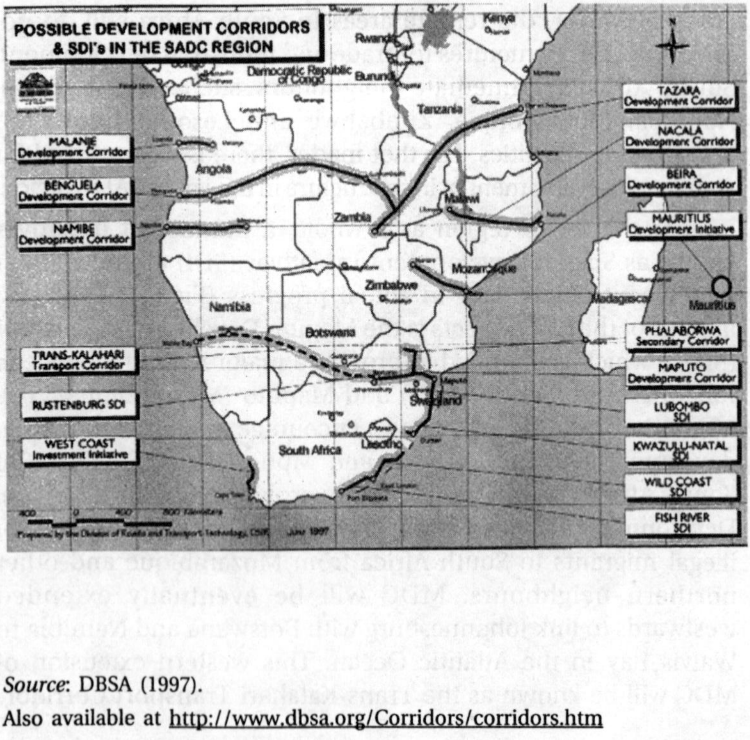

Source: DBSA (1997).

Also available at http://www.dbsa.org/Corridors/corridors.htm

Simultaneously, there are plans under way for a major development of port facilities near Port Elizabeth and Maputo.

The SDI projects have different sectoral focuses. For example, the Kwa-Zulu Natal SDI is primarily intended to facilitate industrial development of this major sugar-producing area; whilst MDC has a sectoral mix of achieving industrial development, promotion of tourism and trade between South Africa and Mozambique, and the opening up of agricultural areas.

Investments needed for implementation of the above SDI projects would run into billions of dollars. The European Union and the Development Bank of Southern Africa have already committed funds for the Maputo Development Corridor project.

Australian companies are very well placed to position themselves in South Africa now in order to have involvement in many of the infrastructure projects in South Africa and the SADC region.

Another major infrastructure project is known as the Lesotho Highlands Water Project. This project, which is one of the most ambitious multi-purpose water schemes in the world, involves the construction of a number of dams in Lesotho — a small land-locked country in southern Africa. This water project is intended to store water and transfer it to the Gauteng Province in South Africa. It will benefit Lesotho by providing hydroelectricity, water, and development in the Highlands region and revenue from the sale of water to South Africa.

The Lesotho Water Project is to be completed in five phases, The total cost of the project will be several billion dollars. Many Australian companies have the expertise to get involved in some stages of the huge multiphase Lesotho Water Project.

2.2.2 *Tourism*

Tourism has emerged as Australia's biggest source of foreign exchange earning. In 1995, tourism income in Australia exceeded $6 billion, which was far greater than the income from exports of wheat, or that of coal. Region-wise, Australia gets the largest number of tourists from Japan and Asia, followed by New Zealand and the UK.

Tourism in South Africa has also been a fast growing industry. In 1994 tourism generated only R7 billion (= Aus$2 billion approximately); but by 1996 it increased to R13 billion (Table 2). At its present rate of growth, tourism is likely to surpass the income generated by the gold and the mining (outside gold) sectors within the next few years.

TABLE 2

Sectoral Contribution to South African Exports: 1994-96

Exports Item	In Billion Rand (1994)
1. Manufactured goods	34.48
2. Gold Exports	22.67
3. Mining (other than gold)	17.68
4. Tourism	13.00 (1996)

Despite the deterioration of the crime situation in South Africa in more recent years (which tends to discourage many tourists, especially from Japan, from visiting South Africa), the wild life and the natural beauty of South Africa, coupled with her world class infrastructure network, offer strong incentives to many tourists, especially the young and the adventurous people. The depreciation of the South African Rand has given an added bonus to tourists. For Australian holidaymakers to Europe, the South African route is an exciting alternative to the European route via Singapore (or Bangkok). Between 1990 and 1996 the number of Australian tourists to South Africa increased from 18,862 to 48,356.

Similarly, South African tourists are now increasingly attracted to Australia because of the large expatriate South African population in Australia, especially in Western Australia. For many South Africans, Australia is a relatively new and exciting country, which might offer them an opportunity to explore the exotic South-East Asian tourist resorts in Indonesia and Thailand. There are also many potential white migrants from South Africa who wish to visit Australia and New Zealand to obtain first-hand impressions before making their final decision. Indeed, the tourism potential between South Africa and Australia is still largely unexplored.

Fig. 2: Growth of Foreign and Overseas Visitors Market: 1990-96

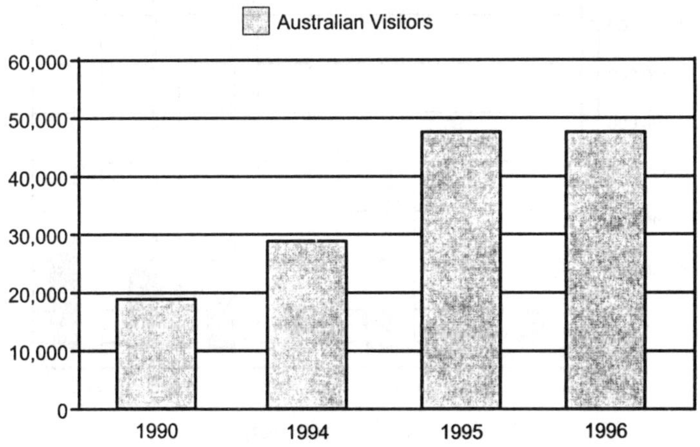

Source: Estimated from SATOUR (1997).

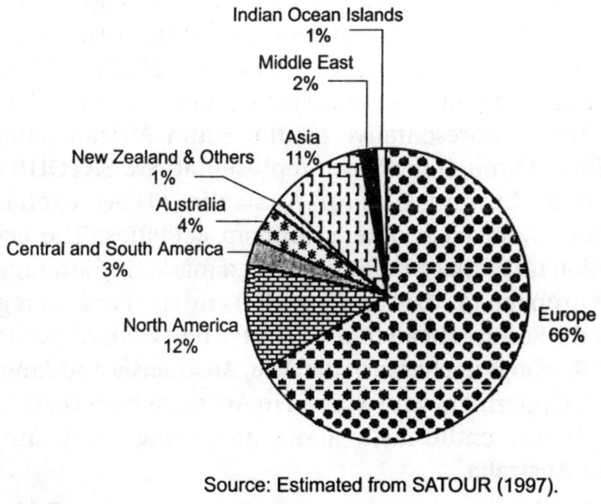

Source: Estimated from SATOUR (1997).

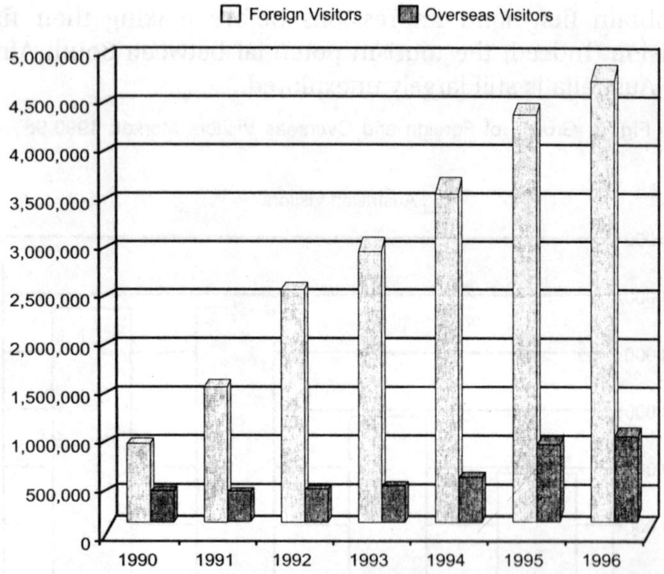

Source: SATOUR (1997).

Currently, SATOUR (South African Tourism Board) has established strong links in Australia. It has an office in Sydney, and it organises regular workshops for potential tourists in Perth, Adelaide, Melbourne, Sydney and Brisbane. One of SATOUR's staff members represents South Africa on the Association of National Tourists Office (ANTO). ANTO in Australia is made up of all heads of state tourist offices. Similarly, Australia has a representative on the South African national tourist office. Through these two representatives, SATOUR and the Tourism Commission of Australia (TCA) exchange information about each other's tourism activities. The actual co-operation takes place in formulating a marketing strategy for enticing European tourists (to Australia) and the Far East region (to follow the South African route). The current General Manager of SATOUR, who is in charge of the Asia, Australasia and America desk is S.A. Opperman, who worked in Australia for 5 years from 1975. He is very enthusiastic about promoting South African tourism in Australia.

SATOUR has been very successful in Germany. TCA can

possibly learn from South Africa about the secrets of its success in Germany. Similarly, SATOUR can learn from TCA about its success in the UK market.

2.2.3 *Direct Investment and Joint ventures*

The South African government has introduced a number of incentives to attract industrial investment in South Africa. It offers a five-year package comprising a two-year establishment grant on operational assets followed by a three-year profit based output incentives. Moreover, attractive industrial financing is available from the Industrial Development Corporation (IDC) of South Africa Limited. IDC was established with the aim of financing new industries and assisting existing industries in expanding, modernising, and generally improving their efficiency. Other objectives of this corporation are to encourage partnerships between local and foreign companies to develop new industries, promote exports and import replacement and regional development.

The Industrial Development and Investment Centre of the Department of Trade and Industry has a network of 56 offices in 49 countries. It provides international investors with the necessary information and support required for the planning and arrangement of investment recruitment initiatives abroad. The centre is the central point of contact for industrial investment related matters.

There has been a fair bit of South African investment in the mining industry in Australia. Gencor Industries Inc. has one of the biggest investments in Australia. Iscor Limited has also been a big mining investor. Barlow Limited of South Africa, which had a turnover of R17 billion (about Aus$5 billion) in 1996, has been investing in a big way in Australia. It has already acquired Taubmans (the painting business in Australia), and is now in the process of acquiring about 80 per cent of the shares of the Australian company, Lanes.

Barlow is indeed a very large business conglomerate, with its main operations in South Africa. There was a time when it produced a wide range of products, from disposable baby nappies to guided missile systems. It is a publicly listed company in South Africa, the UK and the USA. Its current strategy is to take a position in the Australian private sector by taking over controlling shares in some major companies.

Anglo-American Platinum Corporation Limited (AAPCL) is another big South African Company, a big player in the field of platinum production. The current world demand for platinum is about 5 million ounces every year, of which 3.6 million ounces are produced in South Africa, and AAPCL produces roughly one-half of the total South African production.

By comparison, Australia does not have any significant expertise in platinum production – BHP of Australia is only now building up its production of platinum in Zimbabwe. The BHP operation will be in a small mine which is expected to produce 150,000 ounces of platinum a year, about 8 per cent of AAPCL's current level of production.

Australia does have some platinum deposits, none of which so far has proved to be economically viable. AAPCL is currently negotiating with an Australian company to explore the possibility of extracting platinum in Australia through joint efforts. Australia does not have the necessary laboratory facilities and appropriate technology for the extraction and processing of platinum, whereas AAPCL being the largest platinum producer in South Africa is well equipped with all the facilities and technologies required in this regard.

AAPCL also has some association with the Perth Mint, which produces koala coins by using platinum, which are in great demand from collectors in Asia. Perth Mint buys platinum from the open market, but receives co-operation from AAPCL in marketing these coins in the world. Indeed, the man in-charge of Perth Mint's koala project is an expatriate South African. Again, in retailing business, Woolworths in South Africa is reported to have made a move to get into the Australian market. In the services sector, the Rand Merchant Bank has already established its presence in Sydney, and current reports indicate that the ANZ Bank of Australia is planning to establish an office in South Africa.

When we look at the total picture of bilateral direct foreign investment, South African investment in Australia far exceeds Australian investment in South Africa. The exact figures of actual bilateral investments are difficult to obtain. South African investments in Australia are understated by millions of dollars.

By comparison, Australian investment in South Africa is very small. Although the South African government has introduced a number of incentives to attract foreign investors, South Africa has somehow not yet been able to create the "enabling environment" to attract direct foreign investment. In particular the shortage of skilled labour is a major problem as international investors would require an assured supply of skilled labour for effective operation.

Australian investment in South Africa is mainly in manufacturing. There has been, for example, some investment in food processing and electrical equipment. The past studies indicate that in economies with similar profile, as in the case of South Africa and Australia, when trade and investment barriers are removed, exports of manufactured goods to each other are increased; and they actually begin to export more manufactured goods to other countries also.

On current evidence, Australian world-wide exports have risen sharply over the past few years mainly due to the contribution of small and medium-size enterprises. The relatively smaller Australian companies are also well placed to penetrate into the South African market. As the big corporations in South Africa get ready to globalise in a fiercely competitive environment, they would slowly concentrate only on core business and jettison all peripheral activities. This move by big corporations would create enormous opportunities for small businesses in Australia to establish their markets in South Africa, particularly with businesses which are controlled by the blacks.

Small and medium-size Australian companies have until now focused mainly on Asian markets. The current currency crisis in ASEAN, especially in Thailand, Malaysia, Indonesia and the Philippines, might now expose some of these companies to future uncertainty in regard to their exports. They might therefore wish to diversify their markets by re-thinking opportunities in South Africa, especially in collaboration with the newly emerging small businesses under the leadership of the black people.

International business would increasingly find it difficult to establish a long-term foot-hold in South Africa without the support of black people. Labour in South Africa primarily comprises black people not only from South Africa but also from Mozambique, Namibia, Swaziland, Zimbabwe and Lesotho. Some unskilled black workers come from as far as Nigeria and Tanzania.

Now, there is definite antagonism between "white" capital, which controls all the big mining companies, such as gold, platinum, diamonds, coal and other minerals, on the one hand, and "black" labour, on the other. Black workers are organised into strong political unions. Indeed, the national government in South Africa is formed as a coalition with the Congress of South African Trade Unions (COSATU), and cannot therefore take an open anti-labour stance.

Since 1994 a number of "black" companies controlled by the blacks have come into prominence. For example, the New Africa Investment Limited (NAIL), which has a very dynamic black deputy chairman, has gone into gold mining in a big way. The deep-shaft gold mining in South Africa leads to many work-place accidents; every month 8-10 workers die in mining accidents, and many more are disabled. So, black workers are politicised. Australian companies would find it very difficult to effectively function in South Africa without active co-operation of the black people.

Such co-operation would be even more needed for small and medium-size Australian companies which may wish to start an operational base in South Africa, and from there to Southern Africa. This is because the main demand for the products of Australian companies, whether commodities, or financial and banking, or media services, would come from black people. For example, Kagiso Trust Investment Company, which is controlled by the black capitalists in South Africa, is engaged in the business of media and publication. It is now bidding for a new licence for a television channel. Its protracted negotiations with a major television network in Australia were reported to have failed over the issue of employing blacks in the proposed joint venture. It is, therefore, important that small and medium-size Australian companies treat carefully on the sensitive issue of the employment of both "black" capital and "black" labour.

2.2.4 *Health and Education*

The Joint Ministerial Commission (July 1997) agreed that both Africa and Australia could mutually benefit through co-operation in the development of health services. The Ministers identified the following areas of health sector co-operation for early action.

- Health financing systems, including the development of social insurance arrangements and the regulation of private health insurance.
- Schemes to enhance the safety and efficiency of pharmaceuticals in South Africa, and to improve their affordability.
- Means of enhancing access of people in rural and remote areas to health services, including through telemedicine and flying doctor services.
- Health promotion techniques to help and encourage people to adopt safe and healthy lifestyles.
- Rehabilitation of public hospitals through the development of public-private partnership.

Australian health advisors have already started some preliminary work in South Africa which may eventually open the door for commercial opportunities. Aboriginal health care in remote areas in Australia has important lessons for South Africa. Also, the provision of flying doctor services and telemedicine in Australia offers opportunities. South Africans are recruiting Cuban doctors to go to remote areas. Australia has some skills and technology that can be used in South Africa. Designing and construction of regional hospitals is another area in which Australia has considerable experience and expertise.

There is also room for considerable co-operation in the field of education. Lack of education and, consequently, lack of skills are regarded as the main cause of unemployment among black youth. There is a growing recognition in South Africa that the unemployment situation is so serious that the government cannot rely upon free market forces to solve the problem. Welfare measures would also hardly touch the main cause of unemployment. Some welfare measures are already in place. Provisions of free health for babies until the age of 6, free health for all pregnant women, and free food for all school going children up to the age of six, have already been made by the national government in South Africa. But these measures are heavily drawing on the limited budgetary resources. There are just not enough funds to offer schooling to about 2 million children, who are supposed to start their schools. Nor are there funds for high schools, vocational training, and university and higher education. Yet educating black people is the single most important challenge to the South African government. And it is here that Australia has enormous opportunities for exporting her educational services.

Australian educational institutions are now of course slowly moving in to take advantage of the commercial opportunities in education in South Africa. A Victorian institution has already signed an agreement with a number of South African institutions for distance education. An Australian university is planning to start several campuses across South Africa.

However, no overall strategic view has been taken to understand and capture the South African market by Australian educational institutions. Yet any careful observer would notice the need for rapid expansion of education at all levels in South Africa not only to solve the problem of appalling unemployment but also to create opportunities for long term benefits for overseas companies by encouraging them to set up their operations in the South African market.

AusAID may well consider funding research projects which are concerned with the further investigation of the opportunities for "export of education" to South Africa in particular, and the Indian Ocean region generally.

2.2.5 *Housing*

Australia has a world class housing industry. In view of the similarity in weather and topography of South Africa and Australia, it is possible that the two countries might benefit from an exchange of information. The need for good housing in South Africa cannot be overstated. Millions of black people live in appalling conditions in shanty towns. Such people will have to be re-housed. With the growing numbers of people joining the ranks of the middle class, there has also been a demand for better houses in many urban centres. The Australian housing industry can certainly look for opportunities in South Africa. However, the difficulty is that there is no single authority in South Africa to approach on this matter.

2.2.6 *Transfer of Technology*

Australia and South Africa have similar factor endowments in terms of natural resources — coal, gold, diamonds, iron ore, uranium, non-ferrous metals, and agriculture and agro-based industries. With similar factor endowments, any two countries would tend to integrate their economies by means of successful intra-industry trade, which would provide the mechanism for the transfer of technology from one country to the other. It has been argued in more recent economic literature that intra-industry trade is less disruptive in newly reforming and liberalising countries such as South Africa and Australia, which also have a similar economic structure, because intra-industry adjustment requires reallocation of resources mainly within firms in the same industry rather than across firms in different industries.

Let us take some examples. First, the gold industry in which Australia and South Africa jointly control nearly 20 per cent of the annual world production. However, Australia and South Africa cannot work out a common strategy for marketing gold, because of two main reasons: (1) The enormous stocks of gold held by central banks all over the world do not allow South Africa and Australia to have significant control over world supplies in any given year. (2) The rules of WTO, which would not allow a common pricing strategy by any group of countries, as it would clearly defeat the objective of freer world trade.

But the technology of gold production in South Africa is very different from that in Australia. Gold is produced in deep shaft mines, some as deep as 4 km, in South Africa. The technology of such gold production is altogether different from the Australian system of gold production in relatively more shallow mines. In this kind of situation, intra-industry trade can effectively take place to bring about a complementarily of technology. Indeed, reports suggest that South African gold mining companies are buying Australian vehicles, which are very efficient in transporting gold.

Let us take another example: the automobile industry in Australia and South Africa. The motor car industry is a highly capital-intensive industry, with strong forward and backward linkages. Rationalisation of the Australian motor car industry is largely based on the Button Plan. South Africa also has a similar plan for its automobile industry.

There is already an automotive group in South Africa and Australia jointly working on a scheme for exchanging information in development of their respective car plans to maximise their export capacity. The focus of the work of this automotive group would be for the period beyond the year 2000. The work could be directed both to vehicle manufacturing and to trade in components.

There is a great possibility of intra-industry trade between Australian and South African automobile producers. Such intra-industry trade can equally take place in a wide range of industries — winemaking, retail trading, banking and insurance, food processing and other agro-based industries.

Conclusion

The topic "Economic Co-operation between Australia and South Africa" is likely to have considerable practical significance for various industry and could also embrace the health industry and education. Both South Africa and Australia are major economies within the context of the Indian Ocean region. They share a common language and culture. On-going research projects on specific topics such as food-processing, mining, motor cars, health and education will have to get the financial support of governments, business and commerce to enable a better understanding of the complex issues when two large countries, South Africa and Australia, begin to open up for integration in the world's markets.

In view of the emerging new role of South Africa in the Indian Ocean region, there is an urgent need for reorganising Australia's overseas development assistance programme, and in this regard, AusAID has to act as a facilitator.

AusAID may facilitate the study exchanges between SADC countries and Australian educational institutions. Export of education from Australia to the SADC region, with South Africa as the base has enormous potential for many years to come. We wish to reiterate the following recommendation made by Joint Standing Committee on Foreign Affairs, Defence and Trade (1996):

> "AusAID continue to include a focus on education and training in its programmes, with an increased emphasis in the areas of basic education and vocational and technical education."

Under its international seminar support scheme (ISSS), AusAID may sponsor a major seminar on South Africa towards the end of 1998 to bring together academics, businessmen and government officials from both countries so as to examine the full potential for expanded trade and investment, the transfer of technology and development of cultural and educational exchange programmes.

As a preparatory work to the proposed (above) international seminar, AusAID may offer funding support to a research project to study the overall need for educational exchanges at all levels including basic, vocational and technical education between South Africa and Australia. An overall strategic view has to be taken to understand the South African market by Australian educational institutions.

AusAID may also actively support a training programme for small and medium size businesses in Australia, first of all, to create an awareness of the marketing opportunities in southern Africa, and secondly (with the assistance of Austrade), to provide the information needed for trade and investment in South Africa, and the sub-Saharan region as a whole. With better understanding of the markets of the Southern African region, small and medium-size companies in Australia may be willing to geographically diversify their exports and investments.

WORKS CITED

ABS (Australian Bureau of Statistics), Foreign Investment Australia, *Catalogue No.* 5305.0, several issues.

——, International Investment Position Australia, *Catalogue No.* 5305.0, several issues.

——, Balance of Payments and International Investment Position 1995-96, *Catalogue No.* 5363.0, June 1997.

ABARE (Australian Bureau of Agricultural and Resource Economics) (1996), *Australian Commodity Statistics* 1996, Canberra.

Abbott, M.J. (1996), "Australian-South African Trade: Recent Structure and Future Prospects", *Economic Papers,* Vol. 15, No. 4.

Anglo American Platinum Corporation Limited (1997), *Annual Report* 1997, Johannesburg, South Africa.

AusAID (Australian Agency for International Development) (1994), "Background Document for Contractors Bidding for the Australia-South Africa Public Sector Report Programme — the Findings of an Identification Mission to South Africa", Canberra, October.

Barlow Limited (1997), *Annual Report* 1996, Sandton, South Africa.

Brooke, Pattrick S.A. (Pty) Limited (1996), *Mining Mirror,* Vol. 10, No. 2, Bedfordview, South Africa.

Central Statistical Service (1997), *South African Statistics* 1995, Central Statistical Service, Pretoria, South Africa.

Chamber of Mines of South Africa (1996), *Annual Report* 1995-96, Publication Unit, Chamber of Mines of South Africa, Johannesburg, South Africa.

—— (1997), *Statistical Tables* 1996, Publication Unit, Chamber of Mines of South Africa, Johannesburg, South Africa.

Curtin University of Technology (1996), *Indian Ocean Network News,* Vol. 1, No. 4, Perth, Western Australia.

Department of Finance, Republic of South Africa (1997), *Budget Review* 1997.

Department of Foreign Affairs and Trade and the Australian Trade Commission (1997), "Australia and South Africa: A New Trade Partnership", Canberra, June.

Department of Trade and Industry, Republic of South Africa (1997), *Incentive Schemes*, Pretoria, April.

Development Assistance Committee (1995), *Statistical Reporting Directives* 1995 (DAC list of aid recipients 1995, Annex 5), OECD, Paris.

DBSA (Development Bank of South Africa) (1997), *Annual Report* 1997, Midrand, South Africa.

The Economist Intelligence Unit (1991), *South Africa: Country Profile* 1991-92, London.

Financial Review, Sydney, 27 September 1996.

Fukasaku, K. (1992), *Economic Regionalism and Intra-Industry Trade.*

Gold Fields Mineral Services Ltd. (1997), *Statistical Tables* 1996, South Africa.

IMF (International Monetary Fund) (1997), *IFS Data*, CD ROM, Washington, D.C.

Indian Ocean Network News, Vol. 1, No. 4, 1996, Curtin University, Perth.

International Forum on the Indian Ocean Region (1995), Current Economic Characteristics and Economic Linkages in the Indian Ocean, *Working Paper* 2, Australia South Asia Research Centre, Australian National University, Canberra.

Investment South Africa (1997), *South Africa: The Investment Brief*, Sandton, South Africa.

—— (1997), *Manufacturing Development Programme and Tax Holiday Scheme*, Coopers & Lybrand.

Joint Standing Committee on Foreign Affairs, Defence and Trade (1997), Australia's Relations with Southern Africa, The Parliament of the Commonwealth of Australia, Canberra.

Kalirajan, K. and R.T. Shand (1996), "The Australian Economy and Indian Ocean Grouping Countries", *Economic Papers*, Vol. 15, No. 4.

MES (Macroeconomic Strategy) (1996), "Growth, Employment and Redistribution: A Macroeconomic Strategy", Department of Finance, Pretoria, South Africa.

Moody, Alan (1996), "The Economics of Trading Blocks: Application to the Indian Ocean Rim", *Western Australian Economic Review*, Vol. 16, No. 1.

Parliament House (1997), First Australia-South Africa Joint Ministerial Commission, Pretoria, July 9-10, 1997, Joint Communiqué and Action Plan, Canberra.

RSA (Republic of South Africa) (1994), White Paper on Reconstruction and Development, Pretoria: Office of the Minister without Portfolio in the Office of the President, September.

RMB (Rand Merchant Bank) (1997), South Africa: A Country Report, Economic Services Department, Sandton, South Africa, September.

SATOUR (South African Tourism Board) (1996), *The South African Foreign Tourism Market: Some Useful Facts and Figures*, Johannesburg, South Africa, April.

—— (1997), *Satour Annual Report 1996*, South African Tourism Board, Johannesburg, South Africa.

South African Mining Industry (1996), *Statistical Tables* 1995, Publications Unit, Communication Services, Chamber of Mines of South Africa, Johannesburg, South Africa.

—— (1997), *Statistical Tables* 1996, Publications Unit, Communication Services, Chamber of Mines of South Africa, Johannesburg, South Africa.

South African Reserve Bank (1997), *Quarterly Bulletin*, No. 205, September, Pretoria, South Africa.

—— (1997), *Annual Economic Report* 1997, Pretoria, South Africa.

Toit, J. du (1997), South Africa within the Indian Ocean Rim, ABSA Bank, Southern Book Publishers (Pty) Ltd.

UN (United Nations), *Commodity Trade Statistics: Statistical Papers*, New York: Statistical Office of the United Nations, Dept. of Economic Affairs, various issues.

——, *International Trade Statistics Yearbook*, New York, Vol. II, Special Table: B, various issues.

US Department of State (1994), "South Africa: 1994 Country Report on Economic Policy and Trade Practices", Bureau of Economic and Business Affairs.

The World Bank (1997), *World Tables, Baltimore*: Published for the World Bank by the Johns Hopkins University Press.

Contributors

Anita Medhekar-Smith, Faculty of Business and Law, Central Queensland University.

Dhulasi Birundha Varadarajan, Professor, Department of Environmental Economics, School of Economics, Madurai Kamaraj University, Madurai, Tamil Nadu, South India.

K.C. Roy, Department of Economics, University Queensland.

Lawson Smith, Faculty of Business & Law, Central Queensland University.

M.A.B. Siddique, Department of Economics, University of Western Australia.

R. Gabbay, School of Economics & Commerce, The University of Western Australia.

R. James Ferguson, Assistant Professor of International Relations, Assistant Director of the Centre for East-West Cultural and Economic Studies, School of Humanities and Social Sciences, Bond University, Gold Coast, Queensland, 4229, Australia.

R.N. Ghosh, Department of Economics, University of Western Australia.

Rosita Dellios, Bond University, Gold Coast, Queensland.

